ACADEMIC C

# ACADEMIC CHILD

## *A Memoir*

### *by* Hazard Adams

*This copy is for David*

*Hazard Adams*

*March 5, 2014*

McFarland & Company, Inc., Publishers

*Jefferson, North Carolina, and London*

ALSO BY HAZARD ADAMS—*Fiction:* The Truth About Dragons; The Academic Trilogy (The Horses of Instruction; Many Pretty Toys; Home). *Poetry:* The Farm at Richwood and Other Poems. *Nonfiction:* The Academic Tribes. *Criticism:* Blake and Yeats: The Contrary Vision; William Blake: A Reading of the Shorter Poems; The Contexts of Poetry; The Interests of Criticism; Lady Gregory; Philosophy of the Literary Symbolic; Joyce Cary's Trilogies: Pursuit of the Particular Real; Antithetical Essays in Literary Criticism and Liberal Education; The Book of Yeats's Poems; The Book of Yeats's Vision: Romantic Modernism and Antithetical Tradition; Four Lectures on the History of Criticism in the West; The Offense of Poetry. *Edited volumes:* Poems by Robert Simeon Adams; Poetry: An Introductory Anthology; Fiction as Process (with Carl Hartman); William Blake: Jerusalem, Selected Poetry, and Prose; Critical Theory Since Plato (third edition with Leroy Searle); Critical Theory Since 1965 (with Leroy Searle); Critical Essays on William Blake.

LIBRARY OF CONGRESS CATALOGUING-IN-PUBLICATION DATA

Adams, Hazard, 1926–
    Academic child : a memoir / by Hazard Adams.
        p.    cm.
    Includes index.

    ISBN 978-0-7864-4011-5
    softcover : 50# alkaline paper ∞

    1. Adams, Hazard, 1926–   2. Novelists, American — 20th century — Biography.   3. College teachers — Washington (U.S.) — Biography.   I. Title.
    PS3551.D37Z46  2008
    813'.52 — dc22

                                    2008032255

British Library cataloguing data are available

©2008 Hazard Adams. All rights reserved

*No part of this book may be reproduced or transmitted in any form or by any means, electronic or mechanical, including photocopying or recording, or by any information storage and retrieval system, without permission in writing from the publisher.*

Cover photograph: Shutterstock ©2008

Manufactured in the United States of America

*McFarland & Company, Inc., Publishers*
    *Box 611, Jefferson, North Carolina 28640*
    *www.mcfarlandpub.com*

For Diana
Fellow Travailer

# Contents

# *Preface*

Except for the last chapter and the so-called excursuses, this book is mainly about the past, but I hope that the experiences remembered here will have some relevance to the future, if only by offering the opportunity for contrasts that arouse thought. The last chapter repeats and adds to observations I have made before about literary education and the profession and attempts to look toward the future. In it I steal from and insert some parts of an earlier essay in *Innovation and Continuity in English Studies* (Herbert Grabes, ed.; Frankfurt am Main: Peter Lang GmbH, Europäischer Verlag der Wissenschaft, 2001).

Like any book, the writing of this one has a history. My first intention was to give an account of a professional career in education, but I quickly realized that it would mean little if I failed to search back into my own schooling. But even then I couldn't weave a magic circle around what one calls education. My book thus reaches beyond my formal academic career both as student and teacher, voyaging from its beginning into memory of family, teachers, and acquaintances, movement, and anecdote. Attention to my past was interrupted by critical thoughts about the state of academic life; these thoughts I have not wanted to suppress. They appear mainly in the excursuses between certain chapters. I hope my remarks only once or twice descend into diatribe. In defense, I remind the reader that the distinguished philosopher A. N. Whitehead remarked that when he viewed the state of education it was difficult to suppress a savage rage.

In my writing, I found that a passage from W. B. Yeats's *A Vision* (about which I have written a book) lurked in my mind, perhaps as a reminder like a warning from Plato's daimon. Yeats wrote, "I have felt the convictions of a lifetime melt though at an age when the mind should be rigid, and others

1

take their place, and these in turn give way to others." This is, I hope, a good thing, for memoirs have sometimes a tendency toward nostalgia culminating in sour grapes.

*Hazard Adams • Seattle • Fall 2008*

# 1

# Cleveland: Hawken

**1.**

> Now the day is over
> Night is drawing nigh
> Shadows of the evening
> Steal across the sky.

These words floated to the back of the chapel where I sat among the third graders. The older boys were singing, led by the headmaster. Many times later I would join in to sing that hymn, always with the remembrance of that first moment at the Hawken School in a suburb of Cleveland, late in the day, clouds gathering in the great Georgian windows, like the shadows in the hymn. A Wordsworthian spot of time.

> Jesus, give the weary
> Calm and sweet repose.
> With thy tender blessing
> May our eyelids close.

That it was four o'clock and not nearly bedtime made no difference. It was an ending and a beginning. At class day that spring the primary grades were allowed to attend a ceremony in which, among other things, the name of the Head Boy for the year 1933–34 was to be revealed. The headmaster approached the plaque to his left and ceremoniously tore off a piece of paper covering what had recently and secretly been engraved there, announcing simultaneously the senior boy's name. There was applause, and the headmaster called for the passing of the classes.

I moved with my group of seven third-graders in single file to the just-

3

**Hawken School in the 1920s, the old campus under construction and completed.**

vacated pew of the fourth-graders. The seniors were now standing, facing the underclass students who had advanced into their vacated places. Later I would learn that they were not really seniors at all, the Great Depression, as it is now called, having caused Hawken in 1932 to eliminate the top two grades. But it would not have mattered, nor does it for my memory. For an eight-year-old it was a moment of magical solemnity. The chapel interior was one of calm New England church architecture, though with a large curtained stage, simply appointed, clean and white. It provided what must have been my first sense of the beautiful, though I then had no name for what I felt.

It was some years before I ever entered a church. There was a Lutheran church in South Euclid, the suburb of Cleveland where we lived, and what must have been a nondescript Methodist one that I only vaguely remember.

The Lutheran church had a tall, severe, gray-shingled steeple. I heard its bell on Sundays and sometimes when it tolled for a funeral. My grandmother one day explained to me what it was doing. Hawken chapel was all that I knew of religion. The ritual and the calendar of my life were principally those of the school, and my parents' lives as teachers there were part of it. I learned through repetition certain hymns sung at Hawken and then at Lakeside School in Seattle, where my father became headmaster. For me, they were poems, one, "The Recessional," was even by a famous poet, Kipling, who was in my parents' library. For me, it had a vague sense of spirituality, and its words appealed to conscience; I had no idea about "lesser breeds without the law," which passed beyond me. By the time I went to Princeton, just after World War II, compulsory chapel there had been abolished, at least for war veterans. I entered its huge Gothic chapel only once — to look around, a sight-seer more or less.

My parents and grandparents, as I knew them, did not attend church, though my parents had gone fairly regularly, I think, as children. A family story goes that in Richwood, Ohio, my father had transferred from the Presbyterians to the Methodists, or perhaps vice versa because most of the pretty girls were in one or the other, certainly a spirited decision if not exactly spiritual. My mother became as close to being an atheist as possible while still possessing a Calvinist conscience. Either it was a genetic inheritance or it was the result of compulsory attendance at the Presbyterian Church in Logan, Ohio. Perhaps both.

When we had moved to Seattle, my mother, perhaps in a moment of remorse of conscience, sent me to Sunday school at the Episcopal chapel in The Highlands, a gated community where some of Seattle's wealthiest bankers, lawyers, and lumber barons lived. Many of their children attended Lakeside. The Reverend Herbert Gowan, who possessed an impressive white beard and a kind demeanor, taught in a quasi–Socratic style from the Bible something I had never heard of and I could not later remember. The good little girls in attendance seemed able and anxious to answer promptly every question put. I hated their eagerness, correctness, and what seemed to me their clubby self-satisfaction. I informed my parents that I did not care to go back there, and the matter was never again mentioned.

My father was not irreligious. As headmaster at Lakeside, he frequently led the chapel service. Lakeside's chapel was then no more than a long study hall crammed with desks and a small stage at one end before the curtain of which was a lectern. There was nothing to evoke a feeling of the beautiful. My father's readings, especially of the letter of Paul to the Corinthians (I:13) made up for some of that, compelling my attention to the sound and rhythm of the words: "Though I speak with the tongues of men and of angels, and have not charity, I am become as sounding brass, or a tinkling cymbal."

**Hawken School, old campus circa 1930, in a Cleveland winter.**

My father read poetically in a strong voice with a flawless rhythm, characteristic of the poetry he wrote, and without pomposity. I suspect that the religiosity he possessed originated in his poetic sensibility and instinct for the drama of ritual, not the dogma of belief. My father never troubled me with dogmatic thought, and the prayer he apparently had invented for chapel was addressed not just to Jesus but also to "the prophets and saints of all time who trusted in truth, wisdom, and beauty and were not afraid." When I heard these words I thought of the books of poetry and philosophy in my parents' library and not the Biblical prophets, about whom I knew little. It all sounded, in retrospect, more like Plato than Paul. But in my father's act of delivery it was a poem. There was nothing hypocritical about this. My father entered fully and empathetically into the role he played.

Years later, I said idly to my mother, though perhaps with a desire to draw her, that I should have been taught more about the Bible and religion early on. By then I had learned that to read John Donne and William Blake, both of whom I worked on in college, I had to know the Bible. Perhaps defensively but with characteristic logic, she opined (reminding me first of my moment with Dr. Gowan) that I had learned about such matters in the better way, with my own intent and not the coercion insisting on belief. That was not exactly the way she put it, but that is what she meant.

Chapels at Lakeside were enlivened or occasionally deadened by the visit of a genuine Episcopal clergyman, usually Father Horne from The Highlands. We boys endured the sermons at these times with sullen contempt, but Father Horne must have thought us a lively and appreciative congregation. He was given to emitting loud whistles whenever he pronounced an "s." This is clearly a grave cross for a preacher to bear. His most frequent sibilances were, of course, "Jesssusss," followed closely by "Holy Ghossst," and finally "Give ussss thisss day..." and "tressspasssesss againssst usss." Fortunately, the last always came toward the end, preceded by breathless, excruciating anticipation among us boys, already on the verge of hysterical laughter. Those in the front row suffered the threat of the good Father's spit; luckily for them, he had the habit of turning his head to left or right at moments of emphasis, a word he seems not to have used, praise God.

This was not all. Father Horne had a favorite sermon topic the intent of which was to appeal to our youthful primitivism by identifying each apostle with an appropriate position on a heavenly football team. After locating everyone and placing St. Peter at the position of fullback, Father Horne reached the climax of his sermon by naming Jessssussss quarterback and eternal play-caller. We students responded with cheers, and he beamed from the stage's eminence. Then, everyone in good humor, we adjourned to the refectory for lunch.

I do not believe that my father ever witnessed these performances; he seemed to have retired to his office or elsewhere when Father Horne made his visits. I once later recounted the experience to him and to my mother, complete, of course, with as powerful whistles as I could summon. My father responded with appreciative glee, my mother with bemusement.

## 2.

"What is a church, and what is a theatre?" asked Blake rhetorically, implying similarity. The Hawken chapel with its large stage was the scene of dramatic presentations by the students of both the upper and lower schools. My father chose and directed at least one play annually, his major effort being a production of *Hamlet* in 1930–31. The importance of that undertaking was not lost on me, even though I was only four or maybe five years old and did not attend. At home I heard the names Shakespeare and Hamlet, mysterious names spoken with reverence, the mystery to my mind later intensified by a title among my father's books, *Bacon Is Shakespeare*. This sent me down a tunnel of porcine speculation at the end of which was darkness.

My father's *Hamlet* was, from probably biased accounts, a brilliant success, though marred or enhanced, according to your taste, by one notable first-night mishap. It occurred early in Act One and would have threatened serious disruption had not the audience been composed mainly of anxious parents. (I have reported this event briefly in another book, but it is worth repeating at greater length):

> Act I, scene ii:
> QUEEN: Good Hamlet, cast thy nighted color off,
>         And let thine eyes look like a friend on Denmark.

This came out as:

> Good Hamlet, cast thy colored nightie off.

It must have been difficult after that to recapture the audience's full attention. My mother reported a pause and not quite suppressed laughter. Yet Hamlet answered almost as if nothing untoward had occurred, uttering the line that followed ("Ay, madam, it is common") with a grim smile, not the moody sullenness usually intended. The product of a barely adequate effort to suppress laughter, the line provided an alternative gesture, entirely acceptable. By the time that Hamlet was alone on stage, the offending queen, played by a boy, of course, having exited, order reigned once again. Hamlet managed with what must have been deep conviction, "O, that this too too solid flesh would melt." Hamlet was played by Frederick Swetland, from a wealthy family that owned the Isle of Pines in the Caribbean until the Castro revolution. He had no more worry over money and no more responsibility than Hamlet appeared to have. My father later hired him at Lakeside, where he taught briefly, best remembered for throwing erasers at exasperating students, who promptly learned to raise the lids of their desks at the critical moments. During the school year he was ill for a time. An enterprising secretary some years his senior nursed him to health, married him, divorced him, and as far as I know lived well and happily ever after. He later lived a life of ease in Mexico with a second wife. The pedantic Polonius was played by George Armour Craig, who became a professor of English at Amherst and served for a while there as acting president. Ophelia was Peter Bellamy, descendant of the author of *Looking Backward*. In his own character he was a person of infinite jest, but by all reports a moving Ophelia in the mad scene:

> How should I your true love know
> From another one?

It is not excessive to declare that this play exerted a lasting influence on its participants, unless it was just good casting. I can think of nothing like it in my experience, though to this day I clearly remember the magical and frightening effect on me of two Lord Dunsany plays that my father directed, both at Hawken and later at Lakeside: *The Gods of the Mountain* and *A Night at an Inn*. In the first, the lasting scene is the appearance of the true gods, who with a simple communal gesture turn the impostor gods to stone statues.

**Hawken School, 1931, *Hamlet*, act one, scene three. Ophelia (Peter Bellamy) and Polonius (Armour Craig).**

I myself was in plays at school, and I recall them fairly well. These were the annual Christmas plays at Hawken and then Lakeside, performed by lower school students. I and a third-grade classmate named Weston Howell had miniscule roles in the first one I performed in. Not quite spear-carriers, we were pages carrying candles leading an opening procession of *The Siege Christmas,* a free variation on or addition to the Arthurian legend. It was written by one of my third-grade teachers, Hiram Haydn, later novelist, publisher, and editor of *The American Scholar*, author of the distinguished *Counter-Renaissance*. The play was somewhat revised, as I recall, by my mother. For me, the main event of the production was my case of stage fright just prior to the performance. Weston and I declared simultaneously that we would not go on. My memory image is that of Hiram Haydn crouching eye to eye with one of us, then the other, and patiently reasoning us out of our fear. We entered, the first actors to be seen, to enthusiastic applause, frightened still. Years later, I had lunch in New York with Hiram and casually mentioned the play. He hardly remembered it, or perhaps he was mildly embarrassed by the thought of it. Perhaps he worried that an old copy might turn up. I reminded him of my stage fright, but he recalled nothing.

The same play was performed a few years later at Lakeside, and I skip ahead to that. I was in the lead role of a young boy who performs some heroic act that I cannot remember. I do recall that the play was about King Arthur and the Knights of the Round Table, wooden swords and shields having been made in the shop by a talented maintenance man. For some time thereafter one of those swords perched desolately in my closet at home.

I remember better the play of the following year, written entirely by my mother. It involved Robin Hood and his Merry Men and was titled *A Stranger Comes to Sherwood Forest*. I had by then retired from my position as junior matinee idol and played the character role of Friar Tuck, to the disappointment of my mother, who had hoped I would try out for the lead. Because I was slight, I had to be generously padded out. I hadn't wanted to be Robin Hood. There were two reasons. I was the headmaster's son and embarrassed to think of standing out again, and the role of Robin Hood was a wooden one compared to that of the more interesting Friar, who had some amusing lines. Robin, it turned out, was played by Sam Savidge, whose father owned a big Chrysler agency in Seattle. Sam looked well in a Robin Hood hat and performed with a woodenness possibly construed by the audience as dignity. Years later I saw him resume his career on television, advertising Chryslers.

One of my best friends at the time was Stanley Osborn. In the play he was Young David of Doncaster, and the two of us had the stage to ourselves for a bit of dialogue that in every one of our rehearsals was a disaster. Stanley's performance repeatedly exasperated our director, Wilford A. Reaper, a teacher whose temper was well-known in lower-school circles and who had richly earned the title Grim. My mother must bear some responsibility in this matter, for she had written the lines that Stanley confronted heroically but with no success. In retrospect, I imagine that she or Reaper might better have decided to change them. They went:

> FRIAR TUCK (anticipating the appearance of the villainous Sheriff of Nottingham and his lackeys): Do you see anything as yet?
> DAVID: Only a flock of field fares flying over the hill.

This never came out right for Stanley. It was always a spoonerism: "Only a fock of field flares," "only a fock of flield fares," "only a field of fock flares," etc.

Through all the rehearsals we would wait in joyful anxiety for Stanley to approach and conquer this line. Through all the rehearsals he never once let us down. The whole cast would collapse in helpless laughter, wandering about holding our heads, falling and writhing on the stage floor, pounding on each other in glee. Despite the fear he had instilled in us, Reaper was unable to control what became an entirely predictable outbreak; one time he himself was infected by the laughter and joined us in lost composure.

On the night of the performance, there was the usual tension, heightened by the knowledge of what was at stake in the scene between David and the Friar. I prepared to face Stanley on the stage. I wore a tonsured wig and a brown habit with a belt of rope around my ample artificial girth. I held in my hand something like a crozier. Planted there, I observed Stanley approach from the wing, clad entirely in green with a feathered cap. Friar Tuck did not know what message he brought. I knew only too well.

In a show of breathlessness from running, far superior to anything he had accomplished in rehearsals, Stanley responded to me perfectly: "Only a flock of field fares flying over the hill." He swept his arm in an impressive arc in the direction of those fictional birds. I think it was in triumph.

Backstage I and others smothered him with congratulations as if he had just homered against the Yankees. He was laughing and declared that I had looked so odd to him that he had altogether forgotten the difficulty of the line.

When my mother died in 1995, I thought that I might find a copy of one or both of these plays in her papers. There was no sign of them. Perhaps they lie somewhere hidden away and forgotten in a file at Lakeside. For some reason, in my later years at Lakeside there were no plays for the older boys to perform. A pity.

## 3.

In the third grade and in the summer day camp at Hawken, there had been hide-and-seek, kick-the-can, red light, and treasure hunts in Mrs. Bolton's woods beyond the ample playing fields. She was a benefactor of Hawken, later a congresswoman. There were baseball games in which Weston Howell and I, by virtue of superior ability, were allowed to play with the older boys. And there was the Authors' Club. I had already written some poems, carefully preserved by my mother, and so was admitted to membership. In the following year, 1934–35, when I had moved to Seattle, a book of our work with the astonishing title *Prelude to Fame* was privately published under Hiram Haydn's editorship. I had five poems in it. One of them follows, showing, begging your reverence, the influence of Carl Sandburg, whom I had met on his trip to Seattle:

> Right here this street is lazy,
> It has no houses on it,
> But the wind, sighing in the trees,
> Says it has many houses.
> The wind has been farther than I have,
> He has seen many more houses,
> And he ought to know.

My mother had encouraged me to write poems and at bedtime had regularly read to me from Walter de la Mare's anthology *Come Hither*. I regard these moments as the most important and influential of my education, though for years I thought more about baseball than poetry. My favorite poets, in addition to Sandburg, whose collection *Early Moon* I knew intimately, were Blake, Hardy, and the Shakespeare of the songs. I remember third grade with affection. I had imaginative teachers, especially Haydn. There was the usual childish savagery, but it takes second place to better memories.

My very first experiences of school were not, however, so fortunate. The trouble began when my parents decided that I needed to be socialized and that I should attend the local kindergarten. A boy a little bigger, perhaps, and certainly tougher than I took an instant dislike to everything about me, especially my clothes (too neat) and my shyness in new surroundings. He regarded these as signals that I could and should be bullied. I was obliged to fight him daily on the playground to which we were let out as semi-domesticated puppies every mid-morning. I fared not too badly in these fights, though at heart I was certainly a pacifist. It was the verbal abuse that I found intolerable, and this may have inspired me to fight beyond what ability I had, if any. Though I was silent at home, my parents detected trouble. Their solution was to advance me at almost mid-year to the Hawken first grade, where the inestimable Miss Fannie M. Leuhrs valiantly coped with my steadfast refusal to grasp the principle of subtraction. Miss Leuhrs was a very good teacher of what we would now call the old school. She remarked to my mother, who taught second grade, that you could no longer spank the children when they acted up, but you could still sit them down hard in their chairs.

When I went to kindergarten, I had not been much around other children except for two little girls, Norma and Evelyn, who lived on either side of our house. My companions had been my Thurness grandparents, who had come to live with us and to take care of me while my parents were at work. My grandfather Thurness was a dignified, kind man of dark complexion and a thick mustache. I remember him as always wearing a dark gray suit with vest and watch chain. He kept in the vest pocket a small silver knife which he used to peel apples. We went on walks together in the afternoons. He was a soft touch for a nickel, easily maneuvered toward the local drug store and an ice cream cone. My other maneuver was to steer my grandfather around toward the local playground, where adult men were often playing baseball, many, I suppose, out of work. My grandfather liked baseball, and we would spend maybe two or three innings watching. Once a one-legged man played. I saw him single and run on one leg to first. Everybody cheered. In the mornings my grandfather often crossed the street to the fire station, there to play cards or just pass the time in conversation with the firemen. I sometimes went to watch, listen, and be near the two great fire engines. One day he returned with a small black puppy named Curly, my first dog. Whether he had won it or simply been offered it I do not know. Curly was succeeded by a young white collie named Victor (Vicky), who died a lingering death from distemper. In his illness, Vicky would deliberately inhale steam from the kind of steamer my parents had for relief from head colds.

Vicky had been given to us by a colleague of my parents, Clifford Bragdon, who wrote some short poems for me about animals. I don't recall the whole of any, but a few lines come to mind:

> The Giraffe, by heck,
> Is principally neck.

And

> O do not ridicule the pig
> Because his bottom is so big.
> 'Tis better to have more behind
> Than not enough before.

Or something like that. Vicky was succeeded by a fox terrier named Scali, full name Scaliwag. Poor Scali took to biting the postman and was sent to the country where he adjusted well to greater space.

My grandfather Thurness, my mother's father, had been mayor of Logan, Ohio. He was a strong Democrat, an admirer of William Jennings Bryan. He was the son of an immigrant tailor from Otweiler in the Saar region of Germany who had become sick of the warfare there. My great grandfather became very patriotic in his new country and influenced my grandfather to public service. My grandfather was partner in a haberdashery and took to people and politics with ease. Later, when walking with him in London, Ohio, where his oldest daughter Grace lived, he never failed to drop by the fire hall there, seeming already to know everyone, though we were but on a visit.

My grandfather had always been prominently present when dignitaries came through Logan. One of my mother's great disappointments as a small child was to discover that William Jennings Bryan did not actually have a silver tongue as her father had claimed. She was also dismayed to learn from a front row seat during Theodore Roosevelt's fiery oration that he spat. She was wearing a new white frock for the occasion. Free passes to the theater seemed to make up for her political disillusionments.

My grandfather Adams was entirely different. He had grown up on a farm in central Ohio near Richwood that had been homesteaded in about 1820 by his grandfather Hazzard Adams and continued by his father Simeon, who by all accounts was a stern moralist and active emancipationist. Hazzard Adams had come apparently from Connecticut and married in New Jersey a daughter of a veteran of the American Revolution. He seems to have covered his tracks quite well prior to marriage, as the family's efforts to trace back beyond him to his parents have failed. In the family mythological history he was the son of a Rhode Island Adams, who married a Hazzard. The history also claims that he was descended from one of two brothers who came from Wales via England, the other brother being ancestor of the famous American Adamses. Hazzard Adams must have revealed this, but whether it is true or not no one knows. My name should really be spelled Hazzard, but a mistake on my birth certificate, which I had quickly to present when I joined the Marine Corps in 1943, caused me to drop one of the Zs.

Another great grandfather on the Adams side was Hugh Perry, also a farmer, also a strong abolitionist who served briefly as an officer in the Civil War, but his regiment was never, I believe, in combat. The family had horses, and one of my great uncles, Henry, successfully raced a trotter named Jenny in the midwest and northeast. My uncle Hugh Perry Adams told of a visit to Henry when he was an old man. Henry had asked him to bring some good home-made whiskey from Kentucky, where my uncle, a career army officer, was stationed. Unable to locate any decent moonshine, he obtained an old hand-blown bottle and a cork, poured some legitimate Kentucky bourbon into it, and presented it. The old man said it was the only good whiskey he'd had in years. This had not prevented him from drinking a lot of the bad stuff.

Grandfather Adams never liked farming and either sold or lost the farm. He went into teaching for a while, invented the Adams Seeder, manufactured by a company in Galion, not much of a success, and was Union County recorder. Like his parents and in-laws, he was a strong Republican. Late in life, running for and losing by one vote an election for a county post, he declared publicly that he hadn't really wanted the job because the Democrats had things in such a hell of a mess. I have few clear remembrances of him. He was a baseball fan, and on July 31, 1932, I attended with him the first game ever played in Cleveland's Municipal Stadium, now torn down. As I recall it, the score was Philadelphia Athletics 1, Indians 0, Lefty Grove winning over Mel Harder. It was at the time the largest crowd ever to witness a baseball game, 80,284 fans. We were in the left-field bleachers, where I had a good view of Joe Vosmik and over in center my favorite player Earl Aver-ill. We were a long way from home plate. In those days deep center field was 450 feet from home. I see my grandfather in shirt sleeves; he is leaning slightly forward, concentrating on the game.

On one of his visits to us Grandfather Adams had an old Essex sedan, as did my parents at the time. My father referred so often to the "damned brakes" of ours that I thought that was what all brakes were called until my mother in a moment of public embarrassment came to understand why my language was as it was. My grandfather did not like his Essex any better than my father liked the brakes and applied the epithet to his whole car. It was his body language as he cranked the Essex as well as his verbal behavior that left me with the impression of his irascibility. This was not, according to my mother, an entirely mistaken judgment, though her word for him was "distant."

It was not long before his visit that my grandmother Adams died in Marysville and we traveled there for the funeral. I may have conflated this trip with another, but as I recall it we had at the time a large green Willys-Knight sedan which decided to demolish itself somewhere not very far south of Cleveland. This it did by leaving a trail of parts on the highway before rolling majestically to a stop. My father sold its shell for junk in the next town.

Of arrival in Marysville I recall only the following: My grandfather, dressed in a dark suit and high stiff white collar, met us at the door. Several people were present. He asked, "Would you like to see her?" We entered the front parlor, and I was lifted to peer over the side of the shiny black coffin. My grandmother, Nell Perry Adams, reposed there. I had known her, but not well.

It was a convenience on both sides that led to my Thurness grandparents living with us. I was taken care of during the day while my parents were at Hawken. My grandparents had a place to live at minimal expense on their very modest pensions. The arrangement, however, lingered on after I began my schooling, and I sometimes think this was one reason — to end it — that my father eventually took a job two thousand miles away. When we went to Seattle, my grandparents moved to London, where they would be near my Aunt Grace. I never saw my grandfather again. He died in his sleep on the evening of Franklin Roosevelt's overwhelming defeat of Alf Landon. He had gone to sleep a happy man.

My grandmother Thurness was very important to me. The worst thing about moving to Seattle was separation from her, to whom I was greatly devoted. In her nineties, when her mind began to fail, she had frightening hallucinations in which I was in danger. My best poems are about her. She cooked and kept our house. She stoked the coal in the furnace. We sat together in summer on rocking chairs in the screened porch, and she fanned herself.

Before Christmas each year she made a dark fruit cake and hid it. I would try to find it, but never did. My father once joined me in the search, but he too failed. Apparently she employed the purloined letter approach. We were presented the cake at Christmas well seasoned in brandy. In Logan she had been a member of the Women's Christian Temperance Union, one of the major social groups of the town, but in later years she kept a decanter of brandy at her bedside — for medicinal purposes, of course. She was given to certain expressions: "For goodness' sake," "Oh, pshaw!," "Don't be cross." She liked the word "provoke": "Now, don't provoke me" or "That is provoking." It was she who convinced me to go to school by pointing through our front window to a poor man rummaging in the garbage cans on the curb. "You'll have to be a tramp if you don't go to school." On the morrow I went with my parents to Hawken to face Miss Leuhrs and the mysteries of subtraction.

## 4.

It seems as if it was always summer in Cleveland because my remembrances center on events of that season. Certainly it wasn't, for Cleveland winters were bitterly cold, often canceling much of Hawken's football season. I remember summers partly because I was interested in baseball from a very early age. Both pairs of grandparents were present when Joe Cronin's Washington Senators were in the World Series. We listened to the games on the radio. A good thing, too, because my parents were thereby able to keep my grandfathers, who were of opposing parties, from debating politics for those hours at least. Every early evening in the summer, Tom Manning would come on the air and in about half an hour narrate the whole of that afternoon's ball game. My father and I would go to League Park to watch the Indians. I saw Babe Ruth hit a home run there. I remember Willis Hudlin warming up and my father saying Hudlin had good stuff but was wild. This proved to be true.

My father once played a game in League Park. He had been a catcher at Richwood High School and later played on some semi-pro teams. He was a good hitter. The *Richwood Gazette* reported his many hitting feats, including a tremendous game-winning blow by Stub Adams to defeat Mansfield. I remember throwing curve balls to him one summer when I was in high school. He murdered them, but by that time he didn't get around too well on the fast ball. He told me of a game after which his team had to leave the field through an outfield gate, under threat by opposing fans who were angry about the umpiring.

In games with my father and uncle in the vacant lot next door to our house I pretended I was Earl Averill. My father had taught me to bat left-handed like Averill on the ground that I would be a step nearer to first base and would have some advantage since most pitchers were right-handers. One day I hit a ball over the hedge into our backyard and proceeded to trot slowly around the bases as I had seen Averill do. My uncle ragged me at once and for days thereafter, claiming that my homer had been a foul ball. I had some doubts when I hit it, but I was determined to do the trot. My uncle was living in our made-over attic, out of a job or in and out of jobs during the depression. My parents had the only steady work in the family.

One spring my mother and grandmother planted a small vegetable garden in the vacant lot. I think this was to have been part of my education. Unfortunately, it was located in our infield. Though I was interested in the growing vegetables, especially the carrots and radishes, I resented that our ball games were postponed until later in the summer.

Summers were hot and humid in Cleveland. My father liked to work in the backyard gardening. One July day, he observed me staring at the chimney of our two-storied house. He asked me what I saw up there, and I replied that Santa Claus could not possibly get down that chimney. Under pressure, my father admitted that there was no Santa Claus. I was three or four years old at the time.

By the time that I was about seven the Essex was gone, replaced by a box-like 1926 two-door Pierce-Arrow, about as wide as it was long. I was greatly enamored of it because of its sloping lights on the front fenders and the shades one could draw over the back windows. It was a gas hog, and its electrical system was sometimes of a hypothetical character. Hiram Haydn had at the same time a quite splendid old Cadillac sedan with a spotlight. Grander in appearance than our car, it nevertheless had similar shortcomings. Hiram's *bête noir* at Hawken was the shop teacher Elmer Sipple, whom he held in arrogant intellectual contempt and with whom he once came to fisticuffs on the wet weather playfield. Sipple had a genuinely new car, of which he was quite proud. One day, to Hiram's great embarrassment, Sipple's car had to be called on to push both Hiram's and then my father's to get them started on the way home from school.

Hiram and my father had a friendly intellectual rivalry, Hiram the fastidious aesthete and scholar, my father the ebullient poetic personality. Hiram's car played a supporting role in an event that years later he took great pleasure in recounting to me. He and my father found themselves late in the day at Hawken engaged in a typical dispute: Who was the more egocentric? After various proofs had been offered on both sides my father departed. Shortly thereafter, Hiram found me disconsolately approaching him in a school corridor, searching for my father, who was to have taken me home with him. Hiram ushered me into his Cadillac and proceeded in triumph to our house.

Among my mother's papers is a playlet written by an anonymous Hawken faculty member. It is entitled *Simlet: Prince of Remark* (my father, who was Robert, went by his middle name of Simeon, shortened to Sim) and was apparently written for a party that seems to have followed his production of *Hamlet*. I quote briefly from it:

> Enter Simlet in Night robe and his train.
> FAMILIA: Sim, my lord,
>> How goes it on this happy, happy day?
> SIMLET: Define your terms.
> FAMILIA: How so? Upon this day?
>> Wilt thou not ease just one sole day the year
>> Thy straining intellect, slough off just once
>> The slush and quaggy adipose of fact
>> Encrusting it? Oh, come, my lord, sweet chuck,
>> See, there's a buss o' the beezer for thee.
>> What say'st thou now?
> SIMLET: Well, now, of course....
> FAMILIA: Marry, my lord! Of course?
> SIMLET: Why, yes, of course. That is to say, ahem,
>> As Spengler hath in his Decline and Fall....
> FAMILIA: Oh, would he had declined and fall'n indeed!
> SIMLET: As Spengler saith, this holiday, this feast,
>> This little play for school boys, pedagogues,
>> And wives — this day when all the world entire,
>> Like to a mob that scrambles for the dimes
>> O' the rich, froths in ecstasy
>> For candy, novels, fancy socks and ties,
>> Forgetting quite the reason in the day —
>> This feast, I say ... I say, this feast ... uh ... uh...
>> A murrain on thee, girl, thou halt'st my mind
>> With my meanderings.

And so on.

My father tended to hold the stage. After his death, John Carney, the former Hawken headmaster, said to me that he was a true Celt: ebullient with an emotional attachment to thought.

The Pierce-Arrow was not a thing of beauty, nor was it to be a joy forever. It took a distant aesthetic second to Hiram's Cadillac, but we loved it. It was deemed, however, unfit to attempt the trip to Seattle. My parents sold it in June of 1934 to a man who intended to convert it into a delivery truck. As he drove it away we all stood on the front porch and cried.

# 2

# Seattle: Where's the Lake?
# Lakeside 1

## 1.

My father was discouraged by what was happening to Hawken School. In 1926–27 the enrollment had been 130. In his last year, 1933–34, the depression and a decision to cut the two top grades had left the school with only 70 students. In spite of its excellent faculty, Hawken had become a less attractive place to teach. Also, headmaster John Carney, a delightful man and good friend, had been invited to resign. My father was not impressed by his replacement and put his name in at the Albert Teachers' Agency in Chicago. He had managed a master's degree in history at Western Reserve in his spare time. A boys' school named Lakeside in Seattle needed a new headmaster and showed interest. Unlike Hawken, it was partly a boarding school and still had the eleventh and twelfth grades, though not grades one through four. It, too, had suffered from the depression, as my father soon learned.

Years later, my mother told me that on the return train trip (of five days' duration, then) from his interview, my father met George Humphrey, father of one of his students and later Secretary of the Treasury under Eisenhower. Humphrey told him that in all his experience the Seattle bankers and businessmen were the most callous and ruthless he knew. It was clear that among these people were members of the board of trustees of Lakeside. More of that later. My father took the job. One board member whom he particularly liked was Frederick M. Padelford, Dean of the College of Arts and Sciences at the University of Washington and a scholar of Edmund Spenser's poetry. My

19

father believed, probably rightly, that Padelford's influence won him the job. We prepared to move to Seattle.

I had heard of Seattle only through the comic strip *Joe Palooka*, which appeared in one of the Cleveland newspapers. Knobby Walsh, Joe's manager, arranged a fight for him in Seattle, a name I thought was pronounced "See-tul." The house in South Euclid was put on the market. It did not sell. Some time after our move, not having been able to sell it and unable to rent it for a decent return, my parents could not afford, and ceased to pay, the mortgage. It was repossessed. Earlier, the bank where they had a checking account had failed and they had lost all the money in it. Nevertheless, they were able to put a down payment on a 1934 Ford two-door. My grandparents moved to London, Ohio. I accompanied my grandmother on that trip, but I remember only her tears as we left the railroad terminal in Cleveland, nothing of the trip itself or of the time I spent in London before we set out for the West Coast. Nor do I particularly remember any fear about the future or regret at leaving Cleveland. Well, one small one. I hated leaving the Indians, but soon learned that Earl Averill came from a town near Seattle. He was called the Earl of Snohomish, and the Seattle baseball team was also the Indians.

My first remembrance of the trip itself is the Sherman Hotel in Chicago, the first I ever stayed in. My parents went down to the College Inn to watch and hear Fats Waller play. We had taken the train from Columbus. The Ford was to be driven west by my uncle, Bernard Thurness, emancipated from living in our attic, but from whom my parents were not to be freed for some time. He was nicknamed Ike, his middle name being Eichor for his grandfather, a farmer in Vinton County who at a relatively young age was, along with his horse, killed by lightning. Ike had been a successful salesman of furnaces and equipment but quit in a huff when told in 1929 that he had to go on the road. He didn't hold another job successfully until my father helped him land one in Seattle, and that didn't last long. In the last year or two in Cleveland he had married and quickly divorced, my father being the go-between in a nasty proceeding. My mother's sister Hazel lived also in Cleveland, married to a man who had an engineering degree from Cornell but was lured into bond sales for the big money and was subsequently wiped out in 1929. Uncle Gene became, or perhaps was always, alcoholic. My aunt kept them alive as a buyer of women's apparel for a department store. She had a good eye for fashion and was herself appropriately handsome, but she was without detectable common sense. Gene's one great talent, which survived his financial setbacks, was golf. When I was about twenty, visiting in Cleveland, Gene, Ike, and I played a round, Gene taking along only three clubs, which he carried in his fist; and he shot 80. Ike took this only fairly well. I was impressed.

The train trip to Seattle was long and slow, longer even than my father's, because to save money we went by way of Canada. Lakeside's largess was not great, and my mother would not be teaching, so the family income would diminish, though the school provided a house on the campus. The Canadian Pacific Railway wanders through the Rockies, as it did then. But then there were open, screened observation cars, from which one saw the impressive mountains and suffered the cinders from the steam locomotive. My mother was a terrible traveler, suffering all her life from an inner ear problem. She spent most of the trip in her berth. My father, on the other hand, was a spirited traveler and enjoyed everything. In World War I he had easily survived the North Sea on the U.S.S. *Arkansas* and the *Aeolus*.

Our first view of Seattle was spectacular. We came from Vancouver, B.C., by the steamer *Princess Marguerite* (later converted to a troop ship and sunk by a German submarine in World War II). Our arrival was in the evening. We had seen the sun set behind the Olympic Mountains, and the lights were shining from buildings in the city. A big sign that said "Port of Seattle" stretched along a pier. Atop a building was a huge Mobil Oil flying red horse and another saying Union 76. There was the smell of salt water mixed with creosote from the pilings, and oil in the water. Seattle was much smaller then than now, and it was long before the tall buildings were built. At the time the tallest, still standing today but now dwarfed, was the L. C. Smith Tower, the tallest building west of the Mississippi when erected. The view at night was magical for me.

On the next morning we were driven to the Lakeside campus north of the city limits. I now wonder what my mother must have thought and whether my father had sufficiently prepared her. The move to Seattle took both of them from origins and family. It cut them off from close friends on the Hawken faculty, which included some very interesting and talented people. The sight that greeted my mother could not have been encouraging. Over the subsequent years, my parents did not find academic friends like those at Hawken and made most of their friends beyond their new school. Partly, I suppose, this was because my father, being the headmaster, was viewed with a certain distance. Both I and my older son, both of us having been in academic administration for a time, have noticed how differently one is viewed even by friends when one becomes an administrator. Also, when young and working together, discussing with colleagues the immediate day-to-day problems of teaching, teachers make friends more easily, partly out of desire for security.

I think the move was less difficult for me than for my parents. An only child, I was not a stranger to being alone and do not remember suddenly being bereft of friends. The move may have enforced an ability or perhaps a tendency to live a sort of detachment when necessary. It was not exactly a quality lacking among the preceding Adamses.

The Lakeside School had been founded in 1919 by a man named Frank

Lakeside School circa 1934, as it looked on the Adamses' arrival. (Courtesy of the Jane Carlson Williams '60 Archives, Lakeside School.)

Moran, shortly to leave it and found another school that eventually failed. The original site was in Seattle in a wealthy residential district on the shore of Lake Washington. The original building had been a house. Later there was a move slightly inland to new frame buildings. The campus was small and constricted by the density of residences around it. Sometime in 1930, the Board of Trustees decided to move again. The proposed new site was also on the lake in what was then an area north of the city. But it was decided that this site was inappropriate, the reason given that it was dangerous to the boys to be on a lakefront. Someone might drown. Or so the story goes. Today this site, in what is now called Windermere, is some of the most valuable property in the city, which eventually expanded its boundaries to include it.

The Lakeside School became landlocked eight miles north of downtown in a totally undistinguished area of logged-off land, gravel roads, and occasional small houses. Between the campus and a public golf course lay a swamp, now covered over by Interstate 5. To the immediate north was an apple orchard and beyond that a hillside of burnt-out stumps. To the south was a hilly area into which several people had driven and abandoned their old Model Ts. Across the gravel road at the entrance to the school campus was its gray rural

Lakeside School, 1999, the Head's house to the far right. (©Soundview Aerial. Courtesy of the Jane Carlson Williams '60 Archives, Lakeside School.)

mailbox. On it someone had scrawled "Puddleside School for Pups." It was one of the first things my mother and I noticed. Seventy years later the current head (no longer headmaster) of Lakeside told me the first thing he asked when he came to the campus was, "Where's the lake?" It was a question I had already heard many times.

I have often wondered who profited from the sale of this forlorn twenty-five acres to Lakeside. Some member of the board of trustees? A friend? Someone with whom George Humphrey had done or tried to do business?

The sight that greeted my mother could not have been very encouraging to her. The campus, except for two tall fir trees, was nearly without vegetation. The driveways were of gravel and dirt. Five Georgian-colonial buildings in the style of New England prep schools stood starkly on the formerly logged-off land. Four of the buildings fringed a large grassed quadrangle adjacent to a dirt football field with a weedy running track. To the north were two unkempt tennis courts. To the south the headmaster's house was separated from the other buildings by a ravine with scrubby trees.

The house turned out to be large and drafty, and we soon learned that it emitted an odd assortment of creaking noises when the wind blew and sometimes when it did not. My uncle Ike, there alone one night when my parents and I were away, armed himself with my baseball bat and prowled the house searching for an intruder, nothing but the wind or the soul of the house itself.

My parents and I spent only one night in the now demolished Benjamin Franklin Hotel downtown, because we didn't have the money to stay longer. Our furniture had not arrived, so we borrowed mattresses from the school's dormitory and moved into the headmaster's house. The house was large by any standard known to us. At the top was a maid's bedroom and bath and an attic space. On the second floor were six bedrooms, three baths, and a dressing room. The first floor had a front hall, a large living room, a study, a dining room, pantry, and kitchen. There were three basement rooms and a two-car garage. Our furniture could not fill more than a part of this space, and we couldn't afford a refrigerator. My mother utilized a large closet cooler that had two screened air passages to the outside. One day she was startled by (and startled) an enterprising mountain beaver that had gnawed through one of the screens and was investigating the contents. These animals were common around Lakeside, and later on our dogs made a practice of hunting them and proudly presenting them on our doorstep. In the first couple of years at Lakeside we could hear coyotes howling somewhere in the desolate land to the north.

Private secondary educational institutions were not a common thing circa 1934 in the Pacific Northwest. Except for the parochial schools and a couple of undistinguished military academies, there were no boys' private schools. Seattle had two private girls' schools and Tacoma one. Seattle was a blue-collar town built on logging and the maritime trades. It was highly unionized and delivered Democratic majorities. In the region, private schools were looked on with suspicion as places for the spoiled rich sons of bankers, lawyers, and businessmen with a sprinkling of so-called problem children sentenced to boarding school. This was, I suppose, true enough. In any case, the depression had reduced drastically the number of students enrolled. Early in July of 1934, my father arrived to learn that only a meager twenty-five families had renewed registration for the coming school year. In the new blue Ford that my uncle had driven west, my father traveled the state and part of Oregon that summer to recruit students. To my knowledge he had no experience in recruitment, but he was energetic and charismatic. At age thirty-seven he had accumulated enough experience teaching boys of almost all ages to know how to impress them without distancing himself. He was very good with parents, both men and women. He had published poems. There was absolutely nothing effete or schoolmasterish about him. He could talk sports enthusiastically with the fathers and charm the mothers. He understood farms and small towns. He was a navy veteran.

That summer my father talked into re-enrolling their sons more than a dozen parents, from the past year, who had apparently decided against it. He convinced parents in Spokane, Yakima, Grandview, Wenatchee and elsewhere that their sons would profit from Lakeside, receive the proper training for college, and get ahead (or stay ahead) in life. He sold the liberal arts, sciences, and high culture to people who had little of it in their lives but came to understand that they would really like it for their children. He did not sell social development and detested what was then known as progressive education. He was deeply skeptical of John Dewey, whom he had thoroughly read, and he had little or no use for colleges of education. In September, the school opened miraculously with 75 students and increased to 150 in five years. I do not think it too much to say that my father's tireless recruiting in those first years saved Lakeside, but it was many years after his sudden death in 1950 that the Board of Trustees decided to name something for him, an academic scholarship that usually goes to a minority student. This was more appropriate than they knew, for years before he had endeavored to enroll a student of Chinese ancestry and was told by the Board that it would be at the cost of his job.

## 2.

I learned that for a year I would not attend Lakeside, which began in the fifth grade. I was to be sent to the Helen Bush School. This was not the most pleasant, but neither was it an intolerable experience. The school occupied the former Lakeside campus. It was coeducational through grade four or five, but then it was entirely for girls. Of the two private girls' schools in Seattle (the other being St. Nicholas), it was regarded as less staid and reactionary. Its upper-school girls were regarded as more free-spirited, perhaps even less corrigible. This was, I think, a direct reflection of the two headmistresses, the dour Miss Fannie Steele at St. Nick and the flamboyant and entrepreneurial Mrs. Bush, who seemed always in a hurry when I saw her in the hall.

My father kidded me about being sent to "the bush leagues" for seasoning. I was irritated but had to laugh, which irritated me more. The fact was that my father and mother had, in a sense, gone to the bush leagues too. Seattle was really a small, provincial town at the time. The Cleveland that they had left was not yet the one in which the economy went dead and the Cuyahoga River caught fire. Cleveland had a history of great wealth, a splendid art museum, and a distinguished symphony orchestra and hall. Royal

Brougham, sports editor of the *Seattle Post-Intelligencer*, referred to Seattle affectionately as a little sawmill town. For some mysterious reason, Sir Thomas Beecham was for a short time director of the Seattle Symphony and became known for stopping a rendition, facing the audience, and shouting, "Look what they give me for a trumpet player!" Before going away unlamented, he referred to Seattle as a "cultural desert." The Seattle Art Museum, the creation of one man, Richard Fuller, had in its pleasant Art Deco building things from his own assortment of Asian artifacts, principally a collection of snuff bottles. There was a repertory theater, but not nearly up to the one in Cleveland. Not too many years later the founders, who were the proprietors and principal actors, were run out of town under accusation of being communists. Perhaps Seattle's most interesting aspect was its labor history. Over the years it had been the scene of violent strikes.

Then there was the baseball team, the Seattle Indians, who got progressively worse from our arrival until their rescue by a local beer baron. The Indians played on a dirt field known as Civic Stadium. Outfielders had to dodge the tall wooden poles that held the night lights. In 1938 Emil Sick, proprietor of the Rainier Brewing and Malting Company, purchased the Indians from a tightwad named Bill Klepper, changed their name to the Rainiers not long after people had begun calling the team the Sick Indians. Of course, later the sportswriters nicknamed them the Suds. Emil Sick built a new stadium and fielded a winning team right away. Even my father enjoyed watching, though he preferred to attend double headers asserting that there had to be two Rainiers games to equal one Cleveland Indians game. Once, looking around the stadium he observed the fans and declared that there had been "a spontaneous generation of idiots." He didn't live to see the crowds at a Seattle Seahawks professional football game.

My experience at Bush School was characterized by continued incompetence in arithmetic, regarded as dullness coupled with moral laxity by the truly disagreeable Miss Fox. Luckily I had other classes that I found stimulating, especially social science, or whatever it was called, which was mainly forays into the history and art of far-away places. My memory of specific information I ingested at the time is, however, nil; but I believe I was not harmed and perhaps even prepared to gain from an expert teacher of the subject later at Lakeside.

In addition to my daily arithmetic class, I had another notable humiliation at Bush, but one that I learned from. It was brought about entirely by myself. Athletics at Bush were presided over by women and reflected their interests. This meant, among other things, that there was no baseball, either hard or soft. I must have brooded about this or resented not being able to show my prowess in the sport. I got the idea that we of the lower grades, composed partly of boys, should challenge the older girls to a game. This was utter foolishness, but it *was*, as we say, a learning experience. We were, of course, soundly beaten. I had no conception of girls of any age playing baseball, and my team was composed of boys who did not know how to play, boys who did not care to play, boys incapable of concentrating from pitch to pitch, and some who failed to anticipate that these girls could *hit*. I was one of these last. My managerial career ended almost as soon as it had begun, the game being called after a rally by the girls that threatened to go on forever. I had always respected the older women I knew. I now respected those Amazons from the upper grades, gracious in victory.

## 3.

When my uncle Ike arrived from Detroit, where he had picked up our new car, he needed a job. It fell to my father to help him. My uncle was a charming fellow when moved to be so, but intervening in the search was, for my father, something of a risk. My father had met Nellie Cornish, the founder of what is now the Cornish College of the Arts. Like most institutions at the time, it was on the ropes, hit harder even than Lakeside. At the time, it was seeking a business manager. Miss Cornish was hardly systematic or even careful with the resources she did have. One might say that she had run the school directly out of what she managed to entice into her purse, and she liked it that way. There was little record of input and output, though more of the latter than the former. So, though the school needed a business manager, Miss Cornish did not really want one. My uncle got the job, but he was regarded by the proprietor as a sort of interloper, perhaps a stern judge, and above all a snooper. When my uncle tried to bring some order to the books he was summarily dismissed. He returned to Cleveland, but came back to Seattle a few years later. Finally, World War II rescued him, and he had a brief career in the Office of Price Administration in Washington, D.C., returning there during the Korean War just in time to avoid financial disaster. Between wars he had decided to market his invention of a device that was clipped over a car visor to hold various objects — the Auto Park-It. Cashing in his accumulated retirement funds, he spent everything on this invention. It failed, of course, partly but by no means entirely because a large company began to market and successfully sell a similar item. Grumbling about patent got him nowhere. After Korea, to the great relief of my parents, he married a reasonably well-off divorcee who worked for Standard Oil of Ohio. After her retirement, they spent their days changing their minds about where to live, moving from California to Florida and back a couple of times. My uncle thrived on his wife's retirement and lived to be ninety-six.

## 4.

Lakeside had gained something of a reputation in 1929 because one of its students competed in an examination to determine the nation's "exceptional boy." As it turned out the Lakesider won the competition and was described as "the smartest boy in America." It was, in any case, not a bad piece of publicity. Indeed, the school did enjoy an increase in enrollment in 1929, but then the depression brought a sudden decline just as the new campus was being constructed. The headmaster preceding my father was Theophilus R. Hyde, about whom there is little information in the Lakeside archives. A shadowy figure, therefore, he seems to have resigned suddenly in mid-year of 1933–34. Subsequently he became head of a school in southern California. I never heard my parents or anyone else talk about him.

Sometime in the summer of 1934 another event of quite different significance occurred at Lakeside. One day a boy of sixteen rang our doorbell and introduced himself as Charles Bechtol. He came, he said, from a small rural community called Redmond to the east, no more than a crossroads. He wanted to come to Lakeside. He explained that his father had a drug store in Redmond but that his family could not afford the tuition. He wanted to play football, and Redmond High School had no team. He would work for his tuition and board.

Well, Lakeside was certainly not overflowing with students. My father was himself a fierce competitor and liked school athletics. He had coached in central Ohio and at Hawken. He'd been an all-league high-school fullback. Charles Bechtol was a fullback. My father sized him up and took him on. To my knowledge, Charles Bechtol became Lakeside's first athletic scholarship student. It wasn't a mistake. He was a better than average student, a powerful runner, passer, and blocker, a talented basketball player, and eventually holder of four Lakeside track and field records. He later captained the University of Washington football team.

In some quarters of the Pacific Northwest, any private school was regarded either as a reform school or a place for sissies. This reputation my father decided not to tolerate. Charles Bechtol's matriculation signaled the beginning of a period of four years in which Lakeside football excelled, mainly through the deliberate recruitment of good athletes. Then, the mission apparently accomplished, no more, or very few, athletic scholarships were offered.

In the beginning it was not always easy for the Lakeside Wolverines to win. In the first game of 1934, played at Poulsbo High School (now called North Kitsap), Lakeside was defeated 6–0, a twenty-yard pass play resulting in a touchdown being called back because the Lakeside halfback allegedly had his knee on the ground when he passed the ball. There were some local referees who clearly favored the public high schools, and there were no other private schools to play. I remember my father's pride when one of the Seattle papers that year featured an article about the team captioned "Only Sixteen Men But They Win." Lakeside had a few more players than that, but by late in the season injuries had taken their toll. I had known nothing of football, but I became a rabid fan of a sport I later did not really like to play; and I regarded Charles Bechtol as a heroic figure, along with two senior boys who came in 1935. Joe Dubsky and Harry Bird were imported from Chicago by a wealthy University of Washington booster and farmed out to Lakeside for a year. The dormitory was full as a result of my father's efforts, and they lived in our house. I remember Harry singing "The Music Goes Round and Round" as he cleaned up in the refectory after a meal, working off his scholarship. Both ended up on the same team with Bechtol at Washington, and Harry Bird later coached football at Lakeside for a time. In 1934, the team lost only once after the Poulsbo fiasco, and in 1935 the team was unscored on by any high-school team, holding the University of Washington freshmen to a tie and losing, mainly because of key injuries, to the Whitman College second team. On the sports pages favorable publicity came to Lakeside, but not as the Wolverines. Sometime late in 1935, by vote of the student council, the Wolverines became the Lions. I have often suspected that the Wolverine name was intolerable to my father, a staunch Ohio State man, whose eyes tended to glaze over when he heard "Across the Field" or "Carmen Ohio" during radio broadcasts of Ohio State games. Michigan players were Wolverines.

In the spring of 1935, *The Lakeside Tatler*, the student newspaper established just after my father's arrival, published an issue devoted entirely to vignettes of all the faculty members. My father's vignette, entitled "The Head is Red," declared, "[He] is to be counted among those few that have enjoyed a liberal education and remained real."


## 5.

I accomplished or rather survived the year at Bush and entered Lakeside in the autumn of 1935 after another summer in the country north of Seattle. There were hardly any children around. On campus was John Lambert, son of the mathematics teacher, later and still a close friend; but he was four years younger than I. My nearest playmate of closer age was at least a quarter mile away on the dirt road that skirted to the south the Jackson Park Golf Course. He was the son of a Lakeside janitor, a year older than I, and physically more advanced. One of his three older sisters lived with us for a while in the third-floor domestic's quarter and was a sort of maid when not in high school. Theirs was a badly depression-scarred family. As I saw myself in relation to most of the Lakeside boys, so they must have seen themselves in relation to me. Their house was a ramshackle shelter reminding me now of pictures I have seen of southern share-croppers' places. They had a cow named Bessie that my friend milked, some chickens, and a dog named Gypsy, who was one of five born to our collie Queen. Queen was a present I had engineered in return for cheerful acquiescence in the move to Seattle. Her previous owner, proprietor of a collie farm, declared that Queen steadfastly refused to allow male collies to breed with her and had never barked. Freed from the farm, she was soon seduced by what seems to have been a large German shepherd and produced five pups. She even began to bark on occasion, though once when I walked in my sleep she roused my parents not by barking but by insistent nosing and whining. I was found at an open upstairs window. We kept one of the pups, Chinook, a splendidly intelligent animal.

On the edge of the golf course my friend's parents had built a small one-room shack from which they sold pop and candy bars. They also collected money from golfers who had driven balls onto their property and wanted them back. No golfer was going to venture beyond their wire fence, past which was Bessie's pasture. Gypsy seemed to stand guard there, but she was really a pacifist. The father was a tall, raw-boned man of a seemingly irascible disposition; I now think he was angered at the fate of himself and his family.

My friend, whom I remember as always in good humor, became an expert golfer. On occasion in the twilight he and I would sneak over to the course and play a few holes out of sight of the clubhouse. I was a poor golfer, but he tolerated my incompetence. He and his siblings pulled themselves up out of their parents' poverty. I saw him many years later on the University of Washington campus, where he was a student leaving an English class. We spoke but briefly, being by then virtual strangers.

Mary Thurness Adams (1902–1995), the author's mother, circa 1947.

# 5.

In a *Lakeside Tatler* for the autumn of 1937, there is a picture of the headmaster's wife, Mary Thurness Adams, my mother. She is seated, her head turned to face the camera as if she were taking the measure of the photographer. Before her on a table is something that looks like a large white cake. She is not quite thirty-five years of age. Her dark hair is parted in the middle and fluffed out. It reaches barely to the collar of her blouse. She is not smiling. For a moment, she is a stranger, a mystery. When we have not seen someone for a long time, we are at first struck by change, but then we adjust and things seem as they have always been. The person we knew has become the person we now know and somehow always has been. My last remembrances of my mother had taken precedence in my visual imagination over the young woman in the picture. I stare at that picture and my visual remembrance is gradually renewed. This young woman, born in late fall of 1902 in Logan, Ohio, will be suddenly widowed in 1950. I recognize her in the picture as a woman of strong intellect and straightforward honesty. She is a bit of an aesthete, though not so much of one as to interfere with a certain practicality of intent and irritation at pretension. She is given to assertions such as "Oh, for God's sake," which she is likely to utter against all mendacity and just plain stupidity. She will, after terrible grief, gather together a new life from what is left of the old, begin a new career, make a new set of friends, and eventually retire. She will live until 1995, the same person in the picture, after all.

# 3

# Lakeside 2

### 1.

In 1937, the last Lakeside football team for which scholarship students were actively recruited completed an undefeated season, winning over, among others, the champions of Portland, Oregon, and the champions of the Hawaiian Islands. The game with McKinley of Honolulu was played in the University of Washington stadium, which between the thirty-yard lines had been churned into mud. Perhaps the field had also been deliberately watered earlier for the USC game, a not uncommon occurrence. The coach at Lakeside was Leslie Wilkins, who had played under the famous Jock Sutherland at the University of Pittsburgh. Wilkins liked to tell of his sudden reassignment from center to end after he had centered the ball over the goal posts.

Lakeside was in a way transformed by four years of football climaxed by the McKinley win. There were no more accusations that Lakesiders were sissies. As for scholarships, I think my father decided that enough was enough, and among some high-school coaches there had begun to be talk of mercenaries. When I have visited the chapel at Lakeside, I have stopped to view the memorial plaque honoring students killed in World War II. Four of them had played on those teams. They had been heroic figures to us seventh graders, and I remember all of them as good people.

### 2.

Eccentricity is often a sign of a good teacher, or perhaps it is the other way around: good teaching is often a sign of eccentricity. The latter is the more dependable guide, though not infallible, for many eccentrics, unable to control adolescent behavior, have been driven out of the classroom. My Lakeside experience certainly led me to identify eccentricity with good teaching. The first eccentric to impress me, evoking both awe and intellectual influence, was a willowy, prissy man named William Henry Eller. He had studied at Wisconsin and Berlin and possessed a doctorate. His dissertation on Henrik Ibsen, undistinguished in my later view, was published according to the manner of the time. He was always referred to and addressed as Dr. Eller. He was to us, I should say, a wizard of nearly mythological proportions. Given a long white beard, wand, and conical cap, he could have performed a significant role in *Lord of the Rings*.

William Henry Eller had been reared by a widowed mother who taught him to weave, sew, garden, and cook. Beyond mastery of these arts, he was a builder of hand looms (one for my mother that I learned to operate), a meteorologist, a teacher of how to construct giant relief maps of the continents, a hypnotist, a believer in and practitioner of mental telepathy and other occult sciences, an expert gardener, specializing in roses, a talented musician, and a painter. Indeed, he believed that he had been in unconscious communion with William Blake, revealed by the presence of certain "wiry bounding lines" in his own work similar to some in Blake's. His paintings were generally given to display of sylph-like figures in filmy dress only a little, if at all, like some of Blake's. Eller was also a reasonably prolific (and I believe unpublished) bad poet who brought over into English with dire results a nineteenth-century German style. These he occasionally inflicted on my mother, who had to comment on them.

Eller taught what was officially called social science from the fifth through the eighth grades. We called it "sock si." In fact, it was universal history as Eller saw it from the so-called cave dwellers through the Renaissance and somewhat beyond. The subject matter ranged through mythology, art, music, sport, geography, climate, and the weather, as well as the daily life of people and exploits of heroes, both mythological and historical, and tyrants. Eller taught all the way from high culture to how people in the streets actually lived, and of course he knew everything, invoking his universal expertise at appropriate moments.

The textbook that Eller used was the multivolume *A Picturesque Tale of Progress* by Olive Beaupré Miller, which I believe was popular at the time in many prep schools. I still possess all of the volumes. Today, reading through the one covering early Crete to the exploits of Alexander the Great, I am reminded of a passage in a prose poem by John Ashbery, musing over his impression of a movie seen as a child and again as an adult:

> Years later I saw it when I was grown up and thought it was awful. How could I have been wrong the first time? I knew it wasn't inexperience, because I was

experienced the first time I saw the movie. It was as though my taste had changed, though I had not, and I still can't help feeling that I was right the first time, when I was relatively unencumbered by experience.

A lot is just plain embarrassing to an adult reader of Miller, but it is not so to a child. She wrote in a style purposely flowery at times and always in a romantic vein that surely exaggerated the wonders of early Cretan life, the rigidity of the Spartans, and the cultural sophistication of the Athenians in their heyday. Now she would be regarded as racist. She made up fictions of the life of the times. She imagined from the evidence of ruins and artifacts the various dwellings, costumes, and implements. She characterized the great political and intellectual figures, the battles and routes of conquest. She retold in condensed form the great mythic stories and sometimes inferred what their sources were: the origins of the gods, the Minotaur, Jason, Theseus, and Oedipus. She told the story of the wrath of Achilles and the wanderings of Odysseus. Miller's volumes contained in brilliant color accurate representations of ancient artifacts and modern original drawings depicting human lives, often quite fancifully. The descriptions that appeared under the artifacts were written, not in the flowery style of the main body of the text, but in a scholarly manner as if in a museum catalog. It is these illustrations that lodge in the memory. Eller must have found Miller's approach useful, even congenial, a ground for a vision of the past that he wanted to convey.

In Eller's classroom we were held in rapt attention by his dramatic presence. Further, if he left the room, all was silence, for we had learned that he would always know by means of supreme mental powers precisely who in his absence had violated decorum. His ability to maintain discipline and attention was absolute, like the power of my grandmother to express such disgust that it was simply not worth experiencing the consequence. I doubt that Eller had ever participated in boys' sports, though he lauded the Ancient Greeks for engaging in such activities. His power of discipline was not in the style of a coach but in that of a wizard. He was a teacher of the art of memory, which for him was a method of self-hypnosis. He succeeded in showing me how to memorize painlessly a whole semester's materials, which he required to be disgorged in clear prose and orderly fashion on the final examination. Eller dominated my academic experience from grade five through eight, and, I must say, what I learned from him and his way of synthesis remained the greatest influences of my formal education.

I do not recall any feats of memory by him, but I vividly remember those of the equally eccentric Frederick W. Bleakney, my high-school English teacher. Once annually, Bleakney would appear at the weekly school assembly and deliver dramatically from memory Robert W. Service's two best known poems, "The Shooting of Dan McGrew" and "The Cremation of Sam McGee," always followed by universally enthusiastic cheering.

More impressive was Bleakney's knowledge of the contents of the school library. Once I asked him about a specific poem, and he told me exactly where the book containing it was and what page it was on. My experience was not unique, as other students reported similar feats. Some years later when I was in graduate school and coaching club football at Lakeside, he discussed with me in detail one of my team's games play by play. Apparently he had viewed the game, played in a downpour, from the distance of the main classroom building. Bleakney had his own visual method for memorization, which he demonstrated to us, using John Masefield's "Sea Fever":

> I must go down to the seas again, to the lonely sea and the sky
> And all I ask is a tall ship and a star to steer her by.

This Bleakney converted to two lines of pictures. You remembered the words because you remembered the signs that you had drawn. Today I remember the words, but not the signs.

Bleakney's eccentricity was quite different from Eller's and covered a wider range of behavior. He was a small wiry man, standing no more than 5'6", yet he was a formidable athlete. He had a habit of appearing casually at athletic practice sessions and astounding everyone with his powers. He could outpunt the best players on the football team. He was an expert shooter of foul shots and a devastating badminton player. He threw as wicked a curve ball as I have ever experienced. In 1934, when Wilford Reaper, who had been ace of the Washington State College tennis team, arrived at Lakeside looking for a competent opponent to sharpen his game, Bleakney offered humbly to help and proceeded to beat him soundly. In the classroom I once witnessed Bleakney leap from a crouching position next to his desk to one on the desktop while making some point.

His greatest subterfuge was not, however, perpetrated on the athletic field. It occurred at the expense of Lynn McCuskey, a new English and Latin teacher arriving at the school in the late summer of 1936. The McCuskeys were to inhabit a tiny suite in the dormitory, arriving by car with their luggage. McCuskey saw as he exited his car a small man in overalls and, assuming he was a janitor, asked him to help with the bags. When the job was completed he tipped the man. At the first meeting of the faculty he learned that the janitor was in fact head of the English department.

Bleakney was a man of a variety of interests and absolutely no intellectual arrogance. He believed that getting a student to read anything was better than the student's not reading. He took each student where he found him and worked from there. As a consequence, many ill-prepared boys developed great affection for him. With all this he was a formal man. He and the chemistry teacher, George Logan, had been roommates at Whitman College, but he always addressed Logan as Mr. Logan. The last time I saw him, when I was in my fifties and he over eighty, he addressed me to my great embarrassment as Professor Adams. He was gallant but also impish. Taking a summer lecture class at the University of Washington, he once rose to defend vigorously a young woman whom the teacher had publicly humiliated. On the other hand, he challenged a flirtatious secretary at Lakeside to carry her behavior to its logical conclusion. My wife and I were once, I think, victims of his impishness when we called on him and were invited into the back yard. There we were induced to engage in a water-witching experiment and found ourselves solemnly pacing across the yard carrying forked boughs, which seemed by their behavior to indicate a rich aquifer beneath. While this was happening I do not believe Bleakney ever smiled. Come to think of it, I don't recall ever seeing a smile on his face. My mother reported to me at about this time that Bleakney declared he had easily mastered doing two things simultaneously and was now working on three.

Of his teaching I remember today not a lot, most clearly a disagreement I had with him over the emphasis to be put on one phrase in a speech I was to give. It was the honors address at graduation of my class in 1943, and he was coaching me. I was quoting from a popular book of the time, Herbert Agar's *A Time for Greatness*. In that book, Agar tells of a Frenchman who, asked what he had accomplished during the Terror, replied, "I survived." Bleakney argued for an utterance expressing strength, determination, and forcefulness. I held out for an ironic, Gallic shrug of a statement. We continued to disagree, and on commencement night I spoke it my way. He never commented. I think now that Bleakney was a man of humor but not of irony. I, who have since lived most of my life among academic ironists or those who have highly valued irony, regard him as one of the most remarkable people I have known.

## 3.

Three of the great, perhaps the greatest, humanistic studies for youngsters are English grammar, Latin, and mathematics, especially geometry. I am sure many readers will be repelled by this assertion, but I don't care. Still, perhaps I could placate by expanding my view, offering a more broadly conceived trivium: study of our own language and that of others, study of the languages of aural and visual forms, and study of the language of number.

A couple of years into my university teaching I attended a lecture by an eminent professor of linguistics, the theme of which was that English grammar was not to be understood as rules but as usages and that the former were coercive, undemocratic, snobbish, and discriminatory against those not trained as we, the audience, had been. People who spoke ungrammatically (incorrectly, from our point of view) nevertheless communicated successfully, and that was what counted. There is something to be said for this view, but only perhaps for what we would now call its political correctness. I remember watching TV news in the late sixties and seeing a young African American facing the camera and pleading, "I din't commit no laws n'order." We understood very well what he meant. Indeed, it was a kind of poetry, expressing a wealth of meaning both political and social as well as being grammatically and dictionally against the grain.

But I think there was something fundamentally mistaken about the linguist's view. First of all, language's end is not just communication. It is indissolubly linked with thought. We have little capacity to make abstract ideas without it. Second, there is a connection between grammar and logic. I conclude the latter from the experience of what we called diagramming sentences in grades six to eight and from studying Latin beginning in the eighth grade. My view was enforced years later when as a beginning teacher of English composition at Cornell University I was ordered to use a textbook called *Thinking Straight* by the philosopher Monroe C. Beardsley, who, incidentally, made his reputation as an aesthetician. At the bottom of the method of this book was the syllogism and deductive logic as it might be applied to English, a hybrid of a word-order and an inflected language.

At that time, English grammar was being viewed by educationists as the enforced imposition of Latin grammar on a language not or no longer, if ever, Latinate in structure. All true, of course. Nevertheless, my classmates, dull or brilliant, came to write and express themselves orally better by their having tormented English sentences on the rack of ruthlessly spatializing diagrams than most of the students who have been in my freshman college classes. Long ago as a teacher, I learned that I was speaking an archaic language of predicate nominatives, direct and indirect objects, gerunds, accusatives, and the like to students who had never heard of such things and had no language to discuss matters of grammar.

What I possess of prose style and clarity of expression began first with my parents' influence and second with my training in Latinate grammar under the tyranny of Wilford Reaper, who drove us to the blackboard to diagram and, in the process, learn something about the variety of English sentences. Further, with respect to word order, Reaper required us to place assiduously in sentences vagrant words like "only" and subsequently utter explanations of each meaning and what was *not* meant: "Only *I* have five fingers," "I have only *five* fingers," "I *only* have five fingers, "I only *have* five fingers." Reaper was a fierce foe of any suspected decline in discriminations of meaning and variety of verbal possibility.

Latin classes extended the spatializing gaze. Oh yes, it later took me some time to free my writing from the overuse of certain participial constructions dulled into me by painstaking construing of the sentences of Caesar and

Cicero, but at least I knew of their possible use. Unfortunately, my series of Latin teachers did not vary from the appointed round, and none made any effort to connect our study of the language to Roman history. Olive Beaupré Miller had given but cursory attention to Caesar's Gallic wars, and it was only years later that I learned that my view of Catiline had been distorted because I had heard only Cicero's side. Nor did I know that Cicero had been the victim of a political murder.

Latin as it was taught to me was important in a way similar to that of mathematics. Both required orderly analytical thought with symbols. Mathematics is a liberal art and not, I think, a science in the specialized sense that the word "science" has taken on both in common parlance and academic life.

My trials with mathematics proceeded into freshman algebra, taught by a male version of the truly disagreeable Miss Fox. However, in my sophomore year I was liberated into the enlightening terror of a remarkable teacher who rivaled in effectiveness William Henry Eller, but with quite different methods and a totally different personality. I had known Jean A. Lambert for some years before becoming his student. He and his family lived in a house on the campus, as we did. He performed numerous duties at Lakeside. He was the assistant headmaster, director of the dormitory, and varsity basketball coach, having been an All-American at the United States Naval Academy. On the floor during the annual varsity-faculty game he was a whiz of activity and a deadly shooter of the now extinct running two-hander, already out of style at the time. He was as intense off the court as on. We endeavored to imitate his purposeful walk, always apparently intent on its destination, left hand in hip pocket, head tilted slightly to the side, as if preparing to glide around a corner, speed rapid and steady. Dormitory students feared his militaristic daily room inspections. He was a disciplinarian and seemed rarely to smile, but when he laughed it was like a seizure, beginning as a suppressed sneeze, and proceeding to an extended guffaw. He was, above all, intensely loyal as a matter of principle, but also, I think, sentimentally so. He was unfailingly polite and with the ladies even gallant. My first academic remembrance of him was shocking. We sixth or seventh graders were sitting in silence in Eller's classroom, he having left briefly for some reason. The door was open. Suddenly there came into the room from next door, which was Lambert's classroom, Lambert himself and a tall senior named Frank Norton, who was one of his math students and basketball players. They were fist-fighting, and both had landed blows to the face that had left red marks. One of them, I do not remember which, asked if the other had had enough. The answer must have been "no," for they sparred back into the hall. This was something even the clairvoyant Eller could not have anticipated, and we reported nothing, being speechless.

At lunch in the refectory that day, Lambert and Norton sat together, both exhibiting shiners and conversing amiably. I never heard the matter mentioned by either of them, or by anyone of us, for that matter, so shocked were we onlookers. But the sight of the two of them together at lunch spoke something to us.

For Lambert, mathematics was an intellectual discipline and a philosophical subject of total seriousness. This is perhaps surprising, since I imagine he had teachers at the Naval Academy who viewed mathematics as little more than a practical skill. His approach was rigorous and his manner severe, but he was also a reckless taker of chances in contract bridge and in later life an avid visitor to the horse races. He liked dialectic, and his conversations sometimes took this form. At meetings my father organized to discuss books, mainly of philosophy, he and Lambert dominated, carrying on their own dialectic, often to the consternation and mystification of the others. Both carried their athletic competitiveness into these discussions. My father reported that once when Kant was mentioned the football coach wryly asked what team he had played for.

Lambert was famous among the dorm boys for apparently knowing everything that went on. One boy sneaked out for an evening and was shocked on late return to find Lambert asleep in his dormitory bed. But Lambert could not know everything. John Leovich, a scholarship boy from Portland and perhaps the most talented athlete ever to attend Lakeside (All-Coast end at Oregon State, ball player briefly for the Philadelphia Athletics and after World War II the Portland Beavers), told the following story: He was a senior on duty one evening in the dormitory office when a call came in from a tavern some distance away. No faculty member was present. The call informed him that a Lakeside student was there, too drunk to be disorderly. It would be best if someone came to get him. Knowing that the boy, a large lineman on the football team would be in serious trouble, perhaps expelled, Leovich set out, walking more than a mile over hill and dale to the tavern. The culprit was by then just able to walk — with help. But as soon as they reached the campus and had yet to navigate the football field and quadrangle, he could go no farther, mumbling that he wanted to sleep there. Leovich carried the 200-pounder across the field, then, exhausted, kicked and pummeled him across the quad, into the dorm, and finally to his bed. This episode was revealed to me only years later. In some way, Lambert had been eluded.

Lambert was my first and only math teacher who insisted on our understanding every step of a problem, not just how we should proceed but why. In his geometry and trigonometry classes we did not do mechanical chores but thought about process. I came to be fairly proficient in these subjects, but unfortunately Lambert left for the Navy in 1942. My approach to calculus in my senior year was cluttered with stumbling blocks. Our newly and suddenly recruited teacher was clearly only a step ahead of most of us and frequently behind some of us.

## 4.

The war took its toll on Lakeside and on my father, who saw much of his faculty enter the services and was hard pressed to replace them with competent teachers. Some wives were pressed into duty, with at best mixed results. Lakeside was a boys' school, and there had been no women teachers for some years. There were discipline problems for the women.

I do not think my father came to find his job as rewarding even after the war ended. A building program was commenced and successfully completed (though one of the buildings was finished only after his death), enrollment continued to increase, and the school's finances were far better, the mortgages now retired. However, some of the best teachers did not return to their old jobs, and the treasurer of the board of trustees meddled in the finances, even insisting on installing a new business manager who had been a lackey in one of his many enterprises. My parents, and especially my mother, found this insulting, and with good reason, since my father had brought the school its first financial stability. At this time, my father began to think he might even be dismissed and made some job inquiries, in the process of which he learned that the board was not willing to give him a strong recommendation. This was a strategy to keep him, a back-handed compliment that must have reminded him of George Humphrey's warning years before. My father told my mother and me about a conversation he had with the treasurer, who asked him why most of his faculty were Democrats. He answered laughing that if the school paid them more they would become Republicans.

I noticed that we began to take vacations and short holidays away from Lakeside. My parents had found Victoria, British Columbia, to their liking, eventually making friends there and buying property. I usually went along. We would rent a house during summer vacations and stay in hotels for shorter periods. We spent a lot of time on bicycle rides on the Saanich Peninsula. It was a good time for bicycling. Victoria was a quiet small city, and during the war there were few cars and little gasoline available. Our dog Chinook accompanied us. Once when forced to remain behind he took revenge by trashing our living quarters. After that, he ran along with us. Frequently we rode downtown to one of the newspaper offices to read the latest war news scrawled on long sheets of paper hanging in the windows. The street was usually crowded with people staring up at them. One evening the Canadian Scottish Regiment in their colorful caps and kilts held retreat on the Parliament lawn. Later most were killed in the ill-fated Dieppe Raid. The British seemed to have a knack for sending colonists into the worst situations.

For us, these were good times in Victoria even though the news we read was very depressing. Always well-dressed, my father became something of an anglophile and on almost every trip added to a good wardrobe of English woolens. Both of my parents scoured the many antique shops for bargains, of which there were many. Victoria was a retirement community for the British Empire, and many former army and colonial officers often on their uppers, disposed of valuable belongings to these shops.

The hotels we stayed in — the Cherry Bank and the Glenshiel — would have been appropriate for use in one of the early Alastair Sim or Alec Guinness movies, complete with authentic living characters. I remember best retired Major and Mrs. Hunton. She was, in her regal demeanor, reminiscent of Queen Mary, wife of George V. The Major was a thin, elderly gentleman with a handlebar mustache, balding head, and a cane. He had been an avid hunter in many parts of the Empire and once told us of a man shooting in the head and killing another hunter when the latter's head appeared just above a large fallen log. He had mistaken the head for a grouse. The Major's comment on this, the moral of his tale, was, "Imagine, shooting at a sitting grouse!"

My parents' forays into Victoria's antique shops resulted in the purchase of many small items; they had been antique hunters even back in their Cleveland days. Having bought the South Euclid house, they had hardly any possessions to put in it, and little money to spend. Their solution was to buy antiques, which were plentiful in Ohio and far less expensive than new furniture. Purchases of early nineteenth-century country furniture generated my father's interest in restoration and refinishing, lasting through his lifetime, our Lakeside basement and garage being his work places. Along with many books on antiques, I inherited my father's interest but not by any means all of his talent for restoration.

My parents bought a house in Victoria in the summer of 1950, but they spent only one night in it, my father dying suddenly a few weeks later. My mother sold as soon as she could, never returning. Soon Victoria began to change and became what it is today: a mecca for tourists tramping between shops selling the usual kitsch. Here and there remain vestiges of the old colonial city, a tea shop here, a china shop there. W. and J. Wilson, where my father shopped for clothes, still has some English woolens, but much space is devoted to sports wear no different from that available in any U.S. city.

# 5.

We made two return trips to Ohio, one by train for Christmas in 1936 and one by car in the summer of 1938. I remember well the visit to London (Ohio), where my grandmother, recently widowed, now lived. My Aunt Grace, thirteen years older than my mother, was intelligent and industrious. She had gone off from Logan to the College of Wooster, the first of the family to attend college. She studied successfully, majored in German, and taught that subject in high school until it was discontinued in World War I. To my mother's great chagrin, she married a man who my mother correctly saw was far below her intellectually. He came from a relatively well-to-do burgher family in London, where she lived the rest of her long life. My mother always thought she married for the apparent security, having too well remembered an insecure period she and her parents experienced. Her husband worked in and expected along with his brother to inherit his father's clothing store. He and Grace moved into the big Victorian frame house on North Main Street to live with his parents. They fell under the domination of the old man, who lived a very long time, never retired, and held the purse strings to the end. Every day until near his death old man Winchester would wheel his Pontiac out of the former stable behind the house and, without stopping to look in any direction, drive the few blocks to his store. That he never caused or was in an accident is reason for wonder. In his later years he became quite deaf, and when he was at home the radio in the parlor blared unmercifully, driving my aunt to a distraction that contributed to years of insomnia and neurotic verbal repetition.

But more devastating to her was my cousin John, her only child, a few years my senior. John was born with what brains his father might have had and none of my aunt's. He was even sent all the way out to Lakeside one year, but with unpromising results. The experiment was not continued. John had one particular talent, which was the construction and operation of short wave radios and transmitters. Indeed, after World War II, which he spent in the army in Italy, he had a decent career as an engineer at a radio station in Columbus. But this was little or no consolation for my aunt, with whom he carried on a verbal battle as long as he could speak. In his last years he was unconscious from a benign but inoperable brain tumor that finally killed him. He left two not very bright adopted children in my aunt's care, his wife having left him years before, learning, I think, that the family was not as wealthy as she had assumed. Indeed, the Winchester clothing store died a slow death, and the building could not fetch much in rent.

I believe that my aunt could not help comparing John's and her life to that of me and my mother, but I am not sure that my cousin was sentient enough to realize this, for we got along quite well. My mother did not help matters that Christmas of 1936 by giving John a book, his response mortifying my aunt. I rode with him on his bike in the snow delivering papers during that visit. He instructed me in short wave radio. Years later, when I visited we would go out for beers, and he would tell me about the days Jonathan Winters worked at the radio station. Jonathan's mother was even funnier than Jonathan, according to him.

In the summer of 1938, we drove across country in our 1936 Ford touring sedan, top down all the way. We must have been an interesting sight, for my parents had equipped us with white pith helmets to protect from the sun. It was hot all the way, but exciting because of the sights and a new and authentic sense of the expanse of the land. We spent much of the time in Cleveland, I with my Aunt Hazel and Uncle Gene while my parents visited old friends. I was able to renew my enthusiasm for the Indians, attending two games in League Park. Early in the first a young pitcher named Bob Feller (of course, I had heard of him) hurled an amazing fastball that connected with some part of catcher Rollie Hemsley's anatomy, forcing him to leave the game. Later, to my great satisfaction, Earl Averill hit a home run over the right field fence, and the Indians won 3–2 over the Philadelphia Athletics. The Indians won the second game, too, against the Washington Senators.

Later that summer we went to the farming town of Richwood northwest of Columbus to visit briefly my Grandfather Adams, with whom I'd seen the 1–0 loss in 1932. He was retired, living in a boarding house, near the farm on which he had grown up. We met him on Franklin Street and went to the local drug store to have a Coke and talk. My mother told me years later that this was the first time he had seemed to take an interest in me, and he asked me about our trip and the ball games I'd seen. I remember it was hot and late in the afternoon when we parted on the street. It was the last time any of us saw him.

Summers when we were at Lakeside were quiet and lazy. After the dormitory boys left, John Lambert and I would search all the vacated rooms for things left behind and sometimes made significant or at least satisfying hauls of assorted objects. In this and other things we were joined by the only other boy around, Bob Strand, who spent summers with his grandparents nearby. In the summer of 1938 (or perhaps 1937) I invented a baseball game played with dice which fairly accurately mimicked the statistics of professional games and was later further perfected. Soon the three of us created a fictional league that took up much of our time, playing games, keeping records, and trading players. Eventually minor-league teams were created and even model stadiums. This activity, which began to look obsessive from the outside, wore on my mother, who complained about the incessant "thrp, thrp" of dice, which she asserted could be heard from any point in the house. The Adstrabert League went on for several years, resumed operation decades later and after another hiatus continues, though at a slower pace, to this day. Its founders, myself and John Lambert, are still active along with newcomers. My mother noticed that almost all participants were Ph.D.s, but she drew no conclusions or at least did not utter them. Not too long ago my wife Diana and I had a visit from John Lambert, now retired in Lake Forest, Illinois. We played a game between two old rivals, the Hanover Orioles and the Brookfield Gas

House Gang. In about the third inning, John looked across the card table and declared that this was a really good game — not just that game but the whole concept.

In that first summer of Adstrabert League activity, sorely irritated and with visions of wasted youth, my mother installed in each day a reading hour. For some reason, now unknown to me, I was set the task of reading *Gone with the Wind*, which I think did me no harm though probably not much good either. Perhaps as a result, I have never embraced popular fiction.

It must have been at about this time that Benny Goodman's band made a record called "Gone with What Wind?" and I either bought it, or it was among some "78" records I accumulated. I remember liking the title a lot. Today a literary critic might say its meaning is undecidable. I had earlier received for Christmas a small radio on which I listened to Jack Armstrong the All-American Boy and other programs for kids that aired late in the afternoon. These broadcasts — Armstrong, Little Orphan Annie, Tom Mix, Buck Rogers — came in fifteen-minute segments begun with the newly invented singing commercials. Jack Armstrong advertised Wheaties, the Breakfast of Champions:

> They're crispy, they're crunchy
> The whole day through.
> Jack Armstrong never tires of them
> And neither will you!

Jack Armstrong was never on a losing team, and always snatched victory from the jaws of defeat. Little Orphan Annie was sponsored by Ovaltine, a chocolaty powder to be added to milk, guaranteeing good health and success in all things:

> Always wears a sunny smile.
> Now wouldn't it be worth your while
> If you could be
> Like Little Orphan Annie?
> Simply drink Ovaltine.

Competitor with Wheaties in behalf of Ralston cereal was Tom Mix:

> When it's Ralston time at breakfast
> Then it surely is a treat
> With good full flavored Ralston
> Made of golden western wheat.
> Wrangler says it is dee-licious,
> And you'll find that 'fore you're through
> With a lot of cream,
> Boy, it sure tastes keen,
> Ralston cereal's best for you.

All of which goes to show that repeated listening rivals the memory techniques of Eller and Bleakney!

I also tuned in to the Benny Goodman band and others, coming from somewhere in the East, on late Saturday afternoons. My first records were Duke Ellingtons, acquired perhaps by my father, who was partial to Ellington's music, which was different. Someone once asked Ellington why he used so much dissonance, and he replied, "*I'm* dissonant." So my musical education began with things like "Drop Me Off in Harlem" and "Baby, When You Ain't There," the classically simple lines of which were sung by the great trumpeter Cootie Williams. These records were made in 1932 or 33, but came to me in 1939 or 40. Over the years I accumulated perhaps 200 Ellington records along with other jazz classics The early experience of Ellington, Basie, and Lunceford made me impatient with most of the popular white bands of the time, especially Glenn Miller.

My mother's taste was toward Bach and early Renaissance music, which I also liked. In later years she became a proficient recorder player, joining a group of mainly eccentric people who attended recorder camps and courses in the summer. At one of these, when she was over ninety years old, a woman sitting next to her at lunch said to her, "Do you know there's someone over ninety years old here?" The recorder players performed together in their respective houses and occasionally in public. My mother's efforts to have me taught to play an instrument failed abysmally. I sullenly resisted the piano and later declined to play the recorder. My own idiosyncratic efforts to play a guitar came to virtually nothing. I am glad to say that my children have done better and one of them far, far better.

For a decade or more we took dinner at the school refectory, probably, I should guess, to save money. The summers were a relief from this, although my mother's culinary repertoire in those days was not great. However, she could put on a good meal for guests. Among those, I remember well the poet Charles Olson and his wife. He seemed to me the largest man I had ever seen, and I feared that an antique dining room chair would collapse under him. Father H. A. Reinhold came several times, and my cousin Richard and I drove ourselves to embarrassed giggles and outright laughter when he said grace — at some length, I might say — in Latin. Indeed, on one occasion we finally dashed from the table, offering in our hysteria not even muffled excuses. I do not believe he or my parents understood what we were laughing about, nor in a way did we. I suppose we had no idea that Latin might actually be spoken. My Latin teacher, Richard Carbray, told me once that he had been at the Vatican for some important event and was thrown together with three priests from different countries. They all spoke different languages and ended up conversing in Latin, this being the only time he had ever actually spoken it in a social situation. As an adult, I was amused by this.

Former students came from time to time. One, George Kahin, later well-known as an expert on Southeast Asia and for his public criticism of the Vietnam adventure, arrived from Harvard to declare gleefully that my father's head, particularly the jaw, was that of a very ancient, primitive shape according to the cephalic index he had just learned about. This pleased him, of course, but it also pleased my father, who attributed it to his Welsh and Scottish, that is Celtic ancestry.

In the summer following my junior year, I had my first job, messenger for the Seattle First National Bank downtown. I would ride my bike two miles to U.S. Highway 99, where I would park it at a gas station and board a bus. I would report to work for an array of vice-presidents who seemed to do little except visit their desks from time to time and attend an occasional meeting. One of them kept a small notebook in his inside pocket. Every day he would send me out with three pennies for the afternoon paper. This expense he would carefully record in the notebook, along, I suppose, with every other of the day's transactions. I knew then that I would not go into the banking profession. The one respite from the dreary experience of running messages and distributing mail occurred weekly when I would travel in an armored car to the Federal Reserve Bank. Not a guard, I was a loader and unloader of cash, lots of it, far more than I've ever seen since. From this excitement I was emancipated when toward the end of summer my father decided that I should accompany him on a trip recruiting students in eastern Washington.

## 6.

It seems to me now that I must have wasted a lot of time in my early teens that could have been spent in reading. Today I feel that I have not yet caught up and never will. Yet the time must have been crowded with activity. The Lakeside daily schedule was full. Classes went from 9 to 2:40, and then there was a period of athletics until about 4:30. In the evenings, except for Saturday, there were two hours of supervised study hall for the dorm boys, and I attended it. During the varsity basketball season, practice began at four and lasted until six with two night games each week. Baseball practice often went on until 5 or 5:30 for many of us. I did not read much imaginative literature beyond what was assigned in English classes. I remember more clearly readings in American history. I became partial to Jefferson and regarded Hamilton as something of a villain as a result of reading Claude Bowers' book on the two of them. Though biased, this book was a distinct improvement over Muzzey's appalling history textbook current in those days. It offered me as distorted a view of modern history as my father claimed he got from reading Dickens's novels in adolescence. I think my father was complaining about sentimentality and happy endings, but at least Dickens got on the better side of many social issues, while the reactionary Muzzey seemed always wrong and fierce as well.

Many of my activities and thoughts were dominated by athletics. The gymnasium was always open, even over vacations, as were the athletic fields. At Lakeside everyone participated at some level. In the lower school, the boys were divided up into two competing societies, the Maroons and Golds. I soon learned that I did not like to play football very much, a dislike confirmed when I was obliged to tackle the bruising Maroon fullback as he bulled his way at gathering speed over my position. Tackling hurt. My most notable achievement was in the fifth or sixth grade when, playing center, in a state of misplaced ardor, I mistakenly caught a pass for which I was, of course, ineligible. This caused a penalty of five or maybe fifteen yards and the embarrassment of learning on the job.

Baseball and basketball were more congenial. Our varsity basketball coach was Jean Lambert, who emphasized conditioning, zone defense, the fast break, but then a disciplined style of play. I was on the second team as a junior, just beginning to grow into my feet. Lambert was gone for my senior year, but the new coach, after some failed experiments and confusion mixed with obstinance on our part, adopted the system we had grown up with. This suited me, for I was a good defender in the zone, but a little too slow to play man-to-man very well. We did not have high expectations for our team. Two of our veteran players entered the army in December, and only one player remained from the season before. But to our surprise we began to win games and ended up in a tie for our league's championship, the first Lakeside had ever won. I don't understand to this day how it happened. It didn't seem to me we were very good compared to our less successful predecessors. I was playing what would now be called point guard, fairly effective on defense and rebounding but not much of a scorer. And I had a tendency to foul out of games in the fourth quarter. Once I even fouled out in the first half as the result of efforts to thwart a 6'5" center in the paint. He didn't score a basket that half, but he did make a couple of his foul shots. In those days, at 6 feet I was, in fact, one of the taller players on our team. Of course, now I would be regarded on the court as a dwarf.

Once basketball season was over we were quickly into baseball, which always in Seattle and environs began and sometimes ended in rain and drizzle. As a freshman I was taken along on most trips, but never got into a game. However, as a result, I was witness to what should go down as a famous event in Lakeside baseball history. We were playing in Marysville, which was then a farming community about twenty-five miles north. In left field was a fence of sorts, no more than a single wire strung on posts separating the ball field from a cow pasture. At some point a Marysville batter hit a ball that got by our left fielder and came to rest just beyond the fence and directly under-neath an imperturbed and probably imperturbable cow staring vacantly toward home plate. Our fielder ducked under the wire but balked at approaching the cow. No rule known to the umpire governed this situation, and the batter proceeded all around the bases.

My baseball career actually began seriously when I was a sophomore. The apparent starting second baseman was to be the talented Lando Zech, who later became a well-known admiral assigned to submarines. He had come to Lakeside as a senior specifically to study for the Annapolis examinations with Jean Lambert, his uncle. However, after starring on Lambert's basketball team, he chose to forgo baseball to prepare for the exams. For want of any-one better Coach McCuskey inserted me at second. I had been in junior high school a shortstop, but that position had already been filled for two years by my cousin Richard Adams, a graceful fielder who could hit a little.

Richard lived with us through high school. His father, my uncle Hugh Perry Adams, was a career officer in the army and moved frequently, being at one time military attaché in Cairo. Richard was parked with us and lived across the hall from me in our house. We got along well and committed only a few minor outrages against each other. Once Richard found my dog Chi-nook with his pajamas on, asleep in his bed. My bed was occasionally short-sheeted. Together in an impromptu wrestling match we broke an antique bed just restored by my father.

Richard was an excellent student when he cared to be. He was extremely adept at foreign languages, quickly fluent in French. Later when he was in the State Department in Egypt he taught himself Arabic and spoke it well enough later to instruct Middle Easterners in English. But in his senior year he got into academic trouble, failing to complete math assignments for Lam-bert. When he was disciplined for this, including brief ineligibility for base-ball, and required to spend certain hours daily on math, he went to Bleakney and declared he was sorry but his English assignments would be late for a while because of his work in mathematics. This puzzled and somewhat alarmed Bleakney until he discovered that Richard had fallen behind and was not simply declaring that the math assignments were too long and hard.

I think my best baseball performance was at shortstop in Richard's absence for a game or two. I made some good plays and got some hits, the latter being fairly rare in my case. When I was a senior Coach McCuskey was in the navy, and my father took over. I would have liked to play shortstop, but my father thought, correctly, it turned out, that more balls were hit to second because the great majority of high-school players were right handed and hit late against decent pitching. I remained at second, being a pretty good fielder. Indeed, I played up to the last game of the season without an error. However, late in the game, which I am glad to say we won, I threw a double-play ball into the stands. I see it yet, taking off over first baseman Bill Jenkins' head, up and up, a slightly drawn out spot of time. Not Wordsworthian, though, for it gives me to this day no comfort to recall it.

That game ended my academic career at Lakeside, for it was played on the day after commencement exercises the previous evening. The reason was that everything except the league baseball schedule was pushed forward that year. Several seniors were about to be drafted, and others had enlisted with call-up pending. Under the circumstances it was perhaps not surprising that as a team of seniors we were a little hung over for the game. Luckily, our pitcher, a sophomore, threw a two-hitter, and we won. There had been an impromptu party off campus, at which I had my first taste of beer or any alcoholic beverage, for that matter. I recall coming back to our house with the world revolving about me. A faculty party was in progress. Several faculty members greeted me, but they were also celebrating, some more than I had, and I was able to make my way upstairs to bed without incident. Either my father never learned about the state of his subsequently successful team or chose to ignore it.

The second half of that school year had been full of distractions, students and faculty leaving, athletic and other schedules disrupted, gasoline rationed, those reaching age eighteen drafted. There was much anxiety about the future and a marking of time that threatened to make school work and everything else seem irrelevant. We all took the usual examinations, including, earlier in the fall, the Scholastic Aptitude Test and others of that ilk. Many years at Lakeside had prepared me for these. With any sense, one learned how to take them, and I thought at the time that they probably reflected prowess in figuring out how to take tests as much as the various abilities allegedly measured. Test literacy is what we might call it today.

Much of my senior year was taken up by my editorship of the fortnightly school newspaper and the yearbook. The latter I took over when the appointed editor Stanley Osborn was drafted at midyear into the army. Both efforts were frustrated by war shortages, and both invaded my work in English. As I look back on this, I recall no encouragement in my English classes to write imaginatively — no poems, or stories. A great pity, I think, though our teachers were spared our deepest adolescent thoughts. My career as a poet, begun at Hawken, died, only to be reborn briefly many years later. My only imaginative work in the interim was a short dramatic farce written and performed in grade eight and providentially not extant. At least I hope not.

Ivy league schools were encouraging interest from students in the West. I won regional scholarships to Yale and Harvard that year but eventually turned down both. The representative from Harvard who visited the school impressed me as an ass, and the Yale representative talked about nothing but sports once he learned that I was interested in baseball. I had another reservation about Yale. Most of the well-to-do Lakesiders who went east to college attended Yale, and I had no enthusiasm for being connected to that group. When the man from Princeton visited the school my father apparently explored with him the possibility of a similar scholarship there, though I had not applied. It was granted. The visitor with the impressive name, Radcliffe Heermance, the admissions officer, struck me as properly eccentric; he was nattily dressed, somewhat portly, with a large mustache and cane. He talked engagingly about academics at Princeton and revealed considerable wit, totally lacking in the earlier visitors. I signed up.

Princeton impressed me by sending me an occasional book from the Modern Library. It made a habit of sending such books to Princeton students in the service: Dostoyevsky, Thoreau, and others, as I recall. This was my first connection with the institution and the only one for three years into 1946, when the United States Marine Corps no longer required my services. My history teacher at Lakeside, perhaps thinking that I did not work hard enough or up to my abilities, warned me that when I got to Princeton I'd find many students as smart and smarter and at least as well prepared. He was probably disappointed at my casual response, misinterpreting it. The fact was that I fully expected what he had predicted. We were both proved to be right.

# Excursus: The Literate and the Literary

The Princeton books were not sent merely to people who intended to be literature students. Neither Princeton nor I had any idea what I would study. They demonstrated, as I now understand it and then only sensed it, commitment to a liberal education as it was then regarded. It assumed, as it still should, a connection between literacy and the literary, which needs to be made early in childhood and sustained through secondary education. There follows here an excursus. I see it as a conclusion to the account of my early education, from my mother's reading to me from *Come Hither*, through Hiram Haydn's author's club at Hawken and Lakeside teachers, to Princeton's gift of books of high culture. I regret the times when encouragement to read broadly was not strong, ignored, or rejected. Blake said that time is the mercy of eternity, but it is so only if one values it.

First the literary, then the literate. We think there is a thing called literature, but it seems impossible to draw a firm bounding line around it. In some usages literature is any writing, in others it includes oral performances. Certain professions have what is called a literature — medical literature or sociological literature, usually referred to in these professions as "the literature." However, when we think of literature in the literary sense we are thinking of what was collected under that term early in the nineteenth century and has now taken on the status of an institution or, in contemporary parlance, a canon. Before that, people talked about poems, plays, etc., but rarely about them all together under a single term. Perhaps the term "literary" is better in that it does not have the pretension of the noun, a container that inevitably and perhaps arbitrarily excludes any disreputable poetical camels from getting their noses under the tent.

If we want to talk about the literary, we soon come to see that its earliest manifestations must have been oral and mythical. Many scholars used to think that myths were primitive forms of science, that is, crude attempts to interpret the natural world. In the eighteenth and nineteenth centuries there

51

were many theories of this sort advanced. They vied with theories that regarded myths as history distorted by time and linguistic change. However, it became clear to some that it made more sense to see myth not as an attempt to explain or interpret an external world, but rather an attempt to assert the *relation* of human beings to the world and each other. This effort, in its essence, resists the opposition of a so-called perceiving human subject to an object and expresses itself in a language of identity, taking its metaphors and other figures of speech seriously as conveying relation rather than alienation. The mythical, then, acts to bind the community together and the community to nature. The literary we can call a development out of mythical thinking that is freed of belief and intellectual stultification. Giambattista Vico, in his remarkable book *The New Science* (first edition 1725), thought that what he called "poetic logic," the producer of myth, preceded the invention of abstract logic. William Blake, working with a similar notion, saw the matter vertically, conceptualization standing on the base of myth, rather than everything being horizontal in time. This means that the literary grows out of myth. It is not constituted as a single story or even a great mass of stories but rather as a way of thinking and expressing in and by means of tropes and narratives.

The most literary of works are of the sort strongly committed to taking their tropes seriously, that is, literally. It is worth noting that the term "literal" is commonly used to mean anything *but* literary. It is usually coupled with "minded," to describe someone who can't understand a tropological utterance, especially one that employs the trope known as irony. But, as Northrop Frye argued over fifty years ago, the term "literal" *ought* to have something to do with "literary" and not refer to its opposite. I adopt here Frye's use of "literal" to mean something radically literary. This would certainly mean that it is fictive and "centripetal." By "fictive" I mean something *made* (in the old sense of *fictio*), not just an attempt to represent or interpret nature. By "centripetal" I mean what Frye meant: something the parts of which are principally definable in terms of their relations with each other, more so than in their relation to something external to which they refer. When we call something literary we tacitly recognize that it possesses a high degree of tropological language, fiction, and centripetality. I add that because of these it may also be judged as literary by its dramatic quality, but this is a subject not to be approached here.

I also add that when there is a high degree of the literary one finds tropological thinking that is self-consciously fictive, calling attention to its nature. James Joyce's *Finnegans Wake* is the most extreme example I know. Most people who have looked at it think of it as out on the dark, far side of literature, artistically aberrational perhaps. I think of it as at the center, the most literary of works, difficult because of its literary density. I taught about it frequently because I had come to think it a literary education in itself, like Blake's major long poems. Almost anything by Theodore Dreiser, though literary, contains a far lesser degree of all three elements. The mythical aspect can be drawn from Dreiser's novels only by what a psychoanalyst might call depth analysis. In such cases, the mythical appears in very abstract form in a shape the reader abstracts from the plot. Émile Zola, in his book *The Experimental Novel*, claimed that as a novelist he wrote on the model of the experimental scientist, purely objectively. But, as Oscar Wilde pointed out in that very literary work of criticism *The Decay of Lying*, Zola's novels proved to be works of art in spite of Zola.

You will have noticed my saying that as things move inward toward the purely mythical (a point one never reaches, a hypothetical fiction) they exhibit a growing degree of self-consciousness about their fictive nature. In fact, all serious creative uses of symbolic structures — including mathematics, music, and the language of visual forms — are fictive. The difference is not between, say, the fictive symbolism of poetry and the somehow real symbolism of science. All symbolic structures are really centripetal and fictive, and physicists will readily admit this except when they are trying to get money from a federal agency. The real question is the nature of the fiction expressed, or what Immanuel Kant called its categories. Some scientific structures tend to project the fiction that they directly express an external reality by simple correspondence and invocation of the laws of induction and deduction. From a fictive point of view, they *make* the object that they then claim to point outward to. The object is made in their terms and answers to their laws, the categories of their particular fiction. The distinction between subject and object is one of these.

Literary fictions tend to admit, at least tacitly, that they point back into themselves or around in a circle which is their shape. All symbolic structures actually do this, but scientific structures turn their insides into the fiction of an outside. The great paradox, at least to our common way of thinking, is that the language of science, or mathematics, turns out to be the means by which this fictive projection of externality is best expressed, even though mathematics is an entirely autonomous system of signs with no even arbitrary referents fictively constructed by it.

This suggests that the scale from the pure language of science to the poetic logic of the purely literary and the mythical is really a circle and that mathematics returns to myth in some way. This may account for the following phenomena: From time to time, a mathematician writes of the "beauty" of mathematical structure, or a poet makes an analogy between his art and geometric design, as did Yeats in *A Vision*. From time to time, a physicist tries to say outside of mathematics what his theory is and produces something that looks like a highly literary work, a cosmology usually characterized by considerable presence of the trope called paradox and presented often as a quest romance. At this point representation and reference turn inside, and the mathematical has completed the circle by returning to the literary and verging on myth. These literary efforts by scientists tend to humanize science, that is, tend to bring scientific fictions into the realm of the immediate concerns of the human community. The more human the work becomes, the less alienated nature becomes. Science fiction and humanizing books about science belong to the genre known to literary scholars as romance, and it is perhaps no surprise that the great poet of English Romanticism, William Wordsworth, came at the problem of the alienation of human beings from nature from the poetic side but saw the possible connection with science. In his famous Preface to the *Lyrical Ballads* of 1800 he wrote, "If the time should ever come when what is now called science, thus familiarized to men, shall be ready to put on, as it were, a form of flesh and blood, the poet will lend his divine spirit to aid the transfiguration, and will welcome the being thus produced...." Because of our presently enormous communal anxiety about this alienation, it is no surprise that much recent literary output is science fiction with both utopian and dystopian tendencies. In it, science turns to myth, which is characterized by expression of the desire for identity represented by metaphor, where one thing is declared identical to another, and by synecdoche, where the large thing is declared identical to the smaller thing that is its part. I earlier described *Finnegans Wake* as a synecdoche of the literary. The early stories about sun, moon, stars, and animals were not attempts to explain or analyze these things but to erase the anxiety of alienation.

Next, literacy. What is literacy? The common notion of literacy, of course, is that it is the ability to read and write; we now have metaphors spun from that view: computer literacy, media literacy, and so forth. A college professor's meaning for "illiterate," even when one eliminates the hyperbole with which such a person is likely to use it, is different from a social worker's meaning. The former's definition probably identifies literacy with literature in some way. For the former, literacy would probably require the ability to read (that is, interpret) something like "Ode on a Grecian Urn." The latter would probably be contented, for purposes of definition, with Dick and Jane. It is a matter of degree. It appears that Bill Clinton is more literate than either of the George Bushes, who, after all, came pretty far with whatever degree of literacy they can be said to have. Adlai Stevenson was more literate than either. I recall a question put to him about a possible presidential opponent, the automobile executive George Romney. He said only that he thought George Romney a good eighteenth-century painter, but he believed that the Republicans would nominate a nineteenth-century man. In the end, of course, the overwhelming majority of English professors voted for Stevenson, but General Eisenhower defeated him twice. Eisenhower had a high degree of a certain

kind of literacy not often known outside the military. When this got translated into the language of everyday life, it took on the appearance of a new
kind of aphasic disturbance and generated a number of highly literate parodies, such as the one by Oliver Jensen that imagines Eisenhower delivering
the Gettysburg Address. It begins as follows:

> I haven't checked these figures but 87 years ago, I think it was, a number of
> individuals organized a governmental set-up here in this country, I believe it
> covered certain Eastern areas, with this idea they were following up based on
> a sort of national independence arrangement and the program that every indi-
> vidual is just as good as every other individual. Well, now, of course, we are
> dealing with this big difference of opinion, civil disturbance you might say,
> although I don't like to appear to take sides or name any individuals, and the
> point is naturally to check up, by actual experience in the field, to see whether
> any governmental set-up with a basis like the one I was mentioning has any
> validity and find out whether this dedication by those early individuals will
> pay off in lasting values and things of that kind.

I note that my computer is incredulous and underlines the whole thing in
green. Now, parody is a form of irony, that is, it says one thing and means
another. In this case we have the ironic twist of a text that is literary into
something nearly as unliterary as it is possible to be.

What about the person who is impervious to irony, or nearly so? I believe
a low degree of ability to detect irony is a low degree of literacy, and such
people are what we commonly call literal-minded but what I call unable to
read literally. Years ago on a television program called *Northern Exposure*, itself
a trope, the disk jockey, ordained preacher, ex-con, and autodidactical philosopher Chris, who was himself a most interesting study in literacy, wrote a series
of love letters for a friend, each comparing the beloved to something else. The
last began, "Shall I compare thee to a summer's day?" Is it part of a relatively
high degree of literacy to recognize the curious irony of the literary situation
here, where Shakespeare is plagiarized within a plot stolen from Rostand, and
the viewers, or some of them, are supposed to know this? Recognition plays
a major role in literacy, as T. S. Eliot understood when he said that imma-
ture poets copy but mature poets steal, and as Northrop Frye knew when he
said that anything stolen within fifty years is plagiarism and everything before
that is influence.

Literacy has a lot to do with the literary. The literal level of meaning in
a text, according to John Cassian, St. Thomas Aquinas, Dante Alighieri, and
most medieval theorists of Biblical interpretation, was the referential, specifically the historical level of meaning of a text — what "literally" happened. But
"literal" in Frye's sense is the work's internal literary structure, a *fictio* of relations between words. A significant degree of literacy would be the capacity
to read metaphors, metonymies, synecdoches, and ironies (to name only Vico's

favorite tropes) in a literal way, not to assume their roles are limited to decoration of the historical level of the text. To be literal minded in this sense is to be highly literate and literary.

As an example, let me offer Lewis Carroll's "Jabberwocky," part of my early education by way of my mother. The first and last stanzas both go as follows:

> 'Twas brillig and the slithy toves
> Did gyre and gimble in the wabe:
> All mimsy were the borogroves,
> And the mome raths outgrabe.

Is nonsense verse illiterate? Only when it functions not according to the conventions of the literary. Gertrude Stein's remark about Oakland, that "There's no there there," is highly literate. Mike Jacobs, when he said, "I shoulda stood in bed," was a poet for a fortunate moment, and Sam Goldwyn wrote a whole new Book of Proverbs, one of which you know, the famous, "If that's the way it's gonna be, include me out." But enough of the various figures of speech.

By your own interpretation will your degree of literacy be known. Humpty Dumpty's interpretation of "Jabberwocky" is an example of headlong arbitrariness punctuated by occasional brilliance. The brilliance is not enough to overcome our understanding that Humpty Dumpty has an astonishingly illiterate side, generated by a deep, anxious desire to gain domination over the text. But then, the history of interpretation is strewn with cracked eggheads.

Here is Humpty Dumpty on "Jabberwocky":

> "'Brillig' means four o'clock in the afternoon — the time when you begin *broiling* things for dinner."
> "That'll do very well," said Alice: "and 'slithy'?"
> "Well, '*slithy*' means 'lithe and slimy.' 'Lithe' is the same as 'active.' You see it's a portmanteau — there are two meanings packed into one word."
> "I see it now," Alice remarked thoughtfully: "and what are 'toves'?"
> "Well, '*toves*' are something like badgers — they're something like corkscrews."
> "They must be very curious looking creatures."
> "They are that," said Humpty Dumpty: "also they make their nests under sun-dials — and they live on cheese."

This exegesis is based soundly on, as we say today, theory. Humpty Dumpty's theory goes as follows:

> "I don't know what you mean by 'glory,'" Alice said.
> Humpty Dumpty smiled contemptuously. "Of course you don't — till I tell you. I meant 'there's a nice knock-down argument for you.'"
> "But 'glory' doesn't mean 'a nice knock-down argument,'" Alice objected.

"When *I* use a word," Humpty Dumpty said, in a rather scornful tone, "it means just what I choose it to mean — neither more nor less."

"The question is," said Alice, "whether you *can* make words mean so many different things."

"The question is," said Humpty Dumpty, "which is to be the master — that's all."

Humpty Dumpty, who, as one can see, warms to the power of his own discourse, is beyond redemption — at least for the king's horses and men — by comparison to Alice, who is quite bright but in danger of having Humpty Dumptys as teachers both inside and outside the mirror. What Humpty Dumpty needed to notice before declaring arbitrarily the meaning of the words was that "Jabberwocky's" literal form is a parody of the medieval quest-romance in balladic verse. It is implicated with the myths of heroes, dragon-slayers, and the cycles of nature and human life. We have every reason to believe that the young hero will marry a princess. Humpty Dumpty can't see the forest in his urge to exert mastery over all of the trees.

The point is that a desirable degree of literacy requires *literary* experience. The literary and our literary traditions embody our concerns and bind us together. Shelley made the point when he said in his great essay "A Defense of Poetry," "Every original language near to its source is in itself the chaos of a cyclic poem," and then went on to remark, using the word "poet" in a broad sense,

> ...the pleasure resulting from the manner in which [poets] express the influence of society or nature upon their own minds, communicates itself to others, and gathers a sort of reduplication from that community. Their language is vitally metaphorical; that is, it marks the before unapprehended relations of things and perpetuates their apprehension, until the words which represent them become, through time, signs for portions or classes of thoughts instead of pictures of integral thoughts; and then if no new poets should arise to create afresh the associations which have been thus disorganized, language will be dead to all the nobler purposes of human discourse.

I doubt that by short-term methods the grasp of irony or metaphor can be forced on anyone. Reading experience is not just the best teacher; it is the only teacher. Literary experience should begin at an early age with myths, folk tales, and nursery rimes. Mother Goose is the play of language within its own form with no anxiety about correspondence to exterior nature or recognized thoughts. For English and many other languages this involves classical mythology and Biblical legend. These come to almost all of us in translations, but the translations themselves often lie deep in our culture. They contain and are contained by what Blake called "the bright sculptures of Los's halls":

> All things acted on Earth are seen in the bright Sculptures of
> Los's Halls & every Age renews its power from these Works
> With every pathetic story possible to happen from Hate or
> Wayward Love & every sorrow & distress is carved here
> Every Affinity of Parents Marriages & Friendships are here
> In all their various combinations wrought with wondrous Art
> All that can happen to Man in his pilgrimage of seventy years.

In this sense, as Oscar Wilde told us later on, life and nature copy art.

There are, of course, special languages that deliberately make heroic efforts to avoid the alleged dangers of tropes. They have their uses, but in order to escape the seduction of tropes, the efforts often tie up the tongue. It is interesting to observe how disembodied these efforts turn out to be. I think of reports of medical research that make every effort to avoid the personal pronoun. There are "subjects" referred to, though they are clearly regarded as objects. There is full allegiance to the passive voice, as if the author were attempting symbolic suicide. This is, of course, a discipline dedicated to the saving of lives, but it produces a language of death. My mother in her late years made a new career putting the work of academic physicians, often stubbornly committed to their own illiteracy, into reliable and readable English. This included making sure that the author did not dangerously say the opposite of what he intended.

Of course, there is, as I have suggested, a language that does deliberately achieve complete abstraction: mathematics. I have suggested that mathematics is at the other end of the scale from the literary and from myth but in a sense the two extremes come around to meet. A problem arises when mathematical models are naïvely imposed in areas where the fundamental model ought to be the literary one of fictions and tropes. As far as I know, this problem was given its first full expression by Plato in *Republic*, from which the poet is banished as a dangerous liar and the favored youths of the state are to be trained in mathematics. This is, of course, the illiterate reading of Plato, because he also in the same work finds a connection between beauty, dance, and mathematics, and implies that poets are possessed by gods, which can't be all bad.

But the mathematical model that seems to dominate so many academic disciplines, often at the expense of a desirable degree of literacy, is a rather naïve or maybe simple one, as in the effort to establish objectivity by verbal means; and it goes against the fundamental nature of language, which is why the language of so much social science and educational theory is subject to parody. Literary theory in some of its less life-giving forms is by no means exempt from this criticism and has less excuse. An important question is whether mathematics is not a special and brilliant case of imaginative projection from myth. A fractal looks to me as if it is based firmly on the trope of synecdoche, part for whole. One might also note that it's a term, along with quark, that would have done Lewis Carroll, who was a mathematician, proud.

# 4

# USMC

**1.**

Why I enlisted in the Marines in 1943 is no longer entirely clear to me, if it ever was. I suppose it was to escape being drafted and a late adolescent attempt to assert independence of choice. At the time the choice was either passively to await the draft or join the Marine Corps or the Navy programs leading possibly to officer candidacy. The latter would likely delay my being in combat for at least a year, though I am not sure this entered into my thinking, if thinking it can be called. At the time it was assumed that the war might go on for quite a while, no end being then in sight.

In late June, I found myself in a private's uniform, living in what had been a women's dormitory, from which my future wife Diana White and all others had been evicted. We were on the University of Washington campus along with about 350 other Marine recruits and perhaps 1000 who had joined the Navy. We were under military discipline, early rising, organized calisthenics and running before breakfast, a rigorous schedule of classes, physical training, close-order drill, routine guard duty (though it is unclear what we were guarding), restriction to campus, study periods at night, and taps. We were under the direction of officers, sergeants, and corporals. The corporals took on airs of authority and might as well have been top sergeants from our point of view. Our commanding officer at first was Edward Katzenbach, later a Princeton professor. Then it was Paul Moore, wounded at Guadalcanal and later Episcopal Bishop of New York.

Beginning that summer, the university ran a chaos of two programs simultaneously, which must have driven the faculty nuts. We in the military were by governmental decree on the semester system, while the rest of the student body, by now mainly women, were on the university's usual quarter plan. In many cases, a class would have some students on one plan and some on another working at another rate. It was not a period of great accomplishment in higher education, and one, as far as I am concerned, better forgotten, though here I plow on.

We in the Marines were taking a civil engineering curriculum. It would be unrecognizable to a present-day student, well before the advent of computers. In addition the curriculum was adjusted here and there to accommodate the needs of the Marine Corps. This meant, among other things, a course devoted to the question of how to construct a variety of field latrines, a science that had progressed hardly at all since the days of Julius Caesar. I discover that I have maintained memory of the subject matter of this course far better than that of any other I took, which may say something for the power of scatology to keep one alert. Mathematics was, as still seems to be the case today, badly taught; but in the years at Lakeside I had absorbed all that was being offered to us. I slid through the mathematics courses without grace but with satisfactory grades. Physics was a plodding sequence of abstractions to be endured with desultory acquiescence.

Then there was engineering drawing, to be accomplished in those days long before computers on recalcitrant paper with India ink and wayward pen. I found my control of the ink tentative, and was constantly in fear of executing a blob on a nearly completed design. This I did more than once. My fear was intensified because our schedules were such that there was hardly any time at all to repeat a failed task. Indeed, we achieved two years' academic credit in little over one. In addition to the engineering requirements, we studied military law, English composition and speech, and American history, the last apparently to ensure our patriotism or a modicum of knowledge about what we were to fight for. On the whole, our courses were purely technical and supposedly practical. The material was presented mechanically with the apparent end memorization. The intent might as well have been to rid us of any tendency toward intellectual inquiry. I was able somewhere along the line to squeeze in a course on the modern American novel by an excellent teacher, a remarkable exception. However, the whole experience produced in me an academic lethargy that I barely and very slowly overcame at Princeton after the war. It was a dull and dreary time.

**2.**

My fellow student Marines had been collected from all over the Pacific Northwest. It turned out, I think, that coaches in the colleges and universities had encouraged enlistment in the program with the thought that their players might be able to eke out another year at their institutions. The government had a different idea and decided to put all who enlisted immediately in uniform and collect them in a single program in Seattle. As a result, the University of Washington had for a year a large and formidable group of athletes, but not good enough to beat USC in the only Rose Bowl game played by two west-coast teams. USC had a similar program and trounced Washington 28–0. Living among these athletes and participating in baseball, I had a glimpse of what players, coaches, and the university administration put up with; and I came away with distaste for what I have since considered an irritating and unfortunately ineradicable irrelevance in higher education. Of course, the times being what they were, I could not consider what I experienced as typical. The athletes were under military discipline and were carrying a number and types of courses unheard of under normal circumstances. A coach could not call on a player in the usual way. The players' scholarships were from the government, not the athletic department or boosters, and a professional career was not in the immediate offing for even the best. Some of these people had been athletic mercenaries, not very interested in academic studies and willing to cheat in the more difficult classes if they could get away with it. There was little or no loyalty to or affection for the university, against whom some of them had competed the year before. It seems that everyone was a unit unto himself in a situation in which he was supposed to be made a cog in a machine.

In the early spring of 1944 I turned out for baseball in the usual cloudy, wet weather. Some players from the previous year remained, and some had come from other institutions. Our coach was Dorsett V. "Tubby" Graves, who was already a sort of legend at Washington. Today the athletics office building is named after him. Even then the ball field, since replaced by the building, had his name. It is said that Graves played football for four years at one institution and then, under the name of Dorsett, a year at another. Either he had never been a very good coach or he had lost interest, which was not, I think, unusual at the time. I rarely if ever saw him instruct anyone about anything. He, was, however, a great raconteur, and on the overnight train to Walla Walla, where we played a double header against Whitman College, we were up very late listening to his stories. Come to think of it, I don't believe I learned very much from any of my baseball coaches. We learned from watching professional players when we had the chance. The trip to Walla Walla resulted in two wins, interrupted by a fierce wind and dust storm. I didn't get into either game. I think Tubby forgot I was along.

That spring we players showed up, took a desultory batting practice, fielded some balls, and stood around. There was little camaraderie, and with a few exceptions the older players had little to do with the younger, sometimes acting as if they were threats or totally ignoring them. I got into a few games as an infielder, hit well, and would have played more had I not sprained an ankle in a slide. By chance I doubled as the second-string catcher when the regular got into academic trouble. But I never played catcher except in practice. One day Fred Hutchinson, a Seattle native and later major-league pitcher and manager, showed up to take practice with us, and I caught him in his work- out. It was then that I learned what a fast ball really was, and his curve came faster than the fast balls I had seen then or since. Later we played a team, managed by Hutch, from the Navy or the Coast Guard. I got a hit that day, a little bloop over the third baseman's head. I think Hutch was pitching at the time, but that may be an invented wishful memory. In any case, when I came up again the third baseman was told to play in for a bunt and answered, "Aw, the little kid hit it over my head last time!" I was a skinny kid all right, just 18, but six feet tall.

In the summer of 1944, those of us remaining in the program were given the opportunity to be sent to the University of California in Berkeley to complete degrees in civil engineering. All that remained of the Washington and California military programs was to be combined there. I opted against this, foreseeing completion of college in a subject that did not interest me. The result was that I was sent with others to Parris Island, South Carolina, the eastern Marine Corps boot camp, which was the second step toward a commission, if you survived it.


## 3.

The trip to Parris Island on a troop train took eight days. We traveled slowly, stopping frequently. At one station in South Dakota, USO ladies fed us pheasant sandwiches. In Chicago, someone in my car slipped into the station and returned with a bottle of imitation whiskey appropriately labeled "Silver Flash." This he and a couple of others downed rapidly, all becoming heroically sick. At the time, any liquor other than this and Southern Comfort was in extremely short supply.

Of our dull, dirty, and increasingly smelly trip I remember little beyond this except for the dreadful slums inhabited by blacks near the railroad tracks in South Carolina. Somewhere in the boondocks near Parris Island we disembarked. I doubt we had any idea of just where we were.

It did not matter. For the whole time we were at Parris Island we did not leave the base. It was a large flat expanse of sand spit with old frame barracks and vast parade grounds on which we marched interminably day after day in close-order drill. The idea was apparently to reduce us one and all to cogs in a machine, our mental apparatus trained to group response. I wrote back to my parents, "The theory is to wipe out all individuality and encompass everyone in a gigantic machine.... You have just got to stop thinking. The whole idea is to do what you are told and _nothing_ else." But as a group we were different from what our drill instructors, noncommissioned officers, expected from the usual bunch of recruits. We were far more formally educated, better disciplined, and capable of learning everything much more quickly. It seemed that the drill instructors were used to assuming that a recruit would be stupid or at least innocent and would have to be kicked around to absorb any discipline. We all qualified with the M-1 rifle, which was almost unheard of for a whole company. (I, however, had a bad day on the range and almost didn't.) We did things so quickly and efficiently that our instructors were hard pressed to think up new tasks.

One task that was routinely performed by all companies of recruits during their training was to convey our mattresses to and from the delousing center, lice and cockroaches (of enormous size) being the principal permanent inhabitants of Parris Island. The delousing center was presided over by Sergeant Lew Diamond, who had gained fame as a heroic, eccentric character at Guadalcanal and was immortalized in _Guadalcanal Diary_ and later the _Reader's Digest_. It was said that he deigned to salute no one under the rank of colonel. Always troublesome, he had obviously been put away in an ignominious position. But this wiry little man with a billy goat beard made the best of it, lording over all who came near. We fell out one morning, each with a rolled-up mattress over his shoulder. Under Diamond's direction, which included the commands "Back, back!" and "Up!" loudly shouted, we were to march to the delousing center. The command of "Right face" created a chaos of traffic similar to what a rear-ender would accomplish on Interstate 5. After regrouping under a hail of curses, we struggled on.

# 4.

It was quite different, and for the worse, at Camp Lejeune in North Carolina, where we were finally sent to await space in the Officer Candidate School at Quantico, Virginia. At Lejeune we were called Officer Candidate Applicants and wore OCA badges on our collars, the lowest of the low. We were divided into companies by age, and I was in the youngest group, which was destined to gain a certain fame on the base for the severe treatment it suffered. The NCOs we were assigned may have decided that we needed more discipline as the result of our extreme youth. It was either that or simple sadism which led to our torments. Some of these were trivial and some even comical, but they added up over time to fatigue and anger. Rarely did we have an uninterrupted night's sleep, for we were often awakened and called out to muster, fall into ranks, and drill for some obscure purpose or

**Parris Island, USMC, 1945. The author is in row 4, fourth from the right.**

punishment. Once, we were called out, and all of us immediately ordered back into the barracks to find and bring back one penny each. We were to pay collectively for a six-dollar compass lost in the field that day. After the chaos of a desperate hunt for six hundred pennies, we returned to our formation and were then sent at double time past a water bucket to the tune of "Over the Waves," played on an accordion. There we each dropped in our penny and returned to rank. This task completed, we drilled for two hours with water buckets over our heads, clanging our rifles against each other's improvised helmets.

One week of relief occurred when we were assigned duties in the mess hall, away most of the day from our NCOs and under direction of a former New York chef, a Frenchman who contrived to serve quite good, hot fried eggs at breakfast to over a thousand people. This required a huge griddle, many cooks, and waiters at the ready to carry the eggs on huge platters to the eaters. During that week we were the cooks, waiters, and scourers of dishes, pots, and pans. The mass production of good fried eggs may have been the most efficient thing I participated in or witnessed in the Marines. Mess duty also gave us illicit entry into the pantry, where lemon extract was a famous item of theft because of its alcoholic content.

Torment extended to the one time in these months when we were given week-end liberty to leave the base. There had been promises of liberty before, but for some trivial or obscure reason they were always rescinded at the last moment. On that one week end, I and some others went to the nearest town of any size, Wilmington, only to discover that our two most detested NCOs were in the same hotel, drunk, and determined to harass us through the night, and they would have done so had they not eventually fallen into drunken slumber. The commissioned officers either condoned or were ignorant of our treatment. Unfortunately our immediate commander, a first lieutenant, who had been a Big Ten distance runner, was partial to long marches with full packs. These were rather like the one described by William Styron in *The Long March*, though with an officer whose pace was both rapid and steady. He got the nickname of "Peaches," because of a remark someone overheard him making that one of the marches had been peachy.

Parts of our treatment were bad enough that after we had completed Officer Candidate School one of us, the son, I believe, of a general, lodged a formal complaint. I do not know what the outcome of it was. More effective, perhaps, was a colleague who met one of the NCOs later in the beer hall men's room at Quantico and proceeded to give him a good beating. At Lejeune we were G Company, which on the base came to be known notoriously as Gestapo Company.

# 5.

By comparison, Quantico proved to be a vacation. Overnight we became gentlemen and prospective officers. The training was not nearly as physically demanding and wearing as what we had become accustomed to. We took short courses in various infantry weapons, explosives, loading and unloading of boats, and military law. There were field problems. If one were chosen to be in charge of a field problem the chances of bad luck and failure were great, and some of them were famous for being employed to flunk people out of the program. I was chosen twice. In the first instance, somewhere near Manassas, I was in charge of an eighty-one millimeter mortar platoon. We were to set up two mortars on a hillside. Across a valley was an old house and to the right of it a row of trees. We were to fire the two mortars at these objects. I ordered the mortars set up. The one on my right fired at the trees, struck, and nearly demolished the roof of the house. Astonished by this, I ordered the mortar on the left to fire at the trees. There was a perfect hit. Now, mortars were notoriously inaccurate. The captain observing this odd but apparently effective crossfire approached me and asked why I had ordered the mortar on the right to fire at the object on the left. I regard this moment as my finest hour as a Marine: "Sir, it seemed the primary target, and they had set up and were ready to fire earlier than those on the left." The captain regarded me with a wry smile, perhaps indicating skepticism, but he congratulated me and my platoon. To his knowledge no one had ever hit the house, prior to my unerring calculation.

Night problems were the most dreaded. On one of those I was a platoon leader at the far left end of an advancing company. We struggled through trees and brush up a gradual incline in order to set up machine guns, but we soon lost connection with the platoon on the right and struggled back somewhat late to the place of critique to hear the officer declare that it had been the best performance of this problem he had seen. No one noticed that we had become lost and had barely found our way back, tardy as we were.

These two exercises apparently assured my successful completion of Officer Candidate School and a commission as second lieutenant; from that time forward I was not assigned another position of responsibility. A short time after these events, the atomic bombs were dropped on Hiroshima and Nagasaki, and the war was effectively over. We graduated, and I was ordered to report to Camp Pendleton in California after a leave of two weeks.

## 6.

At Pendleton there was a long list of second lieutenants waiting for assignments. Few were any longer going to the Pacific. As jobs came up we were taken alphabetically. I, being Adams, was soon given an order. It was to report to the post exchange officer. The post exchange was a large operation serving a population at the time of over three hundred thousand Marines, most of whom had returned from the Pacific islands. It ran a central store that sold any number of things, including jewelry. It was responsible also for a group of beer halls ("slopchutes") and soda fountains scattered across a large area. I reported to the major in charge of all this in his office at the main store. His first words were, "Adams, do you know accounting?"

"No, sir."

"Well, learn."

The result of this remark was my embarkation on a Marine Corps accounting course, done by correspondence.

I was put in charge of the warehouse that received and then dispensed cases of beer and another that held fountain supplies. I was responsible for the material objects — freezers, refrigerators, tables, and chairs — in the various beer halls and fountains scattered over the huge base. Whole train carloads of beer pulled up to my warehouse, from which cases were distributed to the various beer halls for consumption by veteran Marines. I was in charge of a staff of about fifteen people, from master sergeant to corporal, almost all older than I, not yet twenty. The master sergeant, second to me in rank, was a veteran of the Corps. I learned that he had developed a modestly lucrative business bootlegging beer to bars in neighboring Oceanside. It turned out that if just one bottle of beer in a case was broken in transit, the whole case was written off the books. These cases he put in his car and transported to the highest bidder. I suspect that he also did a modest business in other things.

Learning of this, and without making any specific accusation, I reported to the major that the sergeant ought to be transferred, as I did not like some of the things he was doing. Lo and behold, in twenty-four hours he was gone. Much later, after I had left the Marines, I learned that the major had been court-martialed for embezzlement, mainly of jewelry, I believe. I then knew why the sergeant was so quickly transferred without a question asked. A few years later, I told this story to one of my old Lakeside teachers, who had been a naval officer in the Pacific. Unimpressed, he replied, "Why, hell, after the war ended we were dealing in ships!"

One day, unaccountably and suddenly, I received orders to report to Bremerton, Washington, for discharge. This meant that I had to hand over my command to a successor, and this meant, too, that everything I was responsible for had to be inventoried and acknowledged as received by him. When I had taken over several weeks before, I had participated in an inventory, a process that turned out to be full of mystery. On the books were the furniture of the beer halls and fountains, large beer coolers, freezers, and refrigerators. On my inventory it became clear that some of the largest items had disappeared. It seemed impossible that they could have been spirited out of Camp Pendleton, but they were gone. I do not believe that my predecessor was held accountable, but I was hesitant to sign officially the inventory list and managed to avoid doing so through my period of responsibility. In the new inventory, more items had disappeared, but some of the previously lost items had miraculously reappeared. On my last day, I advised my successor, who was sitting staring disconsolately at a rough draft of the huge list, not to sign anything, to explain, if asked, that the list was still in preparation, and to wait it out. As far as I know, that's what he did.

As anyone may imagine, I had an importance at Camp Pendleton dramatically out of proportion to my youthfulness and inexperience. I was the beer king and catered to by officers who ran the slopchutes, soda fountains, and mess halls. I had two other duties while there. The first was to be the duty officer every so often for the battalion to which I was assigned. This was, as far as I could determine, a purely fictitious entity. It appeared that it was a paper organization composed mainly of young officers waiting for assignment. I would report to an empty office containing only a desk, chair, and phone and sit there for a prescribed period. There was never any work to perform, lists to consult, or reports to be made. Only once the phone rang. It was, I believe, a colonel asking for some information the nature of which I forget. I answered that I could not supply it, whereupon he flew into a rage, berated me for a while, and then hung up. I waited, like a character out of Kafka, worried that someone would come by to whom I would have to give an accounting — of what I could not imagine. Perhaps even the colonel would appear.

Time passed. Nothing happened.

My other duty was occasionally to supervise one of the slopchutes in the evening. In the slopchute would be five hundred or so battle-scarred Marines returned from the Pacific. They would order whole cases of beer at a time and drink all evening, most in a stupor by closing time. When things got too rough we blinked the lights as a warning and ordered the shore patrol to come in and take away the worst offenders. One evening I was obliged to disarm a drunk Marine who had a knife and was threatening someone. After I had accomplished this, a grizzled sergeant from the Fifth Division asked me how old I was. I answered, "Older than I was when I came in here." He laughed amiably, astonished, I think, at how young some officers had become. I was not ordered to testify against the culprit, and I assume he was let out of the brig after he sobered up. He'd been through plenty, I'm sure; and I imagine that no one wanted to punish him.

# 7.

I take the liberty here of skipping ahead six years to my second, luckily brief tour of duty with the Marines. By this time it was 1951, I was married to the young woman I had unknowingly displaced in the University of Washington dormitory, and I had completed a master's degree and was preparing for a set of general examinations for the doctorate. Sometime in 1946 or 1947 the Marine Corps had invited me to join the reserve as a first lieutenant. I went for this bait. Another war did not seem likely, and if it came I would otherwise probably face the draft. Better to be an officer. In the early spring of 1951, during the Korean conflict, I was called up. It was likely that I would go to Korea, but I was granted a delay to take my examinations. When they were completed, I was sent not to Korea but rather, of all places, to Oklahoma.

Diana and I arrived at the sprawling Naval Ammunition Depot near McAlester in the eastern part of the state on a typically hot afternoon in late June. In what was by now a somewhat ill-fitting uniform, I reported to the commanding officer of the Marine guard unit, Major Johnny Jennings, who I later learned was the Marine Corps' champion pistol shooter. He greeted me amiably with two orders. By virtue of previous service, I was to run the post exchange, which also included what was called the farm, home to several horses and a lone pig, referred to as a boar. He allowed that he was tired of waking up at his house on the base and seeing horses peering in the window at him. He suggested that I take steps to see that they were kept where they belonged, and he sure as hell didn't want a boar around.

By virtue of previous athletic record, I was to report to the softball field at seven that evening. He added that otherwise he'd have to play, because the officers' team in the depot league was short a player. He was damned glad to see me because he hated baseball and was no good at it. What I not much later learned was that the commanding officer of the base, a Navy captain, was a baseball fanatic and had organized the base, both civilians and military, into a league. The captain was manager, first baseman, and all-around tyrant of the officers' team. Games were played nightly on a well-lighted, miniature stadium, which was at all times in a beautifully manicured condition. It was kept in shape by prisoners in the brig, who could be observed working on it in the daylight hours. For the good of the whole, they worked off their sins of drunkenness, fighting, and sleeping on duty.

I learned also that Johnny Jennings avoided proximity to the captain whenever he could. The captain was openly critical of his teammates, who, of course, were in no position to respond or to comment on his own somewhat erratic play. I was installed at shortstop on that first evening. After a game or two, I realized the silent contempt in which the captain was held by his teammates. Recognizing that his middle-aged eyes were not what they once were, I threw an occasional curve ball to him in fielding practice. Others enjoyed his efforts to locate the ball. Because my throws were accurate, always eventually reaching first base, he could not complain and never realized what I was doing. A good many others did. A serious silence prevailed.

One evening after a game, I was approached by a tall civilian who worked on the base. He invited me to play baseball, the hard variety, for a team that represented the hamlet of Ashland in what was called the Little Dixie League. Ashland was a town of no more than a few houses and a baseball field several miles southwest on a red dirt road. We would prepare for games at Ashland with no one around, but by game time the whole field would be surrounded by cars, pick-up trucks, and motorcycles, defining its boundaries. Some of our games were played at night on dimly lit fields in towns with names like Krebs and Kiowa, but Ashland's home games occurred on Sunday afternoons, there being no lights there.

I played my last game of hard ball late that summer for Ashland in a town the name of which I forget. I do remember the heat, however — 106 degrees and no wind, unusual for the area, where the wind seemed to blow incessantly. We were having a big inning: I tripled and later scored. We batted around, I came up again, and hit a home run over the right fielder's head. There being no fence, I had to run for it and was overcome by the heat. In this way my career at hardball ended. Shortly thereafter I was discharged.

My principle task as post exchange officer was to check over and sign documents prepared by my assistant, a sergeant. Most of my time I spent at my desk reading books that I hoped would help me with my doctoral dissertation. Occasionally, I traveled out to the farm, which was run by an enlisted man who tended the horses, maintained for recreational purposes, and the boar, who would be slaughtered for the annual barbeque. Boredom was the rule, punctuated by swims in the large officers' pool, which was whipped every morning to rid it of water moccasins, and weekly cocktail parties at a small officers' club near it. These were dreaded by Diana and me. My boredom was nothing compared to what she endured. She made occasional trips to McAlester for provisions at a sadly provisional market, and occasionally we would eat at the local steak house. McAlester was a poor town. It had the state prison, and the naval base was put there during the depression of the thirties to relieve poverty and provide jobs. My Ashland team was scheduled to play at the prison, but for some reason the game was cancelled.

The chief task of the Marine detachment as a whole was to guard and patrol the two hundred square miles of scrub brush, huge jack rabbits, and bunkers housing munitions. The greatest concern was, of course, fire from lightning or a discarded cigarette. The base was divided into four parts, each constantly patrolled by a Marine in a pick-up truck equipped with a sending and receiving radio. An officer had the duty each day and night, and in every stretch of four hours he had to locate and meet each of the four Marines in their trucks, making sure that they were not sleeping or smoking and were actually patrolling the space. This was by no means easy, since the men tended to play hide-and-seek with the duty officer, and the officer was only as a last resort to locate the guards by radio. About once a week I would have this duty for twenty-four hours. In the hot, humid nights there was frequently lightning, but rarely rain. I recall only one small brush fire, rapidly extinguished by the fire brigade.

In late August of 1951, I was unaccountably saved from service in Korea by what must have been a routine review of young officers' records with the intent of thinning the ranks. When I had first enlisted in 1943 I had indicated that I had once or twice had attacks of asthma as a child and had been treated for them for a while. I had completely forgotten about all this, but someone somewhere now noticed it, and orders came for me to be sent home and discharged. To my knowledge I was the only Lakeside graduate to join the Marines who was not killed or wounded. I had never been in combat. The nearest I ever came to danger was in the squad room at the McAlester Naval Ammunition Depot, where in my presence a not very bright private first class accidentally discharged his rifle. The bullet ricocheted around the room, missing me and the culprit, and lodged in the wall.

# 5

# Higher Ed:
# Washington and Princeton

**1.**

Sometime in early January of 1946, after a short time in Seattle, I embarked by train for Princeton, first to Chicago and then New York City, Princeton Junction, and finally the little electric train car that Princetonians called the PJ&B (Princeton Junction and Back). As I walked up the hill from the station I felt for the first time in my life, I think, a wave of anxiety over being alone in a strange place. In the Marine Corps you were never really on your own. Your food and bed were provided and your activities scheduled. You may have been unhappy, angry, or irritated, but you lived a certain kind of order. In this new place I knew no one. Officer in the Marines at age nineteen, beer king of Camp Pendleton, owner of two years of college credit, I reduced myself to the position of a jittery confused freshman. This state passed rapidly, however, mainly by necessity and because of tasks to perform. I had to worry about retrieving from the freight office my grandmother's old heavy travel trunk, which I subsequently employed as a closet, find the room assigned to me, and obtain somehow a bed. I also met with an adviser and discovered with surprise that I had enough credits from my V-12 experience at Washington to be a first-term junior. However, I had studied mostly engineering and the necessary sciences and opted to be a second-term sophomore. This meant that, if all went well I would graduate in the spring of 1948.

Dod Hall, to which I had been assigned, was one of the older dormitories. The rooms turned out to consist of a large living space with a quite splendid bay window, two bedrooms, and a small entrance hall. I obtained a bed at too high a price from a local pirate and installed it in one of the bed-rooms. The floor of the other was covered entirely with empty beer and soft drink bottles left by the predecessors, who had also abandoned an ice box. Over time, when we needed change, my roommate and I redeemed the bot-tles for cash. My roommate, who turned up the next day, had no bed and proceeded to appropriate the large bay window and its cushioned platform, which he used for the rest of the academic year. Other than my bed and the trunk there was no furniture, and neither of us had money to buy even a chair, let alone two. My roommate turned out to be a New Yorker of the class of '46, preceding mine by one year. He was recently back from the war in Europe, and although he seemed to be in good shape, in the middle of the following year he took leave as a result of emotional problems no doubt brought on by his war experience. By that time we had moved to smaller quarters in Cuyler Hall, and he with great pride had acquired a chair, upholstered even.

In that first semester back, most students from war service were wear-ing parts of old military uniforms. I had, in addition, a few things my father had discarded in my favor. We were hardly what the magazines, still bewitched by F. Scott Fitzgerald of two decades before, tried to make people believe Princeton students were like. Indeed, at Princeton I was perpetually broke, living on government handouts from the so-called G. I. Bill of Rights, which took precedence over the scholarship I had won three years before. I had room and board, tuition, and a little spending money. In that first semester we ate sub–Marine corps food in the Commons, attended classes, and in the spring engaged in what was called "bicker," a somewhat less barbaric ritual than "rushing" at schools that had fraternities. My roommate and I joined together in what was known as an "ironbound," which meant that a club wanting one of us had to take both. Quadrangle Club, where we landed, had food that reached civilized standards. This could not always be said of the parties there or elsewhere on Prospect Street.

## 2.

Since the nineteen-sixties, it has been common for college students at the end of every term to evaluate formally their courses and teachers. This was a practice unheard of when I was a student, though, as I remember, the *Daily Princetonian* did put out an evaluation from time to time, the quality of which is perhaps best illustrated by the opening remark about the course "Latin American Affairs," which began with "I have never had a Latin Amer-ican affair, but...." As I think back I am not certain what I would then have said about most of my teachers, and I am quite sure I would have been wrong in some cases about their value for me. And, of course, sometimes there was a difference between the value of a course of study and the contribution of the professor. I have, in any case, been skeptical about student evaluations, mainly because the rhetoric of teaching can be misleading to some and over my teaching career I consistently got very high grades, certainly far higher than I would have given myself. On the whole, it seems to me, students grade the teaching they experience too favorably, although this may have gone hand in hand with the grade inflation that has been rampant in recent decades.

In general, I can say that the teaching at Princeton was quite superior to that at Washington. Perhaps in memory I, too, grade the Princeton professors too leniently, for I can remember only one course at Princeton for its virtually unadulterated badness. It was a large popular lecture course entitled, as I recall, "Social Institutions" and recommended to me by a Princeton athlete. It turned out that it was famous as a "gut" course, chosen by people who filled out their schedules with some easy things. The lecturer was a young professor who liked to be popular and did so by taking iconoclastic positions and hanging out in the gymnasium with students. One of his main views was that all religions were based on the fear of death. Many of his others were equally simplistic, but they were delivered with fiery rhetoric and scorn for the icons of the day. I nearly failed this course, mainly out of lassitude brought on by contempt. To this day I think I was right about the course, but I am certain that this professor scored well in most evaluations by students. He was perhaps even a liberating influence in some cases. I believe that he did not get tenure at Princeton. Thirty years later he could well have been a shoo-in in many places, maybe even there.

On the whole, the teaching at Princeton was pretty good, and where it was mediocre the subject matter carried it along. Almost every course in English was period-oriented. Robert Cawley, who was an expert on Renaissance travel literature, taught the seventeenth-century metaphysical and cavalier poets and had little to say about the poetry even though this was the heyday of the New Criticism, close reading, and fascination with the metaphysical poets. I later wrote my senior thesis on John Donne and subsequently had to unlearn some bad or at least unfashionable critical habits. My graduate teacher at the University of Washington, Arnold Stein, trained in the New Criticism, told me he would not have let me write the thesis I did, which was concerned with Donne's religious and philosophical views as reflected in his poetry. I came to agree with him. Cawley's method when, for example, he taught the work of Andrew Marvell was to discuss Marvell's career, both political and artistic, then read "To His Coy Mistress," comment on its delightfulness, and end the lecture. What he said I found interesting, but I learned little about how to read the poetry of the period.

Better taught was Victorian poetry by Willard Thorpe, though it left me with no enthusiasm for Tennyson and Browning, to whom I had to come back later to appreciate what they were doing. At the time, to what was clearly the disgust of my preceptor, I liked "Idylls of the King" better than Tennyson's shorter and more highly regarded poems. The truth was that no criteria were developing in my mind for deciding what was valuable. Another course, entitled "The Victorian Age" was devoted mainly to prose writers and intellectual history. The lecturer was Dudley Johnson, who appeared always in what I perhaps inaccurately recall as a nearly stiff collar, silk tie with tie-pin, and a dark pin-striped suit. He seemed to keep his distance, his lectures being highly formal performances, with beginnings, middles, and ends (promptly on time), and delivered in a measured, stentorian manner. In some ways he was a figure of fun because of his stiff manner, but he knew his subject and generated an interest in the period. The one poem I remember his discussing was Tennyson's "In Memoriam," and it changed my attitude toward the poet, though I believe his discussion of it was mainly biographical. These courses along with Walter Phelps Hall's nineteenth-century European history converged fortunately to give me a fairly good sense of the period. I wish I had had the same experience with the eighteenth century, but I never put together the courses for that and didn't see any reason to at the time. Hall was already legendary at Princeton, and he is still mentioned fondly on occasion in the *Princeton Alumni Weekly*, which comes out unaccountably about eight times a year and is entertaining particularly for the letters by disgruntled alumni. Over the years they have fulminated about Princeton's rejecting the applications of their children, about women at Princeton, about godless and leftist professors, the architecture of new buildings, the performance of the football team, and so on. Yet in the main they are almost fanatically loyal. Known as "Buzzer," Hall wore a hearing aid, and his voice had been seriously damaged by deafness. He was nevertheless a lively and compelling lecturer. He brandished a cane, which he waved about for emphasis and which sometimes got away from him. He sported almost always a tartan vest and bow tie. He was an advocate, I believe, of the "great man" concept of history. His preceptorials were dramatic encounters. He set the most interesting examination question I ever encountered. The task was to invent a conversation among, I believe, John Stuart Mill, Cardinal Newman, and Thomas H. Huxley. Hall apparently liked the humor in my answer, giving me a first group in the course, and inquiring about me to a student friend of mine.

History was one of the best departments at Princeton at the time. European history of earlier periods was taught by Gordon Craig, later at Stanford. His lectures, as I now vaguely recall them, were brilliant. However, my only clear memory today is that of a verbal slip in which Craig declared that the Spanish throne was in a state of fucks. This he corrected to flux, adding the comment that, come to think of it, the former was not inaccurate.

At Princeton, English drama was well taught from Shakespeare through the eighteenth century. Gerald Eades Bentley did well with Shakespeare, often during his lectures taking various parts for brief performances. Alan Downer did restoration and eighteenth-century drama as well as the moderns. I did not think much about what kind of critical positions my teachers held. Indeed, I was not aware of critical positions as such, and I do not think that there was or is a strong correlation, if any, between critical position and teaching excellence. Among my Princeton teachers I was most impressed by scholarly knowledge (mostly historical and bibliographical), intensity of focus on whatever was at hand, unfailing courtesy, inviting us to regard ourselves as adult scholars, and not pandering to us. Perhaps few of us accepted this invitation to adulthood, reverting to pre-war adolescent behavior on party weekends or in forays to New York City, but it was offered.

There was certainly one time when we all had to put away childish things. Everyone had to write a senior thesis, preceded in the junior year by two independent essays. This was a good idea, but here the Princeton ideal of the undergraduate teacher as universally competent in the whole range of English literature tended to break down. My junior paper choices were the poetry of William Blake and the Gothic romance. I was assigned to Bentley or perhaps he to me. He had an international reputation as a scholar of Renaissance drama. He seemed a rather distant man who projected in a conference the attitude that he ought to or wanted to be doing something else. It is also possible that he did not know a lot about either subject, neither of which was popular at the time. It is, for me, a mild irony that his son became a well-known biographer of Blake.

The result was that I struggled along alone with Blake — and lost. At the time, Mark Schorer's and Northrop Frye's books had recently come out, but I remained ignorant of them, and Bentley gave me no direction. Thus my knowledge was out of date. I fared a little better with the Gothic romances, for Louis Landa, to whom Bentley (in this case) sent me for help, put me onto some helpful if now regarded as odd-ball books. The truth was that I had no idea of how to do the simplest kind of scholarship on my subjects, and the faculty, it then seemed to me, either assumed that by now I should know, felt that I should find out for myself, or didn't care very much. Today I regard the matter as principally my own fault or at least something I could have dealt with on my own.

One course notable for me because of one meeting was at the sophomore-level. It was called "The Nature of Poetry" and the text was Donald A. Stauffer's book by that name. He had apparently invented the course and passed it on to a young instructor, who used Stauffer's book, perhaps by command (Stauffer was chairman of the department). The instructor was a good but nervous teacher who seemed uncertain of himself. One day he was ill, and he was replaced by R. P. Blackmur, the noted critic. The subject for the day became W. B. Yeats, and Blackmur chose to lecture to us on Yeats's eccentric, semi-occultist book *A Vision*, with reference to "The Second Coming" and other poems. My parents had a copy of *A Vision* in their library. I knew nothing of its interior, but I had enormous respect for my parents' books. If they had it, it must be important.

Blackmur walked up and down in front of our class of maybe twenty. He spoke for the required fifty minutes continuously to the wall, to the window, to the ceiling, and always to himself. We did not have to be there. His devotion to his subject was complete and intense. I understood little of what he said. I knew that my parents were great admirers of Yeats, but little more. The lecture was unforgettable. Blackmur later published essays on *A Vision*. I now know that he was working on them at the time. Years later — about forty-five years — I wrote a book on *A Vision*. Toward the end of it I discussed Blackmur's view of the book and concluded that he was in certain important ways wrong about it. But in my experience he was more than either right or wrong. No class I ever had impressed me nearly as much. It has been a lesson to me about the mystery of what great teaching is. Great teaching may sometimes fail to reach some, perhaps touch many, perhaps touch only a few. As far as I can see, to a teacher of pedagogical methods, Blackmur did everything wrong. He didn't relate, as we say, to students; he may not have cared whether they were present; he spoke over their heads, at least mine.

Later I got to know Blackmur a little, meeting him with others occasionally for coffee. In this situation he was approachable and friendly. Some of us called him "the hat" because of a stylish fedora he was given to wearing. I never took his creative writing course, a grave mistake, because he used Joyce's *Ulysses* as a text, finding somewhere in it whatever he wanted as an illustration. A friend of mine who studied with him told a story of an evening class at Blackmur's house. Blackmur apparently had a habit of delivering long perorations similar to the one I'd heard on *A Vision*. During one of these his wife entered the room and after a short while declared, "Richard, no one understands what you are saying." She departed, and returned a little later to say, "Richard, you don't know what you are saying." This marriage, I believe, ended in divorce.

My academic achievement at Princeton was mediocre. What awakened me from intellectual slumber was the writing of a senior thesis. This required real work and a modicum of scholarship, of which I had little. Alan Downer, who was no expert on my subject, was a patient, kindly, but somewhat distant supervisor. I read a large part of the scholarship on John Donne with the unfortunate exception of some key recent essays by New Critics, which, if not entirely on Donne, used him as an example. What I did was out of date. I think that, for the most part, literary education at Princeton had not as yet embraced the critical movements then current and active, for example, at

Yale. Though Blackmur was on the faculty and people like I. A. Richards and Yvor Winters came to lecture, the teaching that I experienced was pre–New Critical. I failed to take Stauffer's course on the history of criticism and thereby delayed my development in a subject that later came to be a major concern. I doubt that I knew what the history of criticism was. Shortly after or perhaps even before I graduated, Blackmur organized an annual series of lectures by contemporary critics. One faculty member is known to have remarked that it was developed so Blackmur could get together with his friends.

I still have a copy of my thesis, but I have not looked at it for fifty years or more. Princeton required that a copy of every thesis be submitted to the library. Surely all of these theses could not be kept, and surely mine was discarded years ago. I certainly hope so. However, the experience of research and writing, flawed as it was, changed my life.

The faults of my Princeton education were mainly my own. What I particularly recall and value, among other things, is the unfailing respect and politeness that characterized the behavior of my teachers toward students and their seriousness about their subjects. We were treated as gentlemen. We weren't, of course, but perhaps some of us became such as a result.

## 3.

Social life at Princeton, if that was what one could call it, was isolated and revolved around the clubs. In those days, Princeton was a men's college with a small graduate school located at a distance from the main body of the campus. By 1946, with return of veterans from World War II, the enrollment had increased to 3800 undergraduates, a few belonging to the class of 1943 and the youngest to 1949. Some old traditions, including compulsory chapel attendance, had been abandoned, but women were still banned from dormitory rooms after seven P.M. and students were not allowed to have cars. The presence of older students, many having been in battle, and the increased number of those on federal scholarships (the so-called G.I. Bill) brought a somewhat greater seriousness to campus life. At least, so I was told by some who had returned. Princeton was no longer quite the college of F. Scott Fitzgerald, if it ever had been.

Princeton seemed to draw a good many students from the South. Indeed, some people spoke of it as the southern university of the Northeast. But most students seemed to me to be from New York, especially the city, and Pennsylvania. There were contingents from the Midwest — Chicago, Cleveland, St. Louis, but few from beyond the Mississippi River. By the chance of dormitory assignment most of my friends seemed to come from St. Louis. I don't recall any friendships I made with people from the Philadelphia "Main Line" or from the so-called elite clubs. My sense of the wealthy eastern students was that most of them were spoiled, somewhat crude and impolite, though I do not think their manner was deliberate, just born of convention and ignorance. On the whole I found them somewhat comical.

Princeton had few Jews and only two African Americans, both readmitted by virtue of their having been sent there as Navy V-12 students during the war. Princeton was obliged to readmit them. One became the basketball captain and was clearly the team's best player in 1946. When I received the name of my roommate it was Jewish. By the time I had arrived, it had been changed, how or why I don't know. Well, maybe I do know. In any case, my roommate turned out to be James Roy Reid from New York City. We got along well enough and together joined Quadrangle Club with some friends from St. Louis.

There has always been much criticism of the Princeton club system, but, compared to the fraternity system at most colleges, it seemed to me superior. For one thing, it eliminated most of the ritualistic silliness and savagery of fraternities. During my presence in the Marine Corps program at Washington, I joined a fraternity, mainly because all my friends had done so. I found the fraternity society stifling, childish, racist, and reactionary. Princeton, itself, was some of those things, and some of the clubs were, as well; but the club I joined had little of what I have mentioned.

I never thought much about being a westerner, at least I never regarded it as a disadvantage, or my lack of money, for that matter. I'd gone to school with wealthy northwesterners and was used to them, though the Princeton wealthy far surpassed most of them in their apparent self-satisfaction. I had never thought of college as being for the purpose of socialization, maintenance of class, or getting ahead. Of course, Lakeside was that for many of the parents who sent their children to it. But I seemed to have inherited from my parents the assumption that college was there to provide a liberal education. I simply assumed that the humanities, though I cannot recall anyone at the time calling them that, should be at its center. Thus, though my record at Princeton was mediocre, I profited greatly from my two and one half years there, and I met other students whom I respected as scholars and intellects, though I knew almost none of them well: among others, William Arrowsmith, the distinguished classicist who was later a colleague at Texas; Sidney Monas, a Russian scholar; Calvin Tomkins, of *The New Yorker*; and the architect Robert Venturi (the last two were in my class and club). In 1947 or 1948, I published two bad stories in *The Nassau Lit*, a sign that there were perhaps not very many good prose writers around. The poets W. S. Merwin and Galway Kinnell were undergraduates at the time, though I met Kinnell only later when he was a visitor at Irvine, probably angry to this day that we neglected to ask him to play on the softball team.

In the spring of 1947, I turned out for baseball and made the cuts, but the coach wanted to make me into an outfielder. I saved him and myself embarrassment by dropping out. My faulty depth perception made a fly ball to the outfield a perilous adventure. I was as good or better than the infielders the coach had from the year before, but they were known to him and I was a newcomer. At the end of the academic year I stayed around to make some money working at the alumni reunion. I am not sure that any other college reunion approaches Princeton's. There is a large parade in which each class marches, in its particular dress for that occasion, usually adorned with tigers and displaying the school colors of orange and black. There are parties, lectures, and other events. There is a baseball game with Yale. In June of 1947, I needed money to get back to Seattle and tended bar for the class of 1929. A small band headed by Joe Bushkin and with Tyree Glenn on trombone entertained. Bushkin, whom I struck up conversations with, didn't much like this gig, and I determined that he resented being regarded as help bought by rich snobs. One evening, when the bar was quiet and the band not playing, some member of the class, in his cups, remarked to me that this had been a nice class, but in 1929 and 1930 all the good guys committed suicide and only those without the guts to do so were left. The group did strike me as somewhat defeated. I escaped one afternoon (or perhaps evening) to hear Norman Thomas deliver a talk to his class next door.

This was the only Princeton reunion that I have ever attended. But Princeton seldom loses track of a graduate. I receive three or more periodic publications from the alumni office, in addition to the *Princeton Alumni Weekly*. In addition, I receive letters from Quadrangle Club asking for money, my class asking for money, and an occasional missive from my class secretary in Arizona, including an annual birthday card. My class is now having mini-reunions in various cities. These days, when the *Weekly* comes, I turn first to the obituaries, where it is most likely I will find names of my friends, then to the class notes, which, as earlier classes die off, march depressingly with every issue closer to the front of the section.

In June of 1948, before commencement ceremonies took place, I boarded the train for Chicago and then Seattle. My diploma came in the mail a month later. By that time I was already a graduate student in English at the University of Washington, having just made it back to Seattle in time for the summer session.

# 4.

My status as a graduate student was "provisional," my grades at Princeton not having been good enough to gain regular admission and certainly not admission to a major graduate school. Though I was no longer provisional after a trial period, I was never during my time at Washington offered a teaching assistantship or any kind of monetary support. Fortunately, my G. I. Bill eligibility had not yet expired. In addition I worked two jobs. In the summers and on Saturdays I worked in downtown Seattle for a clothing store for boys. During the academic year, I coached club sports and junior varsity basketball at Lakeside and drove a Ford station wagon that served as a bus for some of the day students.

It was an interesting but not always pleasant time to be a graduate student at Washington. Long before the Cold War the state legislature had contained many people suspicious of the university faculty. Recent politics had made things worse. First, there was a ruckus over the visiting appointment of the left-wing literary critic Malcolm Cowley. The major effect of this was an immediate increase in attendance at his lectures on the modern American novel. Then the state legislative committee on un–American activities, headed by an eastern Washingtonian named Albert Canwell, began an investigation of the faculty in order to root out suspected communists. As is usually the case when the right goes after the left on a campus, it was thought that most of the culprits were English professors and social scientists. From the summer of 1948 on, I was in classes of some of those being investigated. My first experience of this was in a class in the early history of literary criticism taught by Sophus Keith Winther, author of several forgotten novels about the West. There had been communist meetings that some faculty had attended in the thirties. When Winther was brought before the committee, he testified that he had attended some communist party meetings at that time. Then he named colleagues who had been in attendance and who he thought may have been members. The most excruciating class I can recall ever attending was one in which Winther chose to hold forth on Plato's *Apology*. This was a text not actually assigned, it not being directly relevant to literary matters. The assigned texts were *Ion* and parts of *Republic*. Winther made his discussion of *Apology* into a defense of his actions before the committee. Clearly it mattered to him that he had implicated colleagues, whose careers might be ruined. His discourse reeked with guilt.

Some careers were indeed ruined. In the following academic quarter I was taking a class on *Beowulf* from Joseph Butterworth, a perpetual assistant professor who had been a party member and may still have been, though he might have forgotten for some time to pay his dues. Butterworth was a small mole of a man who walked with a limp, had a slight tremor and physical defect in his hand, wore always the same dirty dark gray suit with vest, had a chronic cough, and was clearly in ill health. He was a terrible teacher though he knew a great deal. His main problem in the classroom was that he would become infatuated with a word in *Beowulf* and fill a whole blackboard with variations, derivations, and connections to words in other languages, failing to get us past perhaps one or two sentences in a couple of hours. One day, without warning, Butterworth was gone, replaced by a professor from the German department, who for the remainder of the quarter drove us relentlessly through the text. To my knowledge, Butterworth never again held a job of any kind. He was frequently seen drinking beer in the Blue Moon Tavern, haunt of writers, academics, and literature students. Robert Heilman, the chairman of English, is known to have said poor Butterworth should have been fired long ago for incompetence as a teacher. Heilman, whose instincts seemed to be on the political right, had found himself obliged, however, to defend Butterworth on grounds of academic freedom.

Winther survived, continued to teach, and lived into his nineties. Two others from other departments were dismissed. I had taken a philosophy course as an undergraduate from one of them, "Scoop" Phillips, a good teacher whom I remember for challenging his freshmen and sophomores to prove that there was not a little green-winged griffin sitting before him on his desk. I cannot recall anything that either Phillips or Butterworth said that could in the slightest be regarded as communistic or un–American utterances endangering Washington's youth. On the other hand, Harry Burns, not a member as far as any anyone knew, was never touched by the investigation. For years he taught a Marxist interpretation of American literature. To my knowledge Phillips never taught again. Some others, no longer party members and perhaps never having been, were deprived of raises in salary. Harold Eby, who taught nineteenth-century American literature, never again received a pay increase, probably because of his early and later rejected communist connections. He could just as well have been punished for inflicting boredom on his students. A course with Eby on a warm summer day in old Parrington Hall was a sure cure for insomnia. I believe his capacity for boring students did not extend to himself. He spent years doing a concordance to the poetry of Walt Whitman that could now be done with a computer in a miniscule fraction of the time. My experience with him had an element of the ridiculous about it. I wrote a paper for him on William Dean Howells as a literary critic for which he gave me an A but wrote a brief caustic comment. It was an essay that sought to uncover Howell's probably unconscious philosophical position. I was openly critical of it. Eby probably liked Howells, though it was difficult to gauge his enthusiasms, which were sober ones.

Another teacher, the philosopher Melvin Rader, was persecuted for a while by the Canwell committee, but he was finally completely exonerated through the efforts of a Seattle newspaper reporter, who proved through a hotel register that Rader was far away and could not have been at a communist gathering where someone swore to have seen him. It turned out that the witness was a consummate liar and eventually became an embarrassment to the committee. The reporter won a Pulitzer Prize, and Rader became the hero of a recent play on the whole affair by my friend, the actor Mark Jenkins, now a professor of drama at Washington. Rader's main subject was aesthetics, and he had written a book on Wordsworth. I took an undergraduate class with him as a graduate student, deciding, because of my growing interest in literary theory, that I needed to know more philosophy. By now, Rader was, of course, locally famous, in part because of his testimony before the committee. He had thoroughly confused the questioners by speculating on their words, indicating that he was confounded by the possibilities of their meanings and expressing respectfully serious worry that he might be misconstruing their intent. I doubt that any legislative hearing or courtroom, for that matter, had ever been subjected to this sort of witness. Alas, Rader's teaching did not live up to this reputation. In front of a class, he could not speak more than a sentence without attempting, apparently unsuccessfully, to clear his voice. He offered little that could be called wit or anything that indicated an original mind. Still, what I read in his class, mainly Locke to Kant, was important to me.

The most celebrated member of the English department at Washington was the poet Theodore Roethke. The chairman suffered a lot for his presence, since he was a heavy drinker and was known occasionally to have to be dried out. He also could become rather violent and trash the furniture at a party. I did not know him, and saw him only when he shambled through Parrington Hall with the gait of a bear. It is said that on one occasion he entered a class through the window and on another entered a lecture room with a large bag, reached the podium, took out a bowling ball and sent it hurtling down the main aisle and through folding doors at the end. It was perhaps the wood floor of the old building that fascinated him, or perhaps the story is apocryphal.

The faculty who were hired in English at Washington in the early thirties were mainly on the left because of their experience of the depression. Their older colleagues were, I think, not. This is interesting because many of them had been students of these older colleagues, having taken their doctorates at Washington and stayed on, probably because there were few other jobs. Not very far on the left was Brents Stirling, a Renaissance scholar. He had been a student of Frederick M. Padelford, who was one of the editors of the monstrous *Variorum Edition of the Poems of Edmund Spenser*. The principal editor was Edwin Greenlaw, and Stirling once said to me, both in earnest and in jest, "Don't buck the Greenlaw trust." That remark provided my first real inkling of the politics of literary scholarship, that there was a jungle out there.

Farther on the left was a younger faculty member, Malcolm Brown, who taught, among other things, Anglo-Irish literature. When older, he wrote a good book on the Anglo-Irish novelist George Moore and, later, *The Politics of Irish Literature*, which took the subject through the nineteenth century. A twentieth-century sequel was begun, but Brown died before he was able to complete it. Under him, I studied Yeats and his Pre-Raphaelite precursors, and this led me back to Blake and eventually my dissertation topic on Blake and Yeats. Brown had a sarcastic streak. At the time I was his student he had as yet published little and was held back for promotion. The principal object of his invective was the chairman Robert B. Heilman, whom he regarded as a politically right-wing interloper and all-around tyrant. Brown called him Prince Robert and probably worse things out of the range of students.

# 5.

My arrival at the University of Washington coincided approximately with that of Heilman. He came from Louisiana State University, where he had become identified as a New Critic, having with Cleanth Brooks edited the textbook *Understanding Drama*, a sequel to the influential poetry text-book *Understanding Poetry* by Brooks and Robert Penn Warren. The latter book was important in making the New Criticism, so named by John Crowe Ransom, Brooks's and Warren's teacher, a major influence in literary studies.

The English faculty at Washington, or at least many of them, were terrified of what Heilman's appointment boded. The department's main lights had been Frederick M. Padelford and Vernon Lewis Parrington, well-known author of *Main Currents in American Thought*. Padelford was a scholar in the traditional mode. In addition to having edited Spenser, he had translated Julius Caesar Scaliger. Parrington was a historian who used literary texts to illustrate American political and intellectual history. Campus buildings are named for both Padelford and Parrington. Heilman was about as far from these erstwhile stalwarts, both by then dead, as could be imagined at that time. The former students of these figures, several of whom were kept on there to teach after their graduate study, managed to push through, before the new chairman arrived, a set of by-laws that limited the chairman's powers and for years frustrated him. However, he did succeed in appointing at once a young man from Yale who had New Critical affinities. This was the seventeenth-century scholar Arnold Stein. Heilman was thought to play favorites among the faculty and to be prejudiced against women and minorities. Whether this was true or not I do not know. It is clear, however, that the department cer-tainly improved during the earlier part of his chairmanship, though it is also true that he stayed in the job far too long, twenty-five years or so, continu-ing to generate resentment among some and, I think, losing touch. In the late years of his reign, I met him on a plane and we discussed the convention of the Modern Language Association, from which we were both returning. He was greatly upset by the decision to shift the convention from Chicago to Denver for political reasons, and it was clear to me that he did not really comprehend why or how such a thing could have happened.

The department was made a livelier place. Theodore Roethke was becoming well known as a poet. Jackson Mathew was doing his translations of Paul Valéry. Young poets Richard Hugo, Kenneth Hansen, and A. Wilber Stevens, who was editing *Interim* at the time, were their students. In Mathew's course, Hugo decided that he liked Baudelaire but hated Mallarmé. One evening when I visited Hansen and Hugo on a houseboat that they shared (along with Hansen's huge cat Wilfred) in Lake Union, Hugo expressed excitement about a new young comedian on television. Watching Hugo watching Jonathan Winters, I realized that they looked alike.

I studied with neither Roethke nor Mathew, and Heilman, for some reason, never taught a graduate course in his career at Washington. I did take a seminar from Arnold Stein on Donne and the metaphysical poets. Stein was the only teacher I had who was what we called a close reader in the New Critical manner. This was a revelation to me and sent me to reading Blackmur and some of the other New Critics. However, Stein was an intimidating teacher, even though I do not believe that he intended to be. I accepted what seemed to me a challenge and came to his office with a proposal to write a master's essay on Donne. He inquired about my Princeton senior thesis, and I was asked to present it to him. Days later he told me that he would never have allowed me to write on Donne in that way. It was too biographical in approach, not attentive enough to style and to the text. Still, I persisted. I had the idea that in Donne's *Anniversaries* there was anticipated in certain ways a later skepticism about experimental and empirical methods. This did not wash with Stein, who wanted a paper of close verbal analysis. He was right, and I do not want to read again my master's paper, which he passed without enthusiasm. It was an act either of kindness or diffidence, one not being able to distinguish the two in his manner. About six years later I was told that when he learned I had brought out *Blake and Yeats: The Contrary Vision*, he remarked, not having read it, that I shouldn't have been allowed to publish it. A few years later, I met him after an MLA session in which I had given a paper on Yeats. From his great height he looked down and opined that it was a "strenuous" paper. I was a little taken aback, not sure whether this was praise. Startled, he made clear that it was. High praise from on high!

Arnold Stein was the only man I know of who could fill, light, and draw an initial puff from what was a huge hooked pipe and speak continuously while doing so. Richard Hugo used to amuse us by simulating a broadcast of a basketball game with faculty members as players. Stein, the center on this mythical (and, I think, undefeated) team, scored well in the paint and swatted away shots of opposing graduate students. Many years later, in the 1960s, the *University of Washington Daily* published student evaluations of undergraduate teaching, and Stein received one of the lowest ratings on campus. A petition went around the country among his former graduate students criticizing this rating. I signed it along with several others I knew. I imagine that Stein had trouble connecting with undergraduates, but his challenge to me, though painful, and his reading of Donne were as valuable as anything I learned in graduate school.

But I did not continue with Donne and the seventeenth century. This was not an act of cowardice. Neither was it simple self-protection or loss of interest. I had been drifting intellectually toward Blake, a favorite since my mother had read to me from *Songs of Innocence and of Experience* before time to sleep. Now, better informed than I was at Princeton, I had begun to read the major books on Blake: Damon, Percival, in whose class my father was at Ohio State, Schorer, and Frye. The last was a revelation that brought about my first true realization of Blake as a poet and thinker.

The principal teacher of English romantic poetry at Washington was E. E. Bostetter, who years later finally published a book, *The Romantic Ventriloquists*, and became a full professor. Bostetter was interested in Blake but later avoided him in his book. This was with good reason, since Blake was really of an earlier generation and did not come into Bostetter's view of what was then the "big five": Wordsworth, Coleridge, Byron, Shelley, and Keats. The so-called lesser romantics — for example Clare, Lamb, Hazlitt, and Mary Shelley — rarely appeared on syllabi. Blake's works, at least his long poems, were generally avoided. At Princeton, Carlos Baker taught Blake's *Songs* and briefly *The Marriage of Heaven and Hell*, but said nothing about the longer works or Blake's visual art. Across the country and in England as well, the romanticists regarded Blake either as an anomaly or properly belonging in the eighteenth-century course, and the eighteenth-century professors thought him a romantic. This was convenient for both, as neither group was obliged to teach him. Northrop Frye's *Fearful Symmetry* and later David V. Erdman's *Blake: Prophet Against Empire* challenged all that, beginning a Blake movement aided and abetted by my generation of young scholars. For a while Blake threatened to become the major romantic poet as well as the principal one of the late eighteenth century. Only after a good while was he accepted by art historians, grudgingly by many, for he did not fit the categories popular at the time. Even when it became obvious that he was a significant influence on certain later artists there was little effort to include him in the history of art.

Bostetter taught a seminar of which half was on Blake and half on Keats. He was also teaching the twentieth-century criticism course, which began with Eliot and Richards and came up through the New Critics and Kenneth Burke. He had the valuable ability to describe and clearly analyze the theories and practices of these critics. His Blake-Keats seminar invited us into Blake's longer poems, but I remained pretty much alone with these works. Frye was my main help, especially his location of Blake as a critic of John Locke and the tradition of empiricism that by now I knew something about. Above all, Bostetter was patient and encouraging. He never imposed his views, and, I think, partly for this reason he was the most popular dissertation director in the department. Only after his book came out did I understand his reservations about the romantic poets. He greeted with enthusiasm my proposal to study Blake and Yeats

Meanwhile I still had the general examinations and a German language requirement to pass through. The latter became the more onerous task. I had studied French and Latin, but chose not to be examined in Latin but rather to begin a crash course in German. Early in the morning for two quarters I and about twenty others would assemble daily in a damp, mildewed room in the basement of old Denny Hall, the campus's first building, since mercifully remodeled. A pleasant instructor tried to buoy our spirits by leading us in a German song at the beginning of each hour. After the ordeal of all this I presented myself for examination and achieved a grade of 49, one point below passing. I had successfully translated a German essay on Donne but failed the grammatical half of the test. A few weeks later, my continuation in graduate school hanging in the balance, I scored 51 and passed.

Bostetter's wife, Betty, née Elizabeth Benton, was the terror of the department and its environs. Heilman regarded her as one of his principal administrative problems, as she was a vicious gossip who drew no line between fact and fiction, favoring the latter whenever possible. Though people she disliked were usually her victims, she was capable of inventing damaging stories about her friends. She had been teaching in the department until her marriage to Bos, as he was called by everyone. The nepotism rule then in effect barred her from further employment. She was a talented writer but never finished anything. Awarded a fellowship by Houghton Mifflin to write a biography of her ancestor Senator Thomas Hart Benton, "Old Bullion," she accomplished little, the book remaining ever "in progress." Much later, after Bos's death, she moved to London, became a denizen of the British Library reading room, and began to write a life of the English physician Thomas Wakley, founder of *The Lancet*. To my knowledge, she produced two chapters written in a breezy journalistic style — and then nothing. Wakley is an interesting subject, and it is a shame she didn't accomplish more. I think she was more interested in the book's being in progress than in finishing it; it kept for her a desk in the reading room, from which she could carry on her London intellectual social life, which involved the collection of English and visiting American academics for occasional display at parties. Her book as a fiction won out over her book as a fact. In the time she appeared to be at work she claimed to be having an affair and to have married. She was, of course, no spring chicken, but in her late sixties. The affair she declared to be with a wealthy Japanese business man, whom none of her friends ever met. The marriage was to an Oxford don known only to her friends as John, who also never made an appearance. She told stories about traveling to "Spitzenberg" (Spitzbergen) with John for his geological research and to other places. She managed to convince some acquaintances of the existence of both of these men. I believe that she imagined herself as a character in a Henry James novel.

Betty sublet a flat illegally near the British Museum from a much younger Irish woman who was subletting it (illegally) from someone else. She had convinced the young woman that she was a wealthy heiress as well as a writer of importance. As she became feeble, forgetful, and unable to take care of herself properly, the woman took over her care and allowed few, if any, visitors to see her. My wife may have been the last of her American visitors and gained admittance only with persistence. What she found was a Betty with hair dyed flaming red and made up like a character in a Toulouse-Lautrec painting. She was uncertain who was calling on her. On her death, her sister learned that she had been talked into changing her will and leaving everything to her keeper. Betty's fiction of wealth and royalties, however, had deluded this Irish schemer. There was not much to inherit, no big manuscript for a publisher to read, no income from royalties. There may have been a bank account somewhere that contained enough to cause her sister to contest the will. Betty and her sister had not gotten along well, especially in the last years, and their final meeting was a disaster. Thus Betty succeeded in making a Jamesian fiction of her life.

My mother, who had known Betty for years in Seattle but kept her distance, told me of the efforts of Betty and some other faculty wives to have a woman friend committed to a mental hospital. It seems that this woman had deluded herself into thinking she was going to marry one of Bos's colleagues, who already had a wife. She harassed both of them with phone calls and other messages. Finally she arranged a wedding, to which, of course, the prospective groom did not come. At the hearing having to do with her competence, the judge found himself faced with an unexpected challenge. After testimony from Betty and her friends, he apparently concluded that it was not at all clear to him just who should be committed. The woman walked free to harass again.

# 6.

Social life at Princeton, at least with young women, had been of a nearly hypothetical character. At least for me. With little spending money, I made

Seattle

RADIO GUIDE

PROGRAMS For Week of FEBRUARY 16-22

5c

Radio

Screen

Stage

Sports

News

Features

DIANA WHITE, THE "STORY GIRL" (See Page 4)

Diana White, the Story Girl (and Rapid Rabbit), 1947.

few forays out of town. When I returned to Seattle and entered graduate school, I had lost touch with most old acquaintances. Luckily for me, in the summer of 1947, before my senior year, one of my old Washington baseball teammates, a fellow Marine, arranged a blind date for me. I later learned that the young woman had drawn straws with two roommates, lost, and was thus condemned to spend the evening with me. Her name was Diana White. She had a degree in English from Washington and was working at a local radio station on which she had her own program for children, "The Story Girl." It was written and acted by herself with the addition of recordings. She also appeared on commercials, the most impressive being one on which she played a rabbit in behalf of Al Phillips' Sudden Service Dry Cleaning. Phillips' several stores around Seattle each displayed a large neon rabbit resembling Bugs Bunny. Disguising her voice, she greeted the listener as follows:

> [whoosh]
> Hello folks, welcome to town.
> Be right back to show you around [whoosh].
> I'm the rapid rabbit with the sudden service habit.
> [etc.]

Al Phillips advertised, "in at ten, out at five."

She was pretty, talkative, stylishly dressed, and possessed of a considerable, sometimes sarcastic sense of humor. Indeed, she later said that I told her she was the most sarcastic person I had ever met. This may actually have been true before I formally entered the academic profession. I had another year at Princeton, but in the late summer of 1949 we were married. I doubt that I would ever have completed graduate school successfully, especially the dreaded German examination, had I not married her. As I write this we are about to celebrate our fifty-seventh wedding anniversary.

## 7.

In early October of 1950, a little over a year after our marriage, my father, aged 53, died suddenly and unexpectedly of a heart attack, leaving my mother devastated, forcing a complete change in her life. She had to move out of the headmaster's house at Lakeside, divest herself of many belongings, and seek employment. About a month before his death, they had bought a house on the water at Ten Mile Point in Victoria, British Columbia. It was the first house they had owned since losing the one in Cleveland. Diana and I passed with them the single night that they ever spent there. When my father died, my mother sold the property as soon as possible. She needed the money, but also she never wanted to return.

My father was a smoker who had several times given it up but always returned to it. This, no doubt, contributed to his death. In aftersight I realized that he was tired and even concerned that he might lose his job as headmaster. The job always had challenges, which he had met with success. Lakeside was now well established and without debt. Its enrollment was growing, and new buildings had been or were in the process of being constructed.

The war had brought real difficulties, for many of his faculty departed and the substitutes were often not adequate. I think that the stresses had begun to outweigh the satisfactions. He once spoke of wanting to be a philosophy teacher in a liberal arts college, and he invented a philosophy course for seniors which in his last few years he taught at Lakeside. He was a reader of philosophy, saying that it relaxed him and took his mind away from the problems of the day. His library provided me with important books I almost certainly would not otherwise have come across: Ernst Cassirer's *An Essay on Man*, *Language and Myth*, and *The Myth of the State*, Susanne K. Langer's *Philosophy in a New Key*, books by Santayana, Russell, and Kenneth Burke's *Attitudes Toward History* and *A Grammar of Motives*.

He had early ambitions as a poet, published a few poems here and there, and part of his most ambitious work, a sonnet sequence entitled "Animus Redundant." He wrote poems right up to his death. One can find lines and notes for poems in books he owned, usually inside the covers, generated by what he had read there. These books comprise a sizeable collection of modern poetry, including, for example, first editions of Wallace Stevens' *Harmonium*, John Crowe Ransom's *Chills and Fever*, and much Robinson, Eliot, and Frost. It impressed the poet Richard Eberhardt when he visited my mother.

Most of my father's work remains in typescripts made by my mother over the years. It was she who sent out his poems to magazines. About a year after his death I began to edit a selection of his poems, which was published by Bobbs-Merrill in 1952. The book received only two reviews, one of which I print here in its entirety:

> That so fine a poet as Robert Simeon Adams could have lived and died among us practically unknown might be a cause for melancholy. But the good poem is its own fulfillment, and if anything, withers a little under too much publicity. It is our good fortune that Adams' wife has preserved his poems in this volume.
>
> The poems are those of a mature and curious mind, somewhat staid at times, rarely excited, but always deeply engrossed in the subject at hand. The spirit is contemporary, but attached to the timeless natural earth rather than to the constructions of man. The technique is largely without flaw, though Adams himself apparently did not select the poems to be contained in the volume. The several sonnets, composed almost entirely of end-stopped lines, display a certain lack of variety in phrasing. One suspects the author would have eliminated some of them.
>
> Adams has a remarkable compass, handling both the exceptionally complicated theme and the simple with sure skill. He shuns a singing cadence for the most part, but gives ample evidence of a grasp of song. The spare brief poems excel in the rightness of word and phrase; there is no cloudiness or dustiness about them and an utter absence of mawkishness [William D. Barney, *The Dallas Times-Herald*, December 7, 1953].

Barney was wrong about the preponderance of end-stopped lines, but otherwise right.

My father had an undeniable talent and wrote some moving poems, among them a powerful sequence of sonnets and evocative poems about his youth on a farm in Ohio. It is probably accurate to say that he was a poet of the twenties and thirties and that by the time the poems were collected and published the style seemed a little out of place. Nevertheless, they well express his thoughtful, deeply emotional nature. I found the following poem scribbled out on a piece of paper casually marking a place in one of his books. I think he would eventually have revised it, had he come across it:

> Here are the shreds of many things forgotten
> A dusty snapshot, pages torn from Lear
> A fragment of some thing that I had written
> On yellow paper, torn and much less clear,
> A broken pen, a pock-marked pewter platter,
> Some crumbling shells, a dry and shrunken bone
> Within a box where ink had left a splatter:
> Strange panorama that a child might own.
> And as I look at them I can't remember
> How long ago it was I placed them there,
> Yet in my brain there must be one live ember,
> But as I look my mind goes wandering where
> Beyond our farm a weed-fringed path had led —
> And I was late to supper — sent to bed.

My father enjoyed life and met new experiences with gusto. He had a lively and inventive wit, enjoying conversation and telling stories. He was sentimental and passionate. He was terrible at managing his own money, always a source of worry for my mother. He was generous to himself and to others and was a sucker for a book salesman. He loved football and baseball and to the end stubbornly held that the stockier linemen of the Big Ten were preferable to the tall, rangy westerners of the Pacific Coast Conference. He regarded Tris Speaker as the greatest of ballplayers. He had been a good player of both games. He became an adventurous collector of early American bottles and a restorer of American antique country furniture. He took up watercolors and produced creditable pictures. Some of the more troubled or troublesome boys at Lakeside were those who in later years were most devoted to him and returned to the campus to visit. He was a man's man whom women liked.

> Our critical day is not the very day of our death but the whole course of our life. I thanke him that prayes for me when the Bell tolls, but I thanke him much more that Catechises mee, or preaches to me, or instructs me how to live.
>
> Donne

## 8.

Sometime in the late forties, The Lakeside School published a new brochure and catalog of classes. The introduction and probably much of the rest was written by my father. I quote in full from the introduction:

> To concentrate on means without envisioning possible and necessary ends in education leads only to training for mechanical objectives. Preparatory education should be all that the name implies. Those engaged in its endeavor should seek a fundamental and guiding philosophy which will build the basis for knowledge, understanding, and growth.
>
> In the long struggle of man to gain freedom from the forces of nature one of the things which stands out in relief is the importance of the sciences in mediating between man and his environment and in revealing to him the mysterious workings of nature's ways. The development of mathematics and science is a tale too often neglected in history and too little understood by the layman.
>
> Failure to understand some of the significance and meaning of man's attempt to comprehend nature scientifically is to remain uneducated, and, in a sense, uncultured. Related to this, and more important, has been man's attempt to comprehend his major purpose and his ultimate destiny in life. Mainly in words has he endeavored to voice his hopes and despairs, his ultimate longings, and his greatest ideals. In poetry and prose is found the expression of his acts and the appearance of his aspirations. Through literature, history, philosophy, art, and music (the humanistic studies) one finds the "proper study of mankind," which has its objective the development of faith in the highest and best hopes of mankind.
>
> We live by understanding and communicating one with another. The ability to understand and to communicate is the essence of good education. To read is not enough, for one should both read and understand meaning and significance. Merely to compute with numbers is not enough, for one should understand the true significance and meaning of computation.

**Robert Simeon Adams (1897–1950), the author's father, circa 1947.**

To be scientific in the narrow sense is not enough, for one must understand science as a human endeavor with ultimate human value. Not only must we learn to do, but we must also understand the meaning and significance of what we are doing. An education of practical routine and punctuality is not sufficient. Vocational or over-specialized objectives, work without understanding, and character without vision lead but to narrowness and mechanization. We do not need to broaden our base — we need to deepen it.

Character is the will and ability to comprehend the full meaning of our lives in the highest sense known to man. It is the profound by-product a man should gain from the totality of his educational experience at home, at school, and in life. It is education's broadest concept and cannot be divorced from anything and everything the boy does. In the classroom, on the field, in the gymnasium, at chapel, in books, sermons, play, precept, and example, the influences exist that communicate to the boy's heart and mind the will, the joy, the pleasure and the purpose of life.

I do not recall having read it until very recently when I went through some old papers and memorabilia in preparation to write these chapters. I have in my career read a good many introductions to university publications. I recall Jack Peltason, the vice-chancellor at Irvine, suggesting to me, who was editing UC Irvine's first catalog, that it would be best to dispense with introductions and their high-sounding phrases. They were, he thought, almost always so much hot air, rarely read, and quickly forgotten. I tried to eliminate the hot air from the catalog. Still, as I read my father's statement I think there is much to be said for it. The time is past when one could imagine that a university would function on the basis of a unified intellectual vision. However, if secondary education had anything near the vision my father expressed, our culture would be far better off.

# 6

# Dublin, 1951, 1962,
# and Beyond

## 1.

*"Oh. And Oy tought he Doyd,"* she responded, as if with disappointment. The two Irish ladies opposite us in the compartment were gossiping about their families. They were dressed entirely in black, gray-haired with round worn faces. They were enjoying their talk. It was October of 1951, Diana and I were on the train from Cork to Dublin, having disembarked from the SS *America* in Cobh with hundreds of Irish-Americans about to visit the old sod.

*"And now why aren't you like ourselves?"* The question came from Nelly Murphy, who with her husband Joe lived in the basement flat of Edie O'Reilly's house on Leeson Street, a floor of which we had just rented. The question was not malicious, but merely inquisitive. It is possible that Nelly had never before met a Protestant. Nelly cleaned all the flats in the house for a very modest fee. She was a stout middle-aged woman from Mullingar with a round face and flaming red hair. We explained that in America most people were not Catholics and we had both been born into families that weren't. To Nelly this seemed to make some sense, but it did not prevent her from thinking us strange. Once I asked her about the Banshee. She warmed to this subject and averred that she had heard it crying once — when a relative in her home had died. I asked if she believed in leprechauns. She was silent for a moment and then with eyes sparkling but then slightly narrowed replied, "I do not," but after a dramatic pause, "but they're there."

My high school Latin teacher Dick Carbray and his wife Mary had found us the flat. For a year they had rented the one above us. Dick liked to tease

Nelly: "Ah, Nelly, you're a fine lump of a girl!" She always blushed, giggled, and cried out, "Oh, Mr. Cahbry, now aren't you very bold!" Carbray was supposed to be studying for an advanced degree at University College, but I saw little evidence that he was. He seemed to be involved in a venture involving sporting goods in addition to becoming a man about town. He called on everyone, as he had when he taught at Lakeside, including that grand dame Maud Gonne MacBride, who kept him waiting for some time before dramatically descending her staircase to greet him. He knew Abbey Theatre players, Dail politicians, and Catholic priests and prelates. He called on De Valara. With him one evening, Diana met the well-known Jesuit Father Martin D'Arcy, at the time darling of Catholic intellectuals. Present also was the Earl of Wicklow.

*"Don't worry. They're happy,"* said the Earl in response to Diana's expressions of shock at the conditions of the many Dublin poor. Silence followed. The Earl was well-known to have converted to Catholicism, but his remark came out as that of a member of the Protestant Ascendancy. Dressed always in a woolen green suit, he had been named by some Dublin wag, of whom there were many, "Billy the Wick." He seemed to spend much of his time strolling between the Gresham Hotel on O'Connell Street and the Shelbourne off St. Stephen's Green.

Carbray once brought home for an evening of talk young Ulick O'Connor, then pole-vaulting champion of Ireland and already well on his way to being a Dublin character. Even then he seemed en route to emulation of Oliver St. John Gogarty. He did not reach the eminence, however, of a man of a few years later who was called "The Pope," though his name actually was O'Mahony. He seemed to have no known home address but was a practicing barrister and could be counted on for an articulate speech on any selected subject at virtually any gathering.

*"That's right, that's right— make a joke about it! That's the Irish people all over—they treat a joke as a serious thing and a serious thing as a joke."* These are the words of the character Seumas Shields in Sean O'Casey's play *The Shadow of a Gunman.* This seems to me an accurate statement, and I later used it as the epigraph for my book on Yeats's *A Vision.* It comments on the special nature of Irish comedy, often so closely aligned with tragedy and vice versa. That play was our first experience of the Abbey Theatre. The marvelous actor Harry Brogan played the role of Shields. During the early part of the first act and part of the second he was virtually invisible in a bed beneath a pile of blankets, from which position he delivered the lines above and many others.

The Abbey Theatre had once again come on difficult times. The made-over morgue off Abbey Street where Yeats, Augusta Gregory, and J. M. Synge founded it had burned, and the company was playing in a larger but old and seedy theater called the Queen's. The name was an irony for the Abbey, which early on had produced Yeats's nationalistic *Cathleen ni Houlihan*. The Abbey still had excellent actors, but it was limited by the decision to produce only Irish plays. The other theater in town was the Gate, which had been founded and was still operated by Micheál Mac Liammóir and Hilton Edwards. They were happy to put on plays of continental origin. Mac Liammóir was a ham, but an engaging one. Later he became well known for his one-man perform- ance of *The Importance of Being Oscar*, a mélange of Wilde's quips.

"*It's a damned outrage.*" This was shouted out by a man sitting behind Diana and Mary Carbray at a presentation of the Irish Film Society. The movie on view was a French documentary about Paris abattoirs, and the scenes were graphic. Immediately the theater erupted in applause, hisses, and cat- calls. "Take it off," someone shouted, and the screen went dark. Not know- ing what might happen next, Diana and Mary made their way hastily to the street. Propriety had won out again in Dublin, as it had with the censorship of books. The event gave rise to a spirited debate over censorship. It exhib- ited no progress but on all sides much good humor as well as outbursts of anger. The Irish minister for education said at about this time that they should burn all the books so that children would have to learn only Gaelic. I am not sure whether this was hyperbole or not. Trinity College, traditionally the bastion of the Protestant Ascendancy, was "censored" as well as periodically censured; the Catholic Bishop of Dublin required that any Catholic desiring to attend there gain his written permission after interview. At the time, the Church governed Ireland with a heavy hand, and its brand of conservatism dominated society. It and the long history of colonial domination created a complex attitude. One frequently heard the remark, "Ah, you can't do that in this country." The statement sometimes had a sarcastic edge, but not always.

One evening I witnessed in a pub a friendly quarrel between Carbray and a genial Dubliner over which was the better education, that provided by the Jesuits or by the Franciscans. There was no declared winner, but I think that the Irish regarded the Spanish Church as preferable to the Italian, which seemed to be suspected of concupiscence. Carbray liked to repeat the statement he heard from an Irish Jesuit, "She's a sure cure for concupiscence."

At a later date Diana and I attended a meeting of a Dublin society, quite amiable, on the subject of the supernatural. The O'Rahilly, son of the O'Rahilly who died in the Easter Rising of 1916, was in the chair. Things went on in an orderly fashion for a while, but evolved into a series of amusingly told stories of encounters with ghosts by elderly ladies and gentlemen, thor- oughly warmed to their subject. I must have been impressed, because a few nights later, deep into Yeats, I saw for a moment a white-draped figure, sus-

piciously Pre-Raphaelite, leaning pensively against the mantel of our marble
fireplace. This creature, perhaps a muse of some sort, said nothing and did
not visit me again.

*"We Irish have such great respect for learning that we seldom approach it."*
Sometime that winter the literary columnist of the *Irish Times* wrote a piece
attacking a work of American literary scholarship. It was the usual American-
baiting that one gradually came to have enough of, made somewhat entertaining by malicious humor. (I think of a recent joke going around Dublin
that today the rarest and most valuable book by Seamus Heaney ["Famous
Seamus"] is one not signed by him.) I responded to the columnist with a
solemn letter, which was published as his column in the next issue. This
response to my effort closed with the remark at the head of this paragraph —
an unanswerable riposte.

> *"Come along now, Trinity!"*
> *"Well held!"*
> *"Oh O'Meara, how could you?"*

These were loud shouts by Trinity graduates at a rugby match on the College grounds. The crowd on the sideline seemed English, dressed in English
sporting fashion that provided a contrast to the world of the Celtic Irish as
sometimes reflected in the *Irish Times*: "Man Drinks 17 Pints, Drives Into Cab-
bage Patch."

My introduction to Trinity came when I called on the professor and
therefore head of the Department of English. There was at that time only one
professor in any department. The other teachers were lecturers, readers, and
those of lower station. The professor was H. O. White, whom Mrs. W. B.
Yeats, I later learned, called H2O. He turned out to be a genial, elderly bachelor who lived in rooms in the College. As far as I know he had no distinction as a scholar, and he seemed to live in pleasant disorder. I discovered that
the department had no office other than his living room. He very kindly
arranged for me to apply for a reader's card at the College library, which was
graced by the grand "long room" with high stacks and many very old books.
I was required to present myself to Dean A. A. Luce, the well-known editor
of the works of George Berkeley. I found him in his office dressed in the
clothes of an Anglican clergyman, all black with white collar and silk black
hose to the knees. He must have looked hardly different from Berkeley, two
hundred years before. I was asked in an austere challenging way my business
in the library. My response that I was writing a doctoral dissertation on Blake
and Yeats was met suddenly by recitation of lines from "The Tyger" followed
by solemn approval. Luce proceeded to administer an oath in Latin that I
was obliged to repeat: I would not steal or deface any library book and com-
port myself decorously at all times. Before this experience, I had thought

Dublin probably little changed, except for motor cars, from Bloomsday 1904.
Now I recognized some remnants even of the eighteenth century. A subsequent visit to Marsh's Library, frequented by Jonathan Swift, enforced this
impression. Dean Luce's response to my subject of scholarship was more favorable than that of a Catholic priest I visited with Carbray. He hoped that I
would say that both Blake and Yeats were "a bit cracked."

The National Library, where I wanted to read some Yeats letters and
consult old newspapers, presented a different picture. Again I needed a reader's
card and in this case the director's permission to consult the letters. The director, Edward MacLysaght, a well-known Irish scholar, was somewhat surprised
at my request. He remarked that just the other day another young American
had come in to study the letters. Why would anyone else want to so soon? I
asked what the scholar's name was. "It was someone named Ellmann, I
believe." It had to have been five years or more since Richard Ellmann, writing *Yeats: The Man and the Masks*, had been there. This experience helped to
educate me to the fact that time and history were different in Ireland: By Irish
historical standards and in the public mind, Oliver Cromwell had been there
only a short while ago.

The National Library reading room was circular in shape, a much smaller
version of the old reading room in the British Library when it was housed in
the British Museum. In the summer it must have been cool and even then
damp. In the winter it seemed colder inside than out. In the dome above, the
windows were always open, perhaps to bring in relatively warmer outer air.
An occasional seagull would enter and fly about. I learned to wear for my
visit long underwear, a wool shirt, a wool sweater, a tweed jacket, an over-
coat, and on rainy days a raincoat. I wore a cap and gloves. Rarely did I
remove any of these garments. I consulted old newspapers piled in disorder
in a separate room, windows also open. Frequently the pages were soot-black-
ened, some pages stuck together by the dampness. The Library had no central heating.

Neither was there any in our flat. There was a grate for a coal fire in our
living room, where occasionally a brown mouse would peek out of a hole in
the baseboard. Miss O'Reilly's front hall was foggy. A bath was a project, for
it took place in a small attached greenhouse converted into a bathroom, still
unheated.

In the recent Irish economic boom of the nineteen nineties, or perhaps
in the decade before, the interiors on Leeson Street were gentrified. Trinity
College has long had a new library, though the long hall where I read remains
much the same. The National Library has been spruced up, and there is central heat. In much of its interior, however, it looks about the same as it must
have when at the end of Chapter Nine of *Ulysses* Joyce had Stephen Dedalus
emerge from it.

## 2.

We came to Ireland following a letter to Joseph Hone from the professor of Irish history at Washington, Giovanni Costigan. Hone and his wife Elvery soon invited us to tea. He was a well-known literary figure in Ireland, having written the first critical study and first biography of Yeats as well as one on George Moore. Hone was a descendant of Irish painters. When Diana and I presented ourselves at their door we learned that the Hones were both upstairs in bed with colds. They had not known how to get in touch, so they ordered their maid, a tiny older woman who could have stepped out of Joyce's *Dubliners*, to prepare a tea for us. From upstairs the Hones endeavored in shouts to carry on a conversation with us, but their voices could not sustain it, and silence ensued. The little maid, who apparently considered herself responsible now for entertaining us, decided to lead a tour of the lower floors. The climax of this tour and perhaps the motive for it came when in the basement she opened a large closet door in which were stacked many paintings, some framed. It turned out that they were by the Hones' son David. In triumph, she pulled out a canvas. Before us was a full-length nude painting of a man. "Can you imagine that now, him parading around in his skin?"

On our second visit the Hones were recovered. Several people from the Dublin literary world were there. The principal subject of talk was Augustus John's new autobiography *Chiaroscuro*, which was treated by everyone except Hone with a good amount of sarcastic wit.

It was Hone who put me in touch with Mrs. Yeats, who invited us to her house on Palmerston Road for evening coffee. She met us at the door, a short round woman with a hawklike purplish veined nose and dark piercing eyes. In appearance she seemed older than her fifty-nine years. Mrs. Yeats was dressed in black sweaters and a black or dark gray skirt that hung to her feet. The costume might have been worn by vendors at the Henry Street market. She coughed frequently a deep unpleasant cough that rattled around in her chest. Seated in a large chair next to a small fire, she seemed rather like what I imagine Madame Blavatsky seemed to Yeats, an old Russian peasant woman. Of course, neither was what she appeared to be. I felt that we were being carefully and shrewdly observed. She poured out coffee and brandy. It was certain that she had already consumed a substantial amount of the latter. Diana had to restrain herself from guiding her hand to the coffee cups.

I was questioned not about my knowledge of Yeats, but about Blake. She was interested that I had apparently read his long poems, but she was not charmed that I was interested in Yeats's occult book *A Vision*. At that time, Mrs. Yeats had not spoken publicly about *A Vision* and her role in it as a medium, automatic writer, and speaker. Her view (and her views were all definite) was that only the poetry was important and the rest quite secondary if not irrelevant. Part of this came from her reluctance to discuss her involvement, which Yeats had finally described in the second version of the book. Only years later did she admit that in the beginning she had faked the trances to keep her new husband's attention from turning back to Maud Gonne and/or Maud's daughter Iseult.

That evening she would not speak of *A Vision*. I remember most clearly a discussion we got into about Ezra Pound. This was dangerous territory for an American, for Pound was still incarcerated in a mental hospital in the States. He had been Yeats's secretary for a time and best man at the Yeatses' wedding. Mrs. Yeats regarded the American treatment of Pound as barbaric: the cage in Italy and then the hospital. In her view this was disgraceful treatment of a great poet. Clearly she was trying to draw me. I had to say something, so I agreed, yes, but under American law his wartime behavior was regarded as treasonous and if he had not been sent to a mental hospital he would have been sent to prison or worse. I quickly added that it was all a messy business and no one had come off very well. There was a moment of silence and then simply a stiff "Yes." We did not discuss Pound again.

Mrs. Yeats was polite in an English way, opinionated in such a way as to intimidate anyone she imagined disagreeing with her. Yet, I believe she was kind; at least she was to me. I seemed to have been judged provisionally acceptable and was invited to come to her house to study in her library, which contained the poet's books. On the visits that followed, she or someone below, where the Cuala Press was located, made sandwiches and tea for my lunch. I first spent a number of days studying the books Yeats had read and his annotations where they existed. Gradually she brought to me manuscripts and typescripts, probably typed by her. On one occasion I was tested and failed. On the wall was a small Rossetti. She pointed it out to me and asked whether I could see anything wrong with it. Supposing she referred to the picture itself, perhaps its technique (for Rossetti's technique was eccentric if not sometimes amateurish), I was unable to respond. She pointed to the lower corner of the frame where, printed out was, "Rosetti." I hadn't noticed the misspelling.

I apparently made up for this failure one day when she casually asked me whether I participated in sport. I replied that I had played as an amateur on a semi-pro baseball team. This, it turned out, pleased her, for that day she gave me the typescript of the unpublished "Michael Robartes Foretells" to take back to our flat to study. I was a bit reluctant and asked her why she should trust me with it. She replied that I was a baseball player and that was enough to prove I was trustworthy. Later she gave me permission to print it as an appendix to my book.

Although Mrs. Yeats faked the automatic writing at first, if ever there was anyone who was a genuine medium, a wizard of sorts, it was she. She was, I think, a shrewd, though opinionated, judge and a competent manager. She didn't care a lot for forced niceties, but still she liked to hold court, as we learned that first evening. In *A Vision*, Yeats wrote that visitations of the "instructors" speaking through his wife were preceded by sharp, apparently supernatural whistlings. Mrs. Yeats was prone to emit loud, startling whistles from time to time. I never had the temerity to query or comment on these eruptions. Perhaps they were reminders to herself of something or they were dramatic presentation to someone interested in *A Vision*. I sometimes have wondered what the response would have been had I said something or reacted in alarm.

On what I intended to be my last visit she stated that she assumed I would not be staying for lunch or returning again. Had something told her this, or was it her way of dismissing me?

## 3.

For anyone interested in writing about Anglo-Irish literature, to spend an extended period of time in Ireland is a necessity. This is as true today as it ever has been, even though the face of Dublin has now changed drastically. Much Irish literature still looks backward. Even Roddy Doyle, who has written mainly novels with contemporary settings, has in *A Star Named Henry* gone back to the years of the Easter Rising, the Black and Tans, and the Civil War. Sebastian Barry in *The Whereabouts of Eneas McNulty* has shown how the days before independence still haunted lives in World War II and later.

In 1951, many of the buildings mentioned in *Ulysses* were standing. The Dublin slums of Liam O'Flaherty's *The Informer* and other books still existed north of the River Liffey. Joyce's Martello Tower at Sandymount hadn't yet been tarted up into a museum. There were still occasional horse-drawn cabs, and herds of sheep and cattle were frequently driven right down Leeson Street. Findlater's grocers, punned on in *Finnegans Wake*, still existed, and young boys on bicycles made deliveries of goods to one's door. There were small food shops — the beef butcher, the pork and poultry butcher, the vegetable shop, and so on. At a nearby vegetable shop one could obtain potatoes and brussels sprouts. It was wise to cut these open to determine whether there were lodgers. The vegetables lay carelessly tossed into boxes, sometimes outside on the street. Near our flat was McGuirk's beef butcher shop. Mr. McGuirk had died, but his widow continued to run the shop. She sat in a screened cubicle in the back and handled all transactions with sometimes bandaged, chilblained hands. Behind the counter stood the impressively large Mr. Monahan, sporting huge handlebar mustaches, a large white apron streaked with blood, and holding a scimitar-like carving knife. He spoke with a Cork brogue difficult to interpret on first hearing. The closest pub was Keough's, where after hours I bought our first bottle of Irish whisky, made by John Power and Sons. An Irish saying tells us that if you want a very good whisky you order Bushmills, a good whisky you order Jameson; if you are thirsty you order Power's. It's a gutsy drink compared to Bushmills, and Jameson is somewhere between. Keough's was dark, smelled of beer and Guinness, and was rarely crowded. Near O'Connell Street was Henry Street devoted to a market, where women sold all manner of things, shouting to each other in rasping voices and hawking their goods: "Ah, sure now you wouldn't want just one of those!"

Children of all ages seemed to be everywhere, prompting one to think that the law forbidding birth-control measures should be rescinded. On the evening when we arrived in Dublin, as we came out of the Gresham Hotel after dinner, we were surrounded by little boys, who seemed to be begging street urchins. Their faces were blackened and they were in ragged clothes, probably not much different from what they usually wore. They seemed to be begging for pennies, though we could not as yet understand the Dublin street accent very well. Convinced that we were beset by the minions of some Irish Fagin, we plunged through them without, I think, surrendering even one penny, quickly boarded a bus that careened in inimitable Irish fashion up the street past Trinity to St. Stephen's Green near our flat. In our excitement at being in Dublin, we had forgotten that it was Halloween.

Ireland 1951-52. Thoor Ballylee, Yeats's tower.

**Author emerging from the National Library.**

## 4.

Travel by car outside of Dublin was always an interesting, sometimes terrifying challenge. If just over the hill there was not a flock of turkeys or a herd of sheep there was an arresting rural view. An Australian acquaintance remarked on the Irish drivers' tendency to proceed four abreast. I was once

**45 Lower Leeson Street, Dublin.**

driven into a ditch by a lorry careening around a turn on a mountain road. The typical rock wall with its sharp protrusions punctured two tires. The driver was down the road and gone before we emerged from the car in dumb terror.

Ireland is a country of great variety of landscape from farmland to mountains to sea. We came upon farmer bikers in old dark suits and caps, who would inevitably nod their heads in a greeting that when first seen seemed disturbingly like a negative gesture. In the towns we were openly stared at. Tourists were few. In the western counties there were women in black shawls as well as colorful tinker carts pulled by horses or donkeys. In some of the market towns on cattle-market day the manure seemed inches deep in the high streets. In Galway the long black dresses were augmented by red Connemara petticoats. Donkeys carried turf for fireplaces. There were stone walls everywhere and distressing poverty.

We traveled to what is now called, for reasons of tourism, Yeats Country, the land between Gort to the South and Sligo and Rosses Point in the North. In the small market town of Gort, where we stayed in an extremely tatty room above one of the two local pubs, we observed a boy chasing a bullock, I presume by mistake, into a tobacconist's shop, where there ensued a loud commotion followed by the bullock's slow retreat as it backed out into the square. It was midafternoon and, as far as I could tell, only we viewed this event, which might have taken place in one of Augusta Gregory's Abbey comedies. A few miles north of Gort were the remains of the Gregory estate.

A long tree-lined drive took us to an opening where once had stood Coole House, made famous by Yeats in several poems. It had been torn down by the government with no thought for its historic value or because its historical connection was to the now-dying and hated Anglo-Irish Ascendancy. It was, in fact, one of the few "great houses" not put to the torch in the Troubles, probably because Lady Gregory was held in respect by those in the area. Nearby was an old tree on the trunk of which the literary famous carved their initials: Yeats, Shaw, Synge and others.

To the East was Thoor Ballylee, the medieval Norman tower which the Yeatses restored and where they spent summers. In 1952, it was in ruins again along with the adjacent cottage. On a stone plaque cemented into the exterior wall was the following, which appears in Yeats's *Collected Poems*:

> I, the poet William Yeats,
> With old mill boards and sea-green slates,
> And smithy work from the Gort forge,
> Restored this tower for my wife George;
> And may these characters remain
> When all is ruin once again.

The tower is now once more restored for the tourist traffic, complete with souvenir shop on the ground floor of the adjoining cottage.

After climbing the narrow winding stone stair, we saw what remained of the furniture built in the rooms and left behind because the pieces when completed were far too large to bring down. We gazed down at the stone bridge and the stream that flowed by the tower. After descending, we gathered up a few of the sea-green slates piled nearby and departed.

# 5.

When we returned to Dublin in 1962, the city did not look very different. It was still more like the Dublin of 1904 than the prosperous and expensive Dublin of 2004, now affluent, corrupted by the drug culture, with signs warning women to watch their purses. In 1962 we could still without anxiety put our children on a public bus to go to school. Trinity College was the same in appearance, but for me it was different. I was in Dublin on a Fulbright Research Fellowship. The new professor of English, Philip Edwards assumed I was there to teach. I did not disabuse him of this illusion and lectured through the year on American literature, in autumn also giving a seminar on Wordsworth. None of this was an onerous task, as Trinity students spent almost as much time in so-called reading periods as in the weeks of lectures. I was spared as a visitor the requirement that all faculty and students wear an academic gown. Many of the ones I saw were tattered, barely wearable, and dating back at least to the time of H. O. White, now in a nursing home. Edwards told me of White's repeated complaint that Dean Luce had stolen his toothbrush. During his and Luce's time White had never been elected a fellow of the College.

I had never taught American literature as such, but soon found that neither the faculty nor the students knew anything about it, and so I was ahead of them. Edwards was an aggressive and ambitious head of the department and had set in motion many reforms, including the conversion of White's rooms in college into offices with a secretary. I soon learned that classic American works were not easily obtainable in Ireland and some, for example Faulkner's, were banned. Students had to get many of the books in England or even France, and I was never sure how many, if any, had.

The ban on attending Trinity remained for over 90 percent of the populace, but this made little difference because the majority of my students were from England or France, probably having failed to gain entrance to Oxford, Cambridge, or the Sorbonne. I lectured to over 100 students (when all were present), and everything I discussed was strange and exciting to them, even if they had not read the books. Hawthorne, Emerson, Thoreau, Poe, Whitman, Melville, and others of the nineteenth century the students regarded as *avant garde* and radical. And so was I! For these students, American literature was liberated and liberating. Groups of them gathered around me after lectures and followed me after class. I was invited to pubs for talk. Never before or since have I experienced such a *succes d'estime*, almost entirely the result of the exotic American subject matter. Edwards asked me to produce three public lectures, which were given to standing-room crowds in a large lecture hall. The first two I based on a book soon to come out called *The Contexts of Poetry*, which I had designed for undergraduate classes. At Trinity they seemed to be regarded as high criticism. In the third, I discussed Yeats's *A Vision*. Some of the faculty present opined that I was all wrong about Yeats's book, principally, I think, because I lifted it out of the biographical criticism they were used to into formal analysis. Not much that was recent, except for Edwards himself, had penetrated the intellectual life of Trinity.

Later in the academic year, students invited me to be in the chair at a debate in the society founded by Edmund Burke. I accepted in ignorance of the topic to be argued. It turned out to be "Resolved: That Columbus should have stayed at home." This was both in my honor and a way to draw me, all in good nature.

My duties were few but of ritual importance. I was enthroned on a handsome chair on a dais facing the debaters and other members of the society, perhaps one hundred in all. There was a central aisle, and on one side were those who supported the proposition and on the other those opposed. The speakers took a position behind a lectern and faced me directly. The speeches were entertaining; many pieces of evidence were offered and some arcane arguments. The deliveries were well beyond the capabilities of almost all American undergraduates, many of whom in my experience have trouble constructing a coherent statement in speech. I was to judge the debate, but only after a vote was taken among the students. I was to award the victory to the side winning the vote.

The debate was climaxed by the oration of a tall handsome young man who offered a unique point of view. Rather than taking the resolution, as all the other speakers had, in the metaphorical sense that implied criticism of America, he took it literally. He had researched Columbus's preparation for his voyage and argued with a wealth of evidence and fiery powers of persuasion that Columbus had been foolhardy ever to have embarked at all and was responsible for misery and loss of life on the Atlantic. Upon completion of his argument he staggered, near collapse toward his seat. Two students rushed to support him, and like an injured rugby player he was helped from the hall. He had been splendidly drunk the whole time.

Mainly on the basis of this stupendous performance I had wanted to award the victory to his side, but the vote went the other way, more students moving over to the con side of the hall than to the pro. Like the Queen before Parliament, I had to acquiesce.

Undergraduate study at Trinity maintained the tradition of debate, but Trinity was gradually changing and being modernized. It had not been too long before that English literary study ended at the seventeenth century. I am not sure that there had been a course of lectures on American literature before I gave mine. I am also not sure that modern Irish literature had yet been taught. The change may have occurred partly because of the competition from University College, which Catholic students attended; but it was also, of course, because of changes in Irish life. In a few years, Trinity would be taken over by the state and Catholics would begin to attend in large numbers. The schedule remained on the English system: Three six-week terms of lectures, punctuated by reading periods. It seemed to me that students spent much of this time skiing in the Alps and elsewhere; at least the affluent seemed to. I was not impressed by the extent of my students' reading. Nevertheless these students were more articulate than Americans of almost any age, and some of them wrote fairly well. I think that their verbal ability could be attributed to emphasis on verbal utterance all through their schooling. The system was driven almost entirely by what we would call comprehensive examinations. Students were not under the stress of the American quarter system with its papers and final examinations. There were papers to be written for tutorials, but they too had to be read aloud. Anxiety was collected at the severe moments when one finally stood for examination.

## 6.

Life for us in Dublin was different this second time. We now had two young children, Sim, just eight, and Perry, six. We enrolled them in Rathgar Junior School, run by the Society of Friends. The teachers were kind and allowed for the difference in preparation. Perry took to learning the compulsory Irish and to reading, helped immeasurably by lessons from his Grandmother Adams, who visited and brought her experience as a primary school teacher into play. I recall her asking him to read a line. He would delay slightly, then with a sly grin whisper, "I see kitty." Perry also excelled in athletics, in a sprint taking second only to a fleet-footed taller girl. The boys experienced many new things. One day Perry reported that a Danish boy, a friend, had brought an open-faced sandwich to school in his lunch!

Sim's greatest moment occurred in a dramatic presentation that required advance preparation, namely the procurement and embellishment of a white rabbit costume. I do not remember the plot of the play, but the costume was greatly admired, being met with gasps of approval by the audience. Perry participated by expertly conducting the rhythm band.

Usually the boys went to school by city bus, a double-decker similar to those in London, but green. They became known to the driver, who delivered them and picked them up. They sat together at the front of the upper deck. During a bus strike Diana managed to secure the daily services of a taxi man, but with difficulty since such behavior seemed to be unheard of. Most Dublin cabbies apparently preferred sitting somewhere in a long queue each morning or afternoon to securing a steady and better than usual fare.

Our landlady on Angelsea Road midway between the house of Brendan Behan and the rugby ground in Donnybrook was a Mrs. Sinnott, who had come to Dublin from Wexford after the death of her husband. She was a pleasant lady, less shy than Miss O'Reilly of the decade before. This time we were without not only central heating but also fireplaces, all blocked up. We got by with two electric heaters and managed fairly well, moving them from room to room when they were needed. We used ceramic water bottles to warm our beds. It was a severe December in Dublin, with snow. One could not meet a Dubliner who did not remark, "Ah, 'tis bitterly cold, is it not?" The post was efficient. One day the postman came to the door with two shot partridges merely tied together and with a tag addressed to Mrs. Sinnott.

On the whole, except for the cold, we lived and ate well. Diana adjusted again to shopping every day, and the Irish stores had excellent meat, cheese, and poultry. The vegetables remained what we today would call organically grown, though now more sparsely inhabited. It was still possible to order Dublin Bay scallops and have them delivered by bicycle.

Dublin television had little to offer with the exception of the Irish counterpart to Julia Child in America. It was Monica Sheridan, equally without nonsense. One day, preparing to cook a pig's head, she held it up for our admiration and intoned, "Alas, poor Yorick" and plunged it into a pot, peered down, and exclaimed, "There's his oye [eye], there's his poor oye!" Beyond Monica Sheridan there was a wasteland of Irish dancing, nothing like "Riverdance," weather-reporting in a particularly pessimistic style, and secular and religious performing heads.

Our social life this time was connected to Trinity College. Through Philip and Sheila Edwards we met and dined with the writer Frank O'Connor and a young Denis Donoghue. The former was a genial, handsome gentleman. Donoghue was a good conversationalist, but O'Connor dominated with his stories. I often took lunch in the faculty common rooms beneath the portraits of Berkeley, Burke, and others. It was the time of the Cuban missile crisis, and I was queried about my views and subjected to a variety of comments, many expressing anxiety and some critical of the United States. In the course of one of these conversations I was reminded that Trinity was still at least partly an English outpost. I was puzzled when one of the faculty referred several times to "we." He did not mean the Irish but the British government.

# 7.

In the winter of that year, I began to write a novel, which eventually became *The Horses of Instruction*. It was not what I should have been doing. I had applied for the Fulbright to do a scholarly project, but since I was now a teaching and not a research fellow, I salved my conscience and went ahead. I think many who knew me and read my novel when it came out in 1968 thought I had written it to let off steam and vent the experience of teaching at the University of Texas, about which experience I write in the next chapter. That was not the motive. It is true that many of the novel's events are adapted from things that happened there, but I did not write to get anything off my chest. Rather, I was looking around for a subject.

The truth was that ever since college I had wanted to write fiction. My efforts at Princeton had gone mainly into the wastebasket. Now, however, I wanted to write to learn about fiction from the writer's point of view. I believe to this day that anyone teaching literature should experiment with writing fiction and poetry in order to find out about its technical problems first hand. I believe that the experience improved my teaching, though from near the beginning it had been predicated on a writerly approach. Perhaps my best book of criticism, the one on Joyce Cary, comes directly out of this experience, and Cary had some influence on how I wrote *The Horses of Instruction*. Today this sort of interest, it seems to me, is confined mainly to creative writing teachers, the tools of analysis by professors having shifted from the art of literature to forms of the political.

One of the more interesting and amusing criticisms of *The Horses of Instruction* was that made by friends and former colleagues at Michigan State University, where I taught after leaving Texas. Their beef was that they could not recognize any of themselves in the novel, complaining that I must have considered them not interesting enough. A similar response did not come from people at Texas.

The first draft of my novel was embarrassing to me. I had created a host of characters, perhaps too many to handle effectively, and there was indecision about the focus of narration. I finally hit on three characters, two to narrate and one treated in the third person, but with his point of view. There was something arbitrary about the decision with respect to the last character. The reason was mainly, I think, to practice that technique. A colleague from Texas, probably recognizing too much that was familiar in the plot, claimed exasperation and wrote that he hoped I didn't teach my students by this example.

*The Horses of Instruction* is about three new young faculty members recruited by an ambitious, fast-talking, big thinking academic dean to help vitalize an English department. I now see the novel as really being about the appearance in the late fifties of the academic operator, the entrepreneur. Were I to write my novel now, the theme of entrepreneurship would be more incisive and pervasive than it is, mainly because I have now had more experience of that type of academic and know better how to handle fictive characters.

The novel I began in Dublin in 1962 appeared after many revisions in 1968. In that early draft and later, I learned a lot about what to do and to avoid as a writer, though the fruit of my knowledge did not always appear in the book. Many years later it was to become the first in a trilogy about academic life in the second half of the twentieth century.

## 8.

Travel around Ireland was not a lot different ten years later. Thoor Ballylee was somewhat cleaned up but not yet the tourist stop that it is today. Coole Park has now also been improved for visitors, a sign that the economics of tourism overcomes old political resentments. Modernization slowly brought realization that the renegade Joyce, the Anglo-Irishman Yeats, and the Old Lady of the big house were money-makers for all.

Our visits to Ireland since 1963 have been mainly to academic meetings, which are the nearest thing to a tax break that academics in the so-called humanities are able to manage. Sometimes the phrase "academic meeting" is rather a misnomer. The Yeats Summer School in Sligo, for example, is more like a two-week party, punctuated by classes and lectures, and the International James Joyce Symposium (occasionally held in Dublin) is much the same, though higher up the social scale. For some years, the Yeats Summer School had as its social and principal sleeping headquarters the Imperial Hotel, now providentially razed but still lamented by those nostalgic for and perhaps at home with seediness. We spent one night in the Imperial. The sink and shower did not drain, the smell of mildew pervaded everything, and the bed hurled the two of us together into the middle, from which only a strenuous scrambling climb to either side would free one. On the next morning, we moved down the river to the Silver Swan. The water of the river was brown, as was that in the hotel. One day later, Roger McHugh, professor at University College, Dublin, had a drink with us in the bar and asked us how the hotel was. We described the room as, relative to that in the Imperial, comfortable. On the following morning we saw, approaching from the Imperial, McHugh carrying two large suitcases. Our friend Rob Garratt of the University of Puget Sound was a couple of doors down the hall from us and told us that every time someone nearby took a shower his sink overflowed. The historian Maureen Murphy had chosen another, smaller hotel and thought it an improvement over the Imperial. It was "up market," she said: Her feet did not stick to the floor when she got out of bed. The climb out wasn't bad either.

We had parked our rented car in the hotel's lot. One evening the ground floor was taken over by a large wedding party, raucous and drunken beyond what academics are capable of. In the morning we found our car neatly side-swiped though it was now nestled between two others, untouched. The lobby was in shambles.

Classes in Sligo ran for two weeks in August from 5:30 to 7 P.M., most of the day being given over to sightseeing tours. There was not a lot of serious attention to the subject matter. One summer I gave a short course on Yeats's *A Vision* and, of course, found it attended by some eccentric Irish ladies intent on turning discussion to stories of the occult similar to those I had heard a decade before in Dublin. Their interest in Yeats was biographical, and they were well informed about his life. My role ended up as a series of attempts to steer the course back to the book. After dinner the parties began and continued late into the night with much drink taken and talk from the literary celebrities brought in for lectures or readings. Stephen Spender, Seamus Heaney, John Montague, Paul Muldoon, Derek Mahon, and Richard Murphy were there at one time or another while we were, along with some American would-be Irish poets. W. B.'s son Michael Yeats and his wife Grainne attended with her harp. Over the years every known Irish poet must have dropped in, along with a mass of critics and scholars from the United States, funded either by their universities or simply taking advantage of a tax write-off.

Academic conferences and summer sessions in Europe depend to a large extent on the modest munificence of university research and travel grants in the humanities and IRS rules. The International James Joyce Symposium is a good example, though it attracts many Europeans. Without the traveling Americans it and others would be reduced to shabby modesty.

Academic celebrities show up at these meetings. Perhaps the most astounding performance I have witnessed at any of them was that of Jacques Derrida in Frankfurt in 1984. The lecture hall was full to standing room. Derrida spoke in French on the subject of one sentence in the work of James Joyce. From time to time, he would pause, and a brave young woman standing beside him would summarize in English. The talk went on and on; people began to leave, but others arrived, apparently just to see the speaker. Derrida had been scheduled for one hour, and two other talks were to take place during the session. But on he went. Another hour and more passed before he stopped. The two academics, who had, no doubt, traveled far at some university's expense were unable to deliver their papers. Later Derrida appeared at a large gathering to respond to general questions. He strode into the hall surrounded by what appeared to be bodyguards, though they were probably acolytes. The impression was of a show of gangster power. The questions were varied and respectful until a young German, who was apparently a hangover from the sixties or even spiritually the thirties, attacked him violently for reactionary, counterrevolutionary views. Derrida, regarded in America as being on the left, answered mildly, insisting on his revolutionary credentials.

In one of our more recent visits to Ireland, we attended the annual meeting of the American Conference for Irish Studies, held that year at University College, Galway. We arrived on a Sunday afternoon. The college was not in session, and participants were to be housed in the dormitories. It was soon discovered that the dormitories were completely devoid of toilet paper. Thereupon there took place the Great Toilet Paper Heist. I rushed to the dining hall and rid the rest room there of its substantial roll. Upon returning to our room, I heard a commotion in the hallway, high-pitched voices, and cheering. Down the hall in triumph came two nuns in full flowing habit each carrying aloft, like successful returning Galahads, a roll of toilet paper.

On returning by car to Dublin airport, we struggled to find our way through the environs. We could see planes landing far to the left, but there seemed no way to reach our destination. A sign we approached said "Dublin Airport" and pointed us straight ahead, but the road veered off to the right. Rob Garratt, who was with us, suggested we stop at a roadside shop for directions. He entered, and after he expressed his frustration the man behind the counter gave complex directions. When Rob remarked that the sign outside said straight ahead, the man remarked, "Ah, now, take no notice of signs around here!" As he said this, his wife appeared from a back room and shouted, "Oh, Seamus, you've got it all wrong," and proceeded to offer a whole new set of instructions. These proved eccentric, and we eventually navigated only by instinct. The whole experience reminded me of a story of a couple driving on a country road in the West of Ireland. They stop to ask directions to Galway of an elderly farmer walking on the roadside. He is silent for a moment as if deep in thought. Then he says, "I wouldn't, now — I wouldn't advise starting from here."

# 7

# Academic Travailer

## 1.

In most respects, seeking an academic job in 1952 was different from today. The main similarity is that jobs then, as they are now, were in very short supply. The returning veterans, who had caused swollen enrollments from 1946 to 1949, were no longer in school and the boomer generation was barely on the horizon. In 1952, The Modern Language Association of America had not yet invented the job list, which today announces all the anticipated vacancies in the country and the specialties desired. The result was that a job-seeker was reduced to the strategy of what Robert B. Heilman called "saturation bombing." Taking his advice, I posted a little over one hundred letters of application, dutifully typed by my wife. My task was made more difficult by being in Ireland, far away from any hope of an interview.

The letters produced discouraging responses, when departments took the trouble to respond. The greater the reputation of the school the more likely to receive a form letter or nothing at all. We docked in New York in May with only a slim hope. Cornell University had written that I might get in touch upon my arrival. It so happened that the chairman of English, Francis Mineka, was going to be in the city, and he would interview me. This he did, and I was invited (at my own expense) to come to Ithaca for more interviews. It seemed that there had been a late resignation and an opening had materialized.

Diana and I took the overnight Lehigh Valley Railroad train to Ithaca, sharing a single bunk that I now like to think of as an upper, though it may have been a lower. The Lehigh Valley moved sideways almost as much as forward. We arrived tired and anxious on a cold gray day with a few snowflakes in the air. After a morning of interviews, Diana and I met for lunch. I reported that I had no idea about my chances. She announced that she had already been offered a job as secretary to the literature program (Cornell's name for what approximated comparative literature elsewhere). This news buoyed me up for an afternoon interview with Arthur Mizener, the F. Scott Fitzgerald scholar, who, it turned out, had a soft spot for Princeton graduates, being one himself. Indeed, I came to think he devoutly wished that he was teaching there. After that, and many questions about Mrs. Yeats, I was offered the job of instructor and was told that I didn't have to accept right away, that I should think it over, consider other offers, and then reply. Ha, ha! There were no other offers, but I responded that I would do as suggested. As soon as we got back to Seattle, we both promptly accepted the jobs.

As it turned out, very late in the summer, the University of Rochester called with an offer, and while we were en route Colby College offered the munificent sum of $2500 per annum. Cornell's was $3500. It was over a year before I learned why I probably got the Cornell job. It seems that, not long before, Robert Heilman had taught summer school at Cornell and became friendly with William M. Sale, a professor influential in the hiring process. Heilman, I believe, wanted very much for someone coming out of the University of Washington graduate program to get a job in the East, particularly the Ivy League. He apparently backed my application once Bostetter had alerted him to it. I believe I may have been the first Washington Ph.D. in English to get a job in the Ivy League. Several years later, Heilman appointed one of Sale's sons to a position at Washington after he was denied tenure at Amherst. Noblesse oblige? At the time, quite a lot of academic business was done in this way. A lot still is, though there are now some stumbling blocks in the way. In those days, much followed from these unspoken questions: From where have you come? Who knows you? Whom do you know?

**2.**

Coming from the West was both a disadvantage and an advantage. The disadvantage, of course, was that western institutions did not have the prestige of the great eastern ones. The West was regarded by some as remote and perhaps only partly civilized. I remember a woman at Cornell asking Diana whether there were kindergartens out there. In fact, there are still professional disadvantages to being in the West. Travel to scholarly meetings is longer and more expensive. The distances between institutions are greater. Lack of proximity to other academics, publishers, and great libraries are all problems.

However, things are better than they were, for some of the western institutions have been improved to the point that only the most snobbish or
provincial Easterner can disregard them.

The advantage I had was more or less psychological. My young colleagues were, for the most part, from Ivy League graduate schools. Although
Cornell was one of these, it was regarded by some as a remote western outpost to which they had been sent as if to a triple A baseball team or to duty
in India. Further Cornell was a partly public institution with an agricultural
college. Though the Mohawks and Eries were long gone, upstate New York
was still alien territory. I, on the other hand, was thankful for a job at all, let
alone in the western outpost of the Ivies. The general unhappiness was comical to me. I soon learned two things: Anxiety was a fairly common characteristic of eastern academics, and even some of the senior faculty seemed to
feel estrangement and dissatisfaction.

Among the young, there were some legitimate stresses. We all knew, having been told, that among the four of us hired as instructors that year, only
one would be promoted to assistant professor — after four years. As far as I
know today, people just out of graduate school today are not appointed
instructor. They become assistant professors right away, and they frequently
teach upper-division courses or even graduate seminars at once. All this was
unheard of circa 1952. The salaries of instructors were barely at a subsistence
level. All of the wives (there were very few women on the faculty) either took
jobs, took boarders into their rented dwellings, or did whatever was available
to make ends meet. Generally, young faculty rented marginal housing below
the campus in the Cayuga flats.

Diana and I were no different from the others. Over four years we lived
in three places in descending order of quality, being sent on from the second
one in advance of the arrival of our first baby. We ended up in the flats in the
small upstairs of a house owned by an elderly widow. Bruce Park, the man
with whom I shared an office, and his wife Lucy Ann had the luxury of a
legitimate apartment in an actual apartment house. This was by virtue of her
getting a job as a librarian at Cornell. Bruce was an affable New Englander,
and we got along well; although our first conversation on intellectual matters
got off to a strange beginning. I was holding forth, for some reason, on Kenneth Burke. As I spoke, Bruce became more and more puzzled, assuming that
I was talking about Edmund Burke. This was eventually straightened out, of
course. It is difficult to think of two more different people than the two Burkes.
Bruce ended up at Brooklyn College, where he experienced the depressing
problems that open admission created, permanently embittering him. He
retired early, moved to Mobile, Alabama, where he happily played jazz piano
and constructed furniture and guitars. In our four years sharing an office we
talked a great deal about teaching English composition, a subject that mon-

opolized our time, as it was the only thing, for the most part, that we were allowed to teach.

In the early fifties, Ithaca was a quiet town with few redeeming features except its setting at the end of one of the Finger Lakes. In Spring we picnicked in the parks, drove out into the countryside, where we viewed early nineteenth-century houses, picturesque but often in very poor condition. We visited the huge pig that belonged to the agricultural college.

The Cornell students I first taught seemed mediocre to me. The reason for this was probably that all freshmen had been classified into three groups according to alleged abilities with English, and I always had middle-group students. Many resented being put into any group at all. One day I was obliged to remove forcibly from class one perpetual troublemaker, who later admitted his resentment. My action seemed to impress the other twenty-two students, who generally behaved with bovine docility. The student in these classes whom I remember best was a sophomore from the agricultural college who had failed the course the year before. He simply could not spell; the best thing one could say about his punctuation was that it was eccentric; and his grammar was erratic enough to be intriguing. But he was in his way the best, most imaginative writer in the class. He had a real subject and wrote convincingly about it. The subject was farm life. Occasionally he would exhibit a charming naiveté, as when he wrote of a young wife that she was "not bred yet." I decided to give him a good grade, following a precedent established by Baxter Hathaway, who taught creative writing and gave a similar student an A to balance his previous failing grade in the same subject. Correctness is fine and to be desired; most, but not all, can learn it. Imagination was rare in my composition classes.

We had what junior university faculty today would regard as a schedule inspiring one to hunt another job. There were three classes per semester, and they were all in freshman composition. There was a highly recommended syllabus and a textbook handed to us. I was told at the outset that in the middle group of classes it would be unusual for anyone to achieve a grade of more than seventy-eight. (Cornell graded on a scale of one to one hundred). There was a weekly paper from each student, meaning sixty-nine papers to grade every week. It was drudgery, but it was also an education for all of us. At no other time in my career did I talk more with colleagues about teaching.

We were fortunate that an assistant professor named Ferris Cronkhite was in charge of freshman English. He was an affable, conscientious person who put a great deal of time and effort into the program. In return, he failed to achieve tenure, ending up at Ithaca College, where I am sure he was a valuable asset. Ferris and I often bicycled around Tompkins County, stopping at graveyards to look at inscriptions. He told me an amusing story about his first lecture before a large class at Cornell. There was an unwritten convention there that dogs were allowed to go anywhere they chose. This was the result of a creative interpretation of the founder's words that anyone could come to Cornell to study any subject. Ferris was lecturing in an amphitheater with a wide central aisle with double doors at the back. As he spoke, suddenly two large dogs entered through those doors, barking, growling, and fighting. The question, as Ferris posed it to himself and stated it to me later, was whether to abandon the podium in an act that seemed a dereliction of duty as well as a loss of professional dignity, or to descend from the dais and endeavor to rid the hall of the dogs, violating Cornell tradition as well as putting one's own well-being in the balance. Luckily two large students bravely separated the beasts and ushered them out. Order was restored and dignity kept. But he admitted to spending the rest of the day in a lingering state of perceived inadequacy.

At Cornell I had reason to think seriously about the freshman composition course, and later I founded and organized such a program at the new University of California, Irvine. I am afraid that my accumulated thought on the subject is depressing. Nevertheless, I am going to summarize here.

Much of every English department's resources and efforts has been and still is expended on composition courses, and the results have not been encouraging. I do not know of many, if any, really effective efforts to gauge success, and there is disagreement about what success is. Yet it may now be doubtful that English departments would survive as more than small isolated programs if most of the rest of the university did not seem to think that composition is the department's sole reason to exist and believe that something needs to be done about the writing of students. The notion of writing as a part of liberal education is very nearly dead. The course is regarded as teaching one to master a skill. Indeed, when I first went to Michigan State University the department that taught it was called Communication Skills. Perhaps that fit in with the fact that until recently the name of the school had been Michigan State University of Agriculture and Applied Sciences. In the contemporary university, as technology has expanded its role the humanistic disciplines have come to be regarded as less and less significant in the corridors of academic power, except as providing service courses to students from other departments. This has resulted in an emphasis on writing English (as well as learning a foreign language) for so-called practical reasons, usually having to do with commerce.

There was a time, long ago, when the freshman course was often fundamentally literary in subject matter. There was also a time, even longer ago, when regular line faculty taught the course. Today, faced with hordes of comparatively unprepared students, universities have turned over the teaching almost entirely to graduate students and lecturers. Both groups provide cheap labor. As a result, graduate programs are overpopulated, relative to the scarcity of so-called tenure-track jobs into which graduate students might advance. The whole thing is convenient to administrations, even as it is annoying. For the senior English faculty it is perfectly all right, since as a result there are graduate students to teach and none of the endless flow of papers to grade that the composition course creates.

But languages are not merely tools of communication; they are means of conceptualization. Teaching to write as if writing were simply a skill is similar to trying to pursue happiness. It is an impossible quest after an abstraction. Writing well and happiness are the by-products of a congeries of specific experiences built up over time. Of course, today the problem of writing has become immensely more complicated, and when we attempt to deal with complexity we usually appoint a committee. Today's specialists in composition are now the committee, and they have gradually created a bureaucracy. There has been a reason for this development. Universities are faced with the entrance of many students whose first language is not English, students whose verbal background has been sadly limited and limiting, and students who simply have not been taught effectively and imaginatively at the stage when such learning is easiest. Everyone knows that a very young child learns a foreign language with much greater ease than an adolescent or adult does. The same applies to learning to read and write a first language. Secondary education has been faced with a very difficult job, and it has failed, partly, I think, because universities have been passively content to accept the poor training of those admitted. All freshman composition is really remedial, a late desperate effort to make up for early lack of success.

For students at any age to become better writers they must become better thinkers. To be better thinkers they need to have the early experience of being read to and of reading things that stimulate imagination and generate thought, that introduce one to the variety of English sentences, grammar, and vocabulary. At the same time learning a foreign language, which should begin at least by grade one, provides a valuable contrast to English. One learns by comparisons. Latin is a so-called dead language, but its study matures analytical skills, introduces a variety of linguistic possibilities, sharpens logic, develops vocabulary, and contributes to the ability to conceptualize. Learning how to write well is mainly by indirection and a convening of different intellectual experiences. When I discover a good writer in my class, I learn almost inevitably that he or she was read to as a child, had a strong English teacher in the primary and later grades, and/or studied Latin.

In addition to this, a literary education, begun early with Mother Goose and proceeding through the great myths and later classics, is essential. All I have mentioned needs to happen before students come to what we call higher education, and universities ought to insist on it.

It won't happen. As I have implied, universities are bogged down in a primitive mode of thought about true literacy, a term that ought, as I have already argued, to have something to do with literature, and they seem to be growing dumber every day.


## 3.

After two years at Cornell, I made an advance. I now taught as one of my three courses per semester "Introduction to Literature," a year-long parade through great books, beginning with Homer and Job, through Greek tragedy and Thucydides to Dante, Cervantes, Shakespeare, and beyond, though we did not reach the twentieth century. Once again the texts were chosen by powers above me. Some of the works I had never read, a sign of inadequacy in my own education and perhaps my own earlier indolence. The year contributed more to my education than any course I had ever taken. But, of course, teaching is always the most intense form of learning, and not just because one is in front of a crowd and doesn't want to make a fool of oneself.

In my first year at Cornell I completed my doctoral dissertation and in the second and third years completely rewrote it into the book *Blake and Yeats: The Contrary Vision*, which came out in 1955. My teaching improved my prose style more than it did that of my students, alas.

In another year I found myself assigned at the last minute to a beginning course in creative writing. This came about in part because of my association with the magazine *Epoch*, edited by its founder Baxter Hathaway, though he never allowed himself to be so-named on the masthead. In the English department he was an outsider; at least he saw himself that way. He thought creative writing was looked down on at Cornell, even disparaged by the department's major powers. He was known to grumble that to teach creative writing was a sure way to avoid promotion. This proved fairly accurate, as I cannot recall any creative writing teacher who made it beyond instructor while I was there. Hathaway himself remained an associate professor for some time, gaining promotion only after he published two well-regarded books on Renaissance Italian literary criticism. Hathaway held the heretical view that creative writers should not have to be better novelists or poets than the other faculty were scholars and critics.

While I was at Cornell a veritable parade of young writers passed through and out of the instructorship. Among them, James B. Hall, an excellent short-story writer, went on to Oregon and then California. George P. Elliott, a novelist, went to Syracuse. W. D. Snodgrass, a poet, went to Wayne State. Robert O. Bowen, an eccentric and difficult man, author of two good but forgotten novels (*Bamboo* and *The Weight of the Cross*), disappeared into Alaska. My experience on the *Epoch* staff, including duties I voluntarily assumed as business manager, was important to my teaching and altered my writing. We read and discussed submissions. Some of these conversations, especially those with Carl Hartman, were the most interesting I have ever had on prose fiction. Hartman was perhaps the best teacher of creative writing that I have known. He had a way of speaking without jargon about a text, using language imaginatively to make his points. He also holds the record, as far as I know, for silence in a classroom, having waited twenty minutes for an answer to a question he had put to a class.

*Epoch* became known for publishing good short fiction, but it was not very successful with poetry. Hathaway himself wrote poems and expressed strong opinions on poetry submitted to us. There were more disagreements on the staff about poetry, some vociferous. Bowen caused consternation when he wrote a two-word rejection note: "Lay off!" This, of course, infuriated an often would-be contributor enough that Hathaway received a fiery letter denouncing all of us. Bowen's rejection note should take its place alongside one Hartman told me about. Sent to *The New Yorker*, a manuscript of a friend of his was returned with a large circular stain on its first page with an appended note: "I am sorry to have spilled gin on your manuscript. E. B. White."

My brief time teaching creative writing at Cornell I recall as unproductive of any good student work, with one exception. I was emphasizing exercises on focus of narration, for want of anything else I could think of to do. My students seemed mainly without talent, or I was unable to bring it out. One member of the class, however, completed assignments promptly, wrote quite a lot, but not verbosely, came and went from class quietly, always dressed in a suit or sport coat, white shirt, and tie. I am sure he learned nothing from me, but he did get in some practice during the semester. His name was Thomas Pynchon. Years later, he told a young colleague of mine, who somehow contrived to meet him, that he had known me when I was wet behind the ears.

# 4.

Although I thought of myself as a scholar of poetry of the romantic period, I seemed to be viewed by the senior faculty as a modernist with an emphasis on poetry. This was all right. I was able to assist Hathaway in an introduction to poetry course. Hathaway was a terrible lecturer, and I spent quite a bit of time in my office hearing complaints. A year later the English scholar Geoffrey Bullough, a delightful man with working-class politics, was visiting, and I assisted him in a modern poetry course. Both of these experiences were useful in different ways. I recall also the presence of other English scholar-critics lured to visit Ithaca for a semester: Basil Willey, Herbert Read, F. W. Bateson, but I had no more than brief conversations with them.

That summer I taught a course on modern poetry after receiving a stern lecture of advice from Professor Walter French, who seemed to own the course and had definite opinions about which poets deserved to be discussed. French was a giant of a man, a medievalist whom students called Grendel. It is said that he squashed an errant bat on his desk during a class session. His advice, offered as if it were a command, was to forgo T. S. Eliot and emphasize Edwin Arlington Robinson and Robert Frost. I do not believe that Wallace Stevens or William Carlos Williams were mentioned, being perhaps beneath French's contempt for Eliot. I taught all of these poets, emphasizing Yeats and Eliot. French was gone all summer and had no thought police under his command. I doubt that French had any idea of how he came across to students and to me.

I had another interesting lesson in attitudes toward professors that summer. I was playing shortstop for the top team in the Ithaca (and environs) fast-pitch softball league. I didn't fraternize with the other players, all of whom worked in Ithaca, most of them at one or the other of the town's two industries, the Ithaca Gun Company and the Morris Chain Works. No one else from Cornell up on the hill was in the league. One evening on the bench I was sitting next to our catcher, who suddenly turned to me and asked, "Say, what do you do?" I answered that I taught at Cornell. He spat on the ground and, looking down, replied, "I thought there was something funny about you." When this news got around, though, the players seemed to take some pleasure in it and began, with good nature, calling me "Professor" and "Prof." Ithaca was gown on the hill but strictly a working class town down in the flats.

# 5.

While all this was going on, Diana was serving as secretary of the literature program. Among her duties was to type Professor Sale's letters of recommendation. Sale was a master of the double negative: "Jones is not unlikely to complete his dissertation by June." "Smith has not been uncooperative." Her advice: Do not ask Sale for a letter. She also worked for Vladimir Nabokov, or rather his wife Vera, who corrected and graded all his papers and examinations. In his lectures, which were apparently very entertaining and well-attended, Nabokov expressed his likes and dislikes. He liked Tolstoy and hated Dostoyevsky. His novel *Pnin* describes pretty well his situation as a Russian professor attached to a German department. The Nabokovs were

**Ithaca, New York, the author suited up to play for Bims (Bill's Luncheonette and International Music).**

perpetual transients. Every year they rented the house of a faculty member on leave. One summer they went to Mexico, and Sale, thinking he could provide an office for a summer visitor, opened the door of Nabokov's office to find it crammed to the ceiling with all their belongings.

Diana shared the department office with Emily Morrison, wife at the time of the physicist Philip Morrison, who later became well-known as a

critic of U.S. policy in Vietnam among other things. We spent one evening
at the Morrisons'. The party included some distinguished Cornell scientists.
The conversation got on the problem of water and wells in upper Ithaca and
never left that intellectual eminence.

There was a lot of traffic in the office. One of the frequent visitors was
George Healey, an affable scholar of the eighteenth century and curator of
the library's Wordsworth collection. One day Healey entered in a state of
excitement, declaring that he had discovered a letter by Wordsworth in one
of Wordsworth's books. He went on about this find, but then suddenly
stopped. "Zall!" he shouted.

Paul Zall was a third-year instructor, a Harvard Ph.D. who acted and
thought otherwise. It was said that he had written in one month his dissertation on the eighteenth-century pamphleteer John Wolcot, who wrote under
the name of Peter Pindar. This, I should guess, is a record of some sort. Zall
was also a practical joker. (Perhaps the dissertation was a joke that no one at
Harvard grasped). His occasional victim was George Healey. The Wordsworth
letter was a fake that Zall had carefully prepared and planted.

Zall liked to do odd things both in scholarship and in teaching. He
found Dorothy Wordsworth's pin cushion in the collection, photographed it,
wrote a brief article about it, and sent it to *Women's Day*. It was published
there, and Zall gleefully added it to his curriculum vitae. He once hid alarm
clocks in his classroom and asked the students to write about their reactions
when they went off. One day, Sale was sitting in his office when students from
one of Zall's classes, all twenty strong, suddenly and apparently unaccountably crowded in, looked around carefully, and solemnly exited. Zall had
assigned the class to write about what they had seen, including Sale. Zall was
not promoted. He went to Oregon and later to Los Angeles State with a stop
as a technical writer at Boeing Aircraft in Seattle. He became a denizen of
the Huntington Library. Whether the Huntington has discovered new and
valuable letters or other documents I do not know.

Diana ran afoul of Zall's tricks, his action being recompense for some
trivial joke she had unwisely played on him. Circulars appeared on bulletin
boards announcing that she would give a dance recital. It was to be self-
accompanied on an exotic musical instrument in the sculpture gallery, a dreary
long room full of copies of ancient Greek and Roman statues and busts.

# 6.

My book on Blake and Yeats came out late in 1955 almost simultaneously with my being informed that I had been promoted to assistant professor. Nevertheless, I went to the Modern Language Association meeting in

Chicago with the idea of testing what remained a poor job market. The motive was not trivial. I wanted to find a job that would pay a living wage. I was making $3900, Diana was no longer working, and we were expecting a second child in the spring. I had sent one letter out to Stanford, which produced a desultory interview that came to nothing. I also entered my name in the MLA job exchange and was contacted by the dean of arts and sciences at the University of Texas.

This initiated a series of rather bizarre experiences that should have warned me off but didn't and brought about my two and one-half years in Austin. At the convention the dean, Harry H. Ransom, interviewed me, or rather discoursed to me about his exploits, present and future. He was a short, somewhat pudgy man with a Texas accent tempered somewhat by a few years in the Northeast. He was a fast talker, full of ideas which poured out about what was going on and would go on at Texas. One of his intentions was to bring to Texas bright young men, to change the university culture, to shape it up, indeed to firm it up, to put the university on the intellectual map. In addition to these vagaries, he declared that he was developing a modern literature collection for the library. Already he had arranged the purchase of a collection of Yeats papers, which, if I came to Texas, I could work with. There would be more.

For the library, that was just the beginning. Ransom had funds at his disposal as he climbed from dean eventually to president (years after I had left). The university had oil money that by law had to be spent only for permanent improvements. Ransom imaginatively took this to include books and manuscripts, not just buildings, concrete steps, and flag poles. He gathered, somewhat indiscriminately at times, a huge collection. No doubt he paid more than he had to for many of these acquisitions. He had, I think, little sense of budgetary restraint. He was ambitious both for himself and for the library, which is now named for him and is massive in its holdings. Ransom's profligacy eventually caught up with him, and he was eased out of power, dying not long thereafter.

In what I call my interview Ransom rapidly mentioned a number of young faculty whom he had or was in the process of recruiting, most from the Ivy League, other collections he anticipated obtaining, a magazine he would establish, and so on. All he knew of me after the interview was from my curriculum vitae, that is, not more than he knew at the beginning. The result was that he invited me to come to Texas to lecture in a program he had established called "The Program in Criticism." He would be in touch with details. This program was a device Ransom employed, it turned out, not just to bring people to Austin to be heard but also to bring people to be impressed with what was going on there, mainly what he was himself doing. He rattled off names of some who had come already: John Crowe Ransom (apparently no relation), Robert Penn Warren, and other critics then in fashion. I returned to Ithaca and reported to Diana on what had been an unusual experience, especially for a lowly instructor of English.

I waited to hear from Ransom, yet nothing came. After a while, I decided to write and ask whether indeed I was to be invited to come to speak and if so when. This evoked a letter of profuse apology sprinkled with expressions of heightened optimism about happenings there. It included an invitation to lecture for the magnificent sum of $500. This was a little more than one eighth of my current salary at Cornell. I doubt that the money came from the fund for permanent improvements unless Ransom had cooked the books to hide expenses for lectures by unknown young scholars.

Then, more surprisingly, came a second letter, this time from the chairman of the English department, whom I had neither corresponded with nor met, offering me a position at $5500 per year, a thousand more than the salary I would make at Cornell. Harry Ransom was a salesman and a buyer, but not, I think, much of a judge. How he got the department and its chairman to accept me, I do not know. He must have either gone around the department or bullied it in a show of power. I came to be quite uncertain that a majority or even a minority of the faculty wanted to appoint me, or appoint several others, for that matter.

Some weeks later, I made the visit to Austin. I believe I spoke on Blake to a fairly large group of professors. I had a forgettable meeting with the chairman, Mody Boatright, who must at the time have explained to me the heavy teaching schedule: four courses in the fall and three in the spring. I was later to learn that Ransom had reduced it to three and three. There would be no chance of my teaching English romantic literature. The department already had three professors competing to teach graduate students, all, oddly enough, specialists on Byron, and all cordially disliking each other. I was apparently to be a modernist. I later learned that the library had a major Byron collection.

The department had a new building with pleasant private offices for all. At Cornell, Bruce Park and I had descended from the attic of Goldwin Smith Hall to a basement office for three. The cost of living in Austin was substantially lower. We were expecting a second child. The young faculty seemed pleasant enough, or at least not outwardly hostile. Some were Ransom's appointments from the year before. Diana and I were not enchanted by life on a shoestring in Ithaca. I had no particular attachment to Cornell and had friends only among the instructors, most of whom were already leaving or would have to. To the surprise of everyone we knew in Ithaca, I took the Texas job. To many it seemed at the time an act of professional suicide, at the least a self-inflicted wound. In one sense, it was, but in another it was what I shall euphemistically call a learning experience.

# 7.

We were called Ransom's Raiders, those whom he recruited and some who seemed to have joined up or been drafted. Located in various departments, we were nevertheless clearly supposed to be his people. I quickly learned that Texas academic politics mirrored Texas politics generally by emphasizing personal power and personal loyalty. Standing on principle did not appear to be a virtue. This meant, under the circumstances, that we were estranged from our departments, not by our own doing but by Ransom's. This meant also that he became our protector and expected full loyalty in return. I do not believe that he ever exerted his power to punish any individual; I do not believe it was in his personality; but the culture made a threat implicit, and he did want loyalty.

Perhaps the young Raider most in the Texas tradition I have just described, recognizable in certain American presidents from the state, was a Kantian philosopher, John Silber. Silber, unlike most of the Raiders, respected power, eventually became dean at Texas, and had ambition for the presidency. Finally, however, he ran afoul of the head of the board of regents, who drove an orange and white Cadillac with huge longhorns adorning the hood. Silber moved on to become president of Boston University, where by an interesting manipulation of members of the board of trustees he became the highest paid university president in the land and stayed on long after he might have retired.

My clearest remembrance of Silber came at a meeting of a club in which faculty members presented papers. A young colleague in English who had never impressed me with either intellectual or social prowess delivered a quite interesting paper that in some ways anticipated Deconstruction. At once, upon its completion, Silber rose and attacked him viciously. The author was unable to respond coherently. But Silber had not bothered to understand the paper. He sensed personal weakness and was out to destroy. I had not seen Silber do that sort of thing before, nor did I later, though many at Boston University apparently did. I had dinner many years later with Helen Vendler, who had moved from Boston to Harvard, and she did not suppress a savage rage at Silber's behavior even as she relished telling about it.

Perhaps the most colorful of the Raiders was William Arrowsmith, the classics scholar, who arrived from Riverside one year after I did. Certainly the tiny Texas classics department, which had almost dried to dust, did not want him. Indeed, they were terrified of him. Within a year Arrowsmith had a large following of students and had recruited by force of personality thirty new majors, up from about six. He was witty, arrogant, theatrical, charismatic. I never saw Arrowsmith teach or lecture, but I am told that in front of a class he became possessed, a different person. Moreover, he succeeded in bringing classics into the arena of contemporary criticism at Texas and founded a journal that spread his word across the country. He set out to use Ransom, who funded it, and he succeeded.

The best-known Raider other than Arrowsmith was Roger Shattuck in French. He did not have a doctorate, but he had been a member of the Society of Fellows at Harvard and had just published *The Banquet Years*, which had given him a considerable academic reputation. In most ways Shattuck was the opposite of Arrowsmith, but he also gathered students. Where Arrowsmith was impulsive, impatient, and effusive, Shattuck was laid back and came on as thoughtful and arty, characteristics that proved to make a hit with the coeds. Several years later he was brought over from the French department to try to bring order to the sick English department, and was apparently had some success. In years after I and others had left, Silber, Arrowsmith, and Shattuck remained until Silber's downfall, perhaps the only survivors among the Raiders. Eventually, they too left. Shattuck first to Virginia, and then (guess where?) to Boston University, where Arrowsmith went, as well.

In my first semester at Texas, I thought it a good idea to have a serious look at the Yeats material. I did not realize that to do this would take some special effort. Luckily I mentioned this intention to a professor who had befriended me, Willis Pratt, one of the Byronians. He informed me that I should proceed to apply to the longtime head curator Fanny Ratchford, and to do this with studied care just short of fawning obsequiousness after an introduction by note from him. Pratt was the only one of the three Byronians entirely acceptable to her. The rare book area was a grand place where Miss Ratchford ruled in the mode of Texan power. I was invited to take tea there with her. Prepared carefully for the occasion, I came with an account of my meeting with Mrs. Yeats and was entirely successful. The Yeats material was opened to me. Much of it I had seen in Dublin. Sometime after I had left Texas, Ransom removed Miss Ratchford from her stronghold. She went on sabbatical leave and is said to have received by radiogram in the mid–Atlantic notice of her termination as curator of rare books. Her replacement had been appointed before she reached Southampton, long before she was able to marshal her dwindling legions.

Ransom had already established firm authority over the departments. It was made clear who held the purse strings and to whom and to what degree loyalty was to be given. In English, the problem of loyalty was complicated by a long-standing feud between two professors. It was clear to the young that one should be either a Cline man or a Graham man. In a superficial way the opposition was one between English and American literature. I was not immediately aware of this internal strife. I knew neither person. When I finally met them, Clarence Cline struck me at once as a somewhat repulsive personality and an untrustworthy character, though I had no experience of his behavior at all. I suspected Uriah Heapish designs and kept my distance. Philip Graham, in manner an old-style Texan, had a somewhat amusing and ironic if mean-spirited way of talking. He held his cards close to the vest. He clearly disliked Ransom and was given to not quite scurrilous comments about him, especially Ransom's suspected connection with certain homosexuals on the faculty. Mrs. Cline, referred to by her husband as Lovey, was an unpleasant sort of southern lady who would declare that she *thought* the kitchen of a colleague's wife was clean. She apparently took a dislike to us when we could not come to her house for dinner because we couldn't find a baby-sitter that night. When we tried to make amends by inviting the Clines to a small gathering, I observed poor Clarence virtually dragging her up our front walk.

The veteran senior faculty had made their way at or their grudging peace with Texas. When the department moved to its new building, a few remained in the landmark library tower. One of these was a crusty southerner Thomas P. Harrison, a scholar who had published what still is and surely will be the only book on birds in Shakespeare. The library tower, affectionately known as Dr. Battle's last erection (he being the president when it was built), had been the scene of a suicide. A story, no doubt apocryphal, is told that a colleague rushed into Harrison's office and shouted that so and so had just jumped from the top, whereupon Harrison calmly replied that yes, he had seen him go by.

Texas social life was divided, for the most part, into either warring or sullenly quiet camps. This was never better demonstrated than when at a garden party celebrating the end of the academic year, people gravitated to separate groups and stayed in them. Cline later became chairman. Shortly after that, Roger Shattuck had to come in from French to bring order. Just before he did this, sometime in the late sixties, he heard a rumor that I was about to publish a novel based on Texas and wrote to me asking whether this was true. He knew that the job he was about to take would be difficult and imagined that my book would make recruiting faculty that much harder. My novel was, in part, based on experience at Texas, but disguised. I told him that I couldn't imagine that it would be an encumbrance. Shattuck, probably annoyed when he finally read it, made clear that he didn't think it very good. He hoped that what I taught my students about prose style wasn't reflected in its technique.

# 8.

It was always hot in Texas. Diana and I found not only the departmental culture but also the weather stifling. It was usual to start out for the campus early in the morning with the temperature already eighty and climbing.

We were there before many houses were entirely air-conditioned. For a while we had what were called evaporative coolers; they were supposed to lower the humidity but seemed to do the opposite. These were about as effective as the device for heat that the Edwards family had in Dublin, which was composed of rocks heated in the night when power was cheaper and cooling gradually as the day wore on. After a while, we could afford a room air-conditioner, which made one area reasonably comfortable.

Social life was partly redeemed by the presence of two other young faculty who were somewhat reluctant or at least skeptical raiders. One was a poet, Frederick Eckman, who played the role in an inimitable way. He was somewhat ravaged looking, grizzled, fully bearded (at times), and bear-like in his motions. He maintained a persona as a small-town Ohio boy. It was my being originally from Ohio that gave me some chance to overcome what would surely otherwise have been either contempt or outright hostility because I came from Princeton and Cornell. He was hostile to all things eastern, including what he considered the American poetry establishment. As a consequence he published in obscure little magazines and put out books from fugitive presses. Over time, after leaving Texas for Bowling Green, he developed a barely above-ground reputation and a group of adoring former students. Eckman's last connection with Texas was a tragic one. His son Tom was killed trying to protect a woman from the killer who went on a shooting spree from the top of the library tower.

Eckman could be tiresome, as he tended, in the manner of some autodidacts, which in certain ways he was, to lecture to me on subjects about which I knew as much if not more than he. However, he knew a great deal about twentieth-century American poetry (he had little use for the English) and wrote a good little book, *Cobras and Cockleshells*, on contemporary verse techniques, almost unknown because of its obscure publisher and its brevity. After his death, the journal *Sagetrieb*, sustained by the National Poetry Foundation, published a memorial edition of his writings with essays about his work, to which I contributed. I called my contribution "The Wizard of Continental." That was the town in Ohio in which he was born and brought up.

The colleague I valued most was James B. Colvert, a Texan who as a teen had played clarinet in the Dallas symphony and later had piloted bombing raids over Germany. Colvert told me once that he had not gone back to a music career because he had decided that musicians were for the most part deeply uninteresting people. Once I was at his house when he came walking into the living room playing flawlessly the solo from Benny Goodman's "Let's Dance."

Colvert had a subtle critical mind with a respect for literary history. While I was at Texas he wrote two brilliant essays on Hemingway and Stephen Crane. At work on a book about Crane, he was sidetracked into editing part of the complete edition of Crane, and his book came out only many years later. When I went to Irvine I sought to have him appointed in American literature, but the powers above me would not approve the appointment on the grounds that he had not published enough to warrant the rank that he then held at the University of Virginia. This turned out to be, over time, a disaster for Irvine. There followed in order two senior Americanists who published a lot and were each in their ways quite unfortunate presences in the department before they wore out their welcomes and moved on. Colvert later served as chairman at the University of Georgia and editor for a time of *The Georgia Review*. Ever since, I have become fully skeptical of committee or administrative evaluations by people who do not really know a candidate's full value, both intellectual and collegial.

It is a demonstrable fact that humanists develop professionally more slowly than scientists and mathematicians, who often have done their best and sometimes only work by age thirty. It is deeply unfortunate that university appointment and promotion policies are mainly oriented to those built up by traditions in science that do not apply well to humanists. But the fault lies in part with humanists, who seem to be content to go along with science-oriented policies. I have not even mentioned the matter of the judgment of teaching, which humanists tend to do more of than scientists, but with little if any reward from the system. Here again, humanists do not insist that teaching be given enough importance.

# 9.

The Texas Program in Criticism, which was advertised in a brochure shortly after I arrived, was really only a series of lectures arranged from time to time by Ransom, who seemed to enjoy inviting academic celebrities to the campus and giving them Texas-size honoraria. Oddly, he rarely attended the lectures or social gatherings that followed. I think his main aim in having the program was public relations. During the time I was at Texas both poets and critics came. Among the critics were Northrop Frye, W. Y. Tindall, and Robert Wooster Stallman, who arrived with a suitcase full of gin, having heard erroneous information or simply thought that Texas was a dry state. Fredson Bowers, who was not a critic at all but rather a bibliographer, came. Speaking of his chairmanship at Virginia, he said it was a "bum's game." I learned about his style of leadership from the phrase he was given to repeating: "Law of the Medes and the Persians!" Bowers apparently took a liking to me and to Colvert. About a year later, I was offered a position at Virginia, but I had just taken another job. Later, he hired Colvert, with whom he edited the Crane volumes. Allen Tate arrived, and Arrowsmith hid a bottle of good bourbon in the kitchen for Tate's exclusive use at a party. Randall Jarrell arrived and genially cracked jokes. Among those I came to know slightly were Dame Edith Sitwell, W. H. Auden, and Robert Graves. It was my assignment to take care of Dame Edith from arrival to departure. I met her train and pushed her around in her wheelchair. She appeared in her usual quasi-medieval costume, draped to the ankles and adorned with enormous jewelry. The effect was more ecclesiastical than royal. She brought with her a reputation for difficulty, but she was gracious with little of the affectation and the tendency to malice with which she had often been characterized. She came to my class and read to the students for an hour from a large book in which she apparently wrote daily, sometimes a diary entry, sometimes general thoughts and observations. When she finished, the members of my large class spontaneously lined up and passed by her as at a reception. They each thanked her, and many, not knowing what to call her, addressed her simply as "Dame." Texas students were the most polite that I have known.

Auden's visit began somewhat comically and ended somewhat unpleasantly. A small committee of Raiders was assigned to meet him in his hotel room and convey him to dinner below. Auden had taken off his shoes and was wearing slippers. As we moved to the door, one of our least sentient colleagues remarked to him in alarm, " Mr. Auden. Mr. Auden, you are wearing your slippers!"

"I know," he replied.

At dinner red wine was ordered, and to his grumbling astonishment it came ice cold, confirming, I am sure, that he had passed beyond the bounds of civilization. The lecture Auden gave was a disaster of dullness. A huge crowd overflowed the auditorium and other rooms, where his voice was piped in. He chose to speak on an almost unknown book called *Lord of the Rings* by a little-known Oxford professor. I suspect that no one in the audience, or perhaps very few, had ever heard at the time of J. R. R. Tolkien. Auden had been deep into the Icelandic Edda and sagas, and spoke on and on about connections to them. He mumbled into his manuscript for over an hour and seemed unaware that people had begun to leave, as if it were a ball game the outcome of which was too sadly predictable. At a party later, Diana had a cordial conversation with him, perhaps because of her Icelandic lineage; but to me he gave the impression that he would be most pleased to be elsewhere — after collecting his check.

It was surprising how many of our visitors were poor speakers and how often their talks were dull. On the whole I doubt that the lectures increased the community's interest in the literary world. Auden mumbled. Tate read directly from a retreaded manuscript. Bowers projected his well-known arrogance in both bodily and verbal language. Most went on too long. A happy exception was Northrop Frye, who spoke flawlessly for fifty minutes without a paper or even notes before him. It was a *tour de force* and can be read today as his essay "Nature and Homer" in his *Fables of Identity.* His was one of the smaller audiences, and Ransom, who actually attended, remarked to me that his talk was disappointing.

In my view, the most disastrous performance, passing beyond dullness into disorder, was that of Robert Graves. In his defense, it was clear to me that he was not feeling well and perhaps running a low fever. Though I was supposed to be in charge of him and his visit, luckily he had along with him an acolyte or, rather, keeper, the young poet Alastair Reid, who was very pleasant, helpful, and well aware of Graves' stubbornness and often cantankerous personality. At our house, Graves complained about our young child's crying, insisting on his being silenced, scorned the ice served in his Scotch, remaining silent about its quality. At one point I was driving a car with Graves and the all-around Irishman Walter Starkie, scholar of things Spanish, seated together in the back. I heard a mumbled conversation that I could not quite pick up, all except the last remark by Graves, "They're all dead now," followed by a short period of silence.

Prior to his lecture, which had been announced to be on a literary topic I don't now recall, I asked him what he would like me to say about him in my introduction. "Say I am a master of all trades and a Jack of none, and by the way I have a different lecture to give." I followed his direction, declaring that Graves had changed the topic of his lecture and would announce it himself. There followed a rambling, incoherent discourse on Mexican drugs and ritual use. Of what the audience, from both town and gown, thought of this I did not like to speculate.

One of Ransom's motives for these lectures was to attract manuscripts to the library. It was partly this hope that brought him to invite T. S. Eliot to speak. The event was well-publicized, and a huge crowd of thousands attended. Eliot, accompanied by his wife, proved to be pleasant, affable in a somewhat formal way that was an expression of good manners. He was a conscientious, interesting, as well as very highly paid lecturer. Diana and I sat directly behind the bare back of Mrs. Eliot in the second row, and I detected that she was a keeper of a different sort.

## 9.

In some ways we were arrogant in our response to Texas. I still think of it as another country and sometimes remark, not entirely in jest, that things would be better if it were. Of course, some Texans think that, too. I recall a woman saying to me that her daughter was doing a year abroad — at Wellesley. The attitude that demanded unthinking personal loyalty and punishment for those who did not provide it seemed to pervade the culture, a morality of sheer naked power. I sensed it in Ransom, otherwise a mild-mannered man not really, I think, well suited to the mores. I saw it in the young Silber, who exported it to Boston. It was present in the enmity of Graham and Cline and the unspoken demand that you had better choose a side. It expressed itself obliquely in the willingness of Shattuck and Arrowsmith to go along with Ransom and then Silber.

I left Austin with relief in January of 1959 for a visiting appointment elsewhere. I have not been back to Texas, though I was once invited to lecture there, and I have no idea what the state of the English department is now. My experience was long ago, yes, in another country, and the players are almost all dead.

## 10.

Texas was an education for someone who would become an administrator — what not to do. The opposite was the case at Michigan State. The chairman there, when I accepted the job, was Russel B. Nye. He was in his last year of several. His reputation as a scholar was actually in history, and he had won a Pulitzer Prize not long before. Nye had seen Michigan State grow from a college of agriculture, the nation's first land-grant college. It was by now Michigan State University, but it had the subtitle "of Agriculture and Applied Sciences." Eventually this was abandoned by the powerful president John Hannah, who knew and cared little about the humanities himself but knew they were a necessity in a major university. Hannah kept up the old "ag college" tradition. Before school began each fall, he hosted a huge reception and party in the student union for all newcomers and talked to every one of them. When he heard complaints about MSU putting up too many new buildings at public expense, he had erected before every building a sign in the school colors describing the private funding and public funds expended, if any, on it. When I sought a half sabbatical (a year before a sabbatical was due) to supplement my Fulbright Fellowship, I was summoned to his office and interviewed about my scholarly intentions. On the next day I was granted the sabbatical in writing. Hannah knew nothing about what I intended to do, but he still thought it was his business as president to decide on the matter. Michigan State profited by his style for some time, but it grew to be enormous. In 1962, when Diana and I went to Ireland it already had 18,000 students. When we came back, there were 25,000, and now I believe it is twice that big or even larger than that.

Through the early stages of this development Nye had run a peaceful department with an assortment of eccentrics, many of whom had been there a long time. The department's morale profited from the fact that Hannah had established a lower-division "University College" offering basic courses that all students took, taught by departments whose only task was to teach a single year-long course: Natural Sciences, Social Sciences, Humanities, and Communication Skills. The last of these was what most English departments taught as freshman composition. To this day, that course remains the major source of problems for English departments, dominating the budget, eating up administrative time and energy, and providing grounds for dissension. Nye and his department were free of this. However, there was an underside. There was little support for graduate students. They could do little teaching because another faculty taught Communication Skills. This had not been much of a problem because there had not been an emphasis on graduate study, but by the time I arrived there was ambition to develop it.

The one most important thing I learned from Nye flowed from a remark he made to me. He said he thought the department got along pretty well because he tried to give everyone a specific responsibility so that each person would have some sense of importance. This, he admitted, required creative imagination at times and willingness to suffer but not to panic when someone not entirely competent erred. What he said reminded me of Bruce Park's story about his navy commander, who insisted that all of his officers learn to dock the ship. He would take the ship out into the bay, order an officer to bring it in, remove himself to his cabin and sit there with his head in his hands. Later, attempting to put the Nye principle into action, I came to understand the commander's feelings as he sat there waiting.

In the year I came, Nye relinquished his chairmanship to David Mead, but his influence and way of acting remained strong. In this respect the department, while growing, did not change a lot. Not many new appointments had recently been made. I and a couple of others were regarded rather as novelties, people to be curious about. Our reception was friendly, just the opposite of the attitude toward northern interlopers at Texas. The new experience, was, in short, a relief, and the department was better than people on the outside realized.

I was back to sharing an office. The department, as is often the case with English, was housed in an old building that had been built for another use, in this case a dormitory for women. The ceilings were high and the rooms large. The furniture was old and oaken, little different from what my grandfathers would have had. I shared my office with Wallace Moffet, who appeared to me as old as the furniture. He was a veteran of many years at MSU and a genial and friendly man who was determined to make me feel at home. This attitude carried over to his wife Lucille. Wallace was not like any college professor I had known, but he was familiar to me, nevertheless, for he could have been a teacher at Hawken or Lakeside. He said one day that all anyone needed to give him was the textbook a little bit ahead of time and directions to the classroom. He knew little, perhaps nothing, of contemporary criticism or, I think, contemporary literature. The notion of specialized scholarship was of little interest to him. He read texts and about their authors and went into the classroom to teach. He never once held it against me that I quickly became the principal force there for the introduction of new literary ideas. Indeed, he encouraged me.

The department had an eccentricity all its own. Nye laughingly said to me that an exception was being made in the decision to hire me, for there was more than one syllable in my name; this was principally a one-syllable department: Nye, Mead, Geist, Heist, Rust, Babb, Struck, Yunck, Waite, Scott, and Smith, and maybe others I have forgotten. The most interesting of these to me was Arthur J. M. Smith, the Canadian poet, an ebullient character in his fifties, who seemed to discover enjoyment in everything. He taught poetry, and it was his honest view that poetry was a very specialized pleasure that few people enjoyed. He meant no disparagement of those who did not appreciate it. Diana and I attended a Duke Ellington concert in Lansing with the Smiths. When we attempted to exit the parking lot we were confronted by the arm of a barrier, no clear way to raise it, and no attendant. Smith leapt from the car, and before we could figure out what he was about to do he tore the arm from its post, bowed to us and ushered us through. Apparently we were the only witnesses to this misdemeanor.

There was not a lot to do in East Lansing. Of course, there was Big Ten football for fanatics and the occasional academic events, but little else. The English department's solution was the Saturday night party with dancing and a midnight supper. A few people from other departments were granted the privilege of attending. One of these was Charlie Pollock, the art professor and brother of Jackson, who enlivened these evenings by subjecting the youngest wives to creative dancing. A few years ahead of his time with respect to technique, he was capable of exhausting all of them.

Diana and I made occasional trips to Ann Arbor to visit our friends from Cornell days, Jim and Joan Gindin. One evening they were the unfortunate hosts for a party at which Nelson Algren and some friends ended the evening by trashing parts of the house. William Styron was there but did not participate in this, nor did the Tigers' third baseman Steve Boros, who had been Jim's student and may have attempted to bring order. By the time that the mayhem had begun we were on our way back to East Lansing. The party had followed a program of speakers sponsored by Arnold Gingrich and *Esquire* magazine.

Michigan State was still dominated in the public eye and in that of most students by agriculture, engineering, and, of course, football. Our department faculty and graduate students made a play to erase the charge of effete-ness by fielding a fast-pitch softball team that astonishingly captured the university's intramural championship. The final game was won over a team composed of MSU football players. There was great consternation among these uniformly massive, fast, and quick players when they learned who we were. Many may not even have known that there was an English department! Our pitcher was the principal cause of our victory. His name was James Calderwood and later made a reputation as a Shakespeare scholar at Irvine. He had been a two-sport star at Oregon, known, a friend said, first, for having the misfortune of succeeding Norm Van Brocklin at quarterback and, second, for having made the shortest punt in Oregon history. He was, nevertheless, a remarkable athlete and had an assortment of pitches that baffled batters, especially free swingers. I was his catcher, the only one in the department both capable of and willing to face catching him. Just for the fun of it I would call for a variety of pitches, but he finally admonished me, saying just to signal for two fastballs and then a riser. This almost always worked. Our victory, of course, in no way changed the culture at MSU, but our self-esteem was raised somewhat.

Until I came to Michigan State I had never been able to teach English romanticism. I don't think this was unusual in my generation. The instructorship and assistant professorships were still rather like apprentice jobs, and the teaching was usually limited to lower-division classes. That is a far cry from today or even from the late sixties, when young Ph.D.s had many job offers and departments had to compete for their services, by offering them upper-division courses and sometimes even graduate seminars. At Michigan State I was suddenly the senior romanticist. My first course took place in a lecture room of the agricultural college. Behind my lectern, reaching to the ceiling, were shelves and shelves of stuffed birds on display. I am sure that there are as many birds in romantic poetry as Professor T. P. Harrison found in Shakespeare, and there they all were, true visual aids, as we say, ready to be gestured toward during discussions of Keats and Shelley, Wordsworth and Coleridge. Yes, an albatross was there, and a nightingale.

Soon I was also teaching Anglo-Irish literature and the history of criticism, having established both courses. As far as I could tell, Michigan State students had no experience studying and thinking about either the history or practice of criticism. The undergraduate students were docile, and some seemed interested enough. Almost anything from Plato to I. A. Richards and beyond was new to them. This was to some degree true of the graduate students, who were uneven in talent and training. They were teachers trying to get a leg up, people who were not admitted to more established programs, and people who had to choose the program nearest to home or work. I recognized that I had myself belonged to groups two and three above. In teaching criticism I tried out a variation of the experiment that Richards described in his *Practical Criticism*, that is, to give the students poems without the names of authors or any other information about them and ask for their judgments of them. The results were sadly about the same as Richards'. It was 1959 or '60, but even the New Criticism was relatively new at MSU, and the students needed to learn how to read a poem. I had to begin the history of criticism with some very practical definitions and introductions, including the assertion that there was such a thing as literary criticism and what it was. Back then I thought I knew.

I do not remember well very many of the students from those days. One who stood out as an undergraduate was W. J. T. Mitchell, who later wrote a fine book on Blake and followed it with interesting theoretical books on literature and art. He became editor of *Critical Inquiry* at the University of Chicago. In my house in Seattle years later he sang Blake's songs to us, accompanying himself on the guitar. Among graduate students, a young Okinawan named Okifumi Komesu unaccountably turned up in my Yeats seminar, and years later from his professorship in the University of the Ryukyus published in English a very good book on Yeats.

There was at MSU at the time a lively minor administrator named Stanley Idzerda. His ambition was to attract better undergraduates to the campus. He invented for this purpose what I shall call "The Great National Merit Scholar Scam." Idzerda sent a personal letter to every finalist and runner-up in the National Merit Scholarship examinations, inviting them to Michigan State for a weekend of activities. They had to pay their transportation, but everything else was on the university. While there, these high-school seniors would hear lectures, participate in forums, sample the athletic facilities, etc. Students came from everywhere in large numbers. Idzerda asked me to lecture on reading poetry. A large crowd was assembled. Following the lecture there was the most vigorous discussion and question period I can remember, complete with mini-lectures from the floor on points I had made, skimmed over, had not made, and should have made.

Idzerda's plan was an immediate and astounding success. That year more Merit Scholars enrolled at MSU than at any other university, and this prominence lasted for several years until other universities caught on and adopted similar programs. Even today, some forty years later, MSU has what would seem to be a disproportionate enrollment of Merit Scholars. But all was not entirely rosy with this influx. A good many of these very bright students were disillusioned, particularly by the size to which the university was growing. There was also some grumbling about the quality of the instruction. I myself did not notice the effects of the presence of the first of these students, since I was in Dublin the following year and not long after that moved to California. However, I was later told that teaching became more interesting with two or three of these students in one's class. Idzerda eventually moved on, no doubt to wave his magic wand elsewhere before impressionable young people.

The English department, too, began to stir with new ambition. Carl Hartman, later to join me at Irvine, arrived to bolster creative writing and founded the *Red Cedar Review*, a quarterly of student writing. Things picked up in the graduate program. Hartman and I established the Conference in Modern Literature, which took place over three days in the spring. Quite a few notable critics and scholars came to talk about everything from the theory of literature to bibliography and textual scholarship. For the first time, I came to realize that problems in literary theory and criticism have parallels in textual scholarship, as they have had over the centuries with philosophy.

The Conference suffered an absurd crisis in its third year, when the modernist scholar Frederick J. Hoffman and some of his followers attempted in what nearly became a coup to bring out of it a formal society of scholars. The move may have been in Hoffman's mind from the beginning, but it was hastened by our including a panel discussion by poets, which, of course, as panels by academic poets usually do, turned out to be an anti-academic attack. This seemed to split the conference-goers and deeply offended Hoffman, who gave the impression of disliking literature (or at least its creators) except as a thing with which to make professional hay. The conference ended peacefully with Hoffman retreating without triumph back to Wisconsin. A few years later, Hoffman, then at the University of California, Riverside, proposed to me moving himself and his tiny band of two or three followers to Irvine, He, though not alone, had managed to split the department at Riverside into warring factions. The proposal died when one of his enemies was hired by us. I never heard from him after that.

The Conference had its social events, but not on the scale of the Yeats Summer School, having but three days to get up steam. Scandal arose, it is said, when a visitor bedded somewhere south of East Lansing a faculty wife. Drink was plentiful, and with his usual wisdom Northrop Frye declared in opening remarks that nine A.M. was a quite too early and uncivilized time to begin sessions.

One of the participants in the first year was Murray Krieger, then of the University of Illinois. He had written the first rigorously argued book about the New Criticism and was important in the development of the teaching of criticism and theory and its history. His was the first book on modern criticism that approached the subject philosophically. He had been a student of the philosopher Eliseo Vivas at Chicago, going with him to Ohio State. Though he parted with Vivas on some points of theory and almost all politics, he respected Vivas's critical work, mainly because it was philosophical in approach. I had written a favorable notice of Krieger's work in *The American Scholar*, and soon an invitation to lecture at Illinois came. Krieger had been hired there at an astounding salary for the time, virtually unheard of for someone so young. He was obviously unhappy with the academic conservatism of the department and wanted to bring in someone who would be on his side. No luck. I lectured on Yeats to what seemed to me hostile incomprehension, and my pseudo-candidacy, of which I was actually unaware, came to an end.

Krieger soon went to Iowa and tried again there. Diana and I drove out to Iowa City in the depths of winter. We decided against the move. The reasons were several. I saw nothing in particular to do there, certainly little of the intellectual pioneering I was doing in Michigan. Critics and theorists abounded at Iowa: Geoffrey Hartman, Rosalie Colie, Ralph Freedman, and others. Paul Engle dominated *his* creative writing program. Krieger already taught theory. Further, Iowa City at that time made Lansing appear to be a metropolis. Finally, uprooting the children and ourselves seemed a bad idea.

Driving back to East Lansing, we hit a tremendous blizzard that marooned us for a full day and night in a lone motel that seemed far from anywhere. By this time, of course, we were veterans of such snows. Trying to pay for our house in the second year in Michigan, I signed up to teach an extension course in the evening in Grand Rapids. Ten out of the ten times I went there I drove back in a blizzard. The last time, in March, I followed the tail lights of a huge truck all the way. If it had gone off into a cornfield, I would have followed. The Midwest, it seemed, was the Midwest, living in one place not much different from living in another.

The Iowa visit had an unexpected bonus. Philip Roth and his then wife (well before Claire Bloom) were apparently dragooned to entertain at us dinner. There followed the funniest dinner I can ever recall having. Roth was a nonstop, sit-down comedian. Everything he said was funny. He declared that he was smitten by the visit of the British novelist Angus Wilson, who, he said, spoke repeatedly of the wonderful American "penal system." Roth kept returning to this, a sort of leit motif in his monologue.

## 11.

Michigan State was a good place when I was there, pleasant, particularly for our children. We would not, I think, have considered a move except to the West Coast. About a year after the Iowa flirtation, I was elected or perhaps appointed to be the next chairman at Michigan State. However, shortly after it became clear that this would occur, I received a letter from the University of California, Irvine, which was still in the planning stage. I could be interviewed for the founding chairmanship of English there. At about the same time I received a similar invitation from the University of California,

San Diego, but not to be chairman. My visit to California begins the next chapter.

Eventually, I took the Irvine job. A meeting of the department at Michigan State had to be called, and I announced that I was leaving and why. It was a difficult and moving moment for me, particularly moving because the response was cordial and understanding. They all seemed to agree that I was making the right decision. One person even responded by saying I should take them all with me.

# Excursus:
# Academic Entrepreneurship

According to the nearest dictionary, an entrepreneur is "one who organizes, manages, and assumes the risks of a business or enterprise." This does not sound much like someone in academic life, but a sort of entrepreneurship has developed there over the past few decades. My first and most stunning experience of the academic entrepreneur was Harry Ransom at Texas. Maybe he was just someone who did business in the Texas way; I don't really know. However, I'll call Ransom ahead of his time, an academic entrepreneur on the grand scale. He made big plans, organized them to his liking, and controlled those involved, though sometimes he managed things recklessly. I am sure he took risks with the college budget. He made ventures for the college his business, though the ventures may have been mainly on his own behalf on his way to the presidency of the university. Again, I don't know. He introduced into departments his own appointees, protected them, arranged teaching schedules, and in other ways favored them, creating around himself a cabal of young people inevitably in his debt. He founded and edited himself a magazine designed to bring importance to the university as an intellectual center. He sometimes used it to publish friends or well-known people he wished to impress or had invited to speak. He created a program of visiting lecturers, who were paid what were in those days large sums for their appearances. His greatest entrepreneurial effort and success was to develop for the library a huge collection of manuscripts and books in modern literature. In all of these matters, especially the last, he was, of course, not risking his own capital, but expending the university's, often, I am told, going over budget and often overpaying for literary materials. There was a risk: his own job security, but he advanced up the ladder from dean to president, reaching a level perhaps beyond his competence and from which he was, I believe, forced to retire. He was a free wheeler and dealer of a type that I had never seen.

Academic entrepreneurship now operates in different circumstances and has appeared even among young professors. Its causes, rooted in the second half of the twentieth century, are not far to seek. Perhaps the most important is the incursion of federal research money into academic science and medicine. Humanists came late to this largess, and their share was but meager scraps from a bountiful table. I recall a young biologist friend at Irvine asking, "Don't you folks get any goodies?" The humanists aped the scientists' National Science Foundation and the National Institute for Health, managing to get the National Endowment for the Humanities established by Congress; but the budget has always been miniscule, and the head of the Endowment has sometimes been hostile to the doings of humanists, as seemed to be the case with Lynne Cheney. Nevertheless, some humanists began to act like their distant academic colleagues. Along with this came the growth of the mega-university. These seem now to be called "research universities," being thereby contrasted to institutions without or virtually without Ph.D. programs and huge investments in expensive equipment. Research universities are now often as large as small cities, with resultant problems of crime, health, traffic, and growth of an administrative and clerical staff developed in part to deal with the bureaucratic complexities of grant oversight, or in some places notorious undersight, as for example in my own institution, where in the medical school the situation became scandalous and even criminal.

In the research university, individual faculty members found themselves more and more attached to their grants and research groups than to their institutions or their academic departments. Inevitably curricular issues took a back seat. Scientists could pay themselves summer salaries from their grants and attend conferences worldwide, writing the costs off as business expenses. Young science faculty began to be judged by committees on promotion and tenure by their success in garnering research money as much as or more than by their actual scientific achievements.

Faculty members began to teach less. This seems to have been a universal development across all disciplines, made more problematic by the difficulty any administrator had (if he or she cared) determining what a faculty member's actual teaching load was, especially in the sciences, or even how to calculate it. Gradually humanists caught on. The decline in teaching load over the years can be illustrated by my own career. At Cornell I taught three courses each semester with 20 to 25 students in each section of freshman English composition and a paper a week from each of them. The load was heavier at Texas: four and three; but through the munificence of Dean Ransom some of us taught three and three. At Michigan State, on the quarter system, I taught two courses each quarter. Irvine began with five courses per year on the quarter system, and I might as well have thought I'd died and gone to heaven. At Washington I had a similar schedule at the beginning, but it was reduced to four courses as the result of having a large number of graduate students to supervise. Now the load has been reduced to four for all faculty, but practically speaking the load is three. Almost everyone has a reduced load for one reason or another, some fairly good and some not so good or incomprehensible. It is only recently that this situation in English came to light. At the present time no regular line faculty member teaches a freshman class, and almost no one teaches sophomores. These courses, the total enrollment of which easily doubles that of the rest of the curriculum, are now taught by part-time lecturers and graduate student assistants, many of whom began with no teaching experience whatever, some with only a little. They are underpaid and without adequate fringe benefits. In some places they seek to unionize. I am sure it is statistically provable that the more one teaches the less money one makes.

The sum result of all this is a growing alienation of faculty from the institution and, I suspect, that of students, too, plus a continuing growth of academic entrepreneurship as the acknowledged way to get ahead. Professors who are well-known enough for their research can sell themselves to the highest bidder and on occasion take their spouses and their lesser research colleagues with them into better laboratories. This puts much emphasis on the so-called networking that is easier to accomplish with the rapid growth of information technology and the many conferences held annually. Differences in professional salaries have grown alarmingly. The entrepreneur tends to gain; the others stand still and lose relative to the cost of living. Bitterness increases. The university's impersonality, the increased pressure from government, both federal and state, the growth of an administrative class with very large salaries compared to those of the actual teachers all make for alienation. In many places the role of the faculty, as a faculty, seems trivial relative to that of the football coach. Presidential salaries can strike one as obscene except when compared to those of the coaches. This is a tangled web, and there does not seem to be much chance of unraveling it.

Personal aggrandizement is a symptom, not a cause of these many developments in academic life, and it is an ugly one. Signs of how entrepreneurship as an assumption has invaded academic life are two columns in the weekly *Chronicle of Higher Education*: "Peer Review" and "Hot Type," devoted respectively to those who have negotiated new positions and those who have published works either deemed important or controversial. In addition to this, the *Chronicle* has a way of seizing on some academic star and repeatedly referring, issue after issue in some cases, to that person's recent exploits or assertions. One is reminded of a gossip column about rock or movie stars in a local paper. To someone from the outside this would seem preposterous or comical, if anyone were noticing.

Some of these developments can be traced back to the greater pressure now publicly exerted on universities to be all things to all people, exacerbated by growing scarcity of funding that has driven most state universities to copy private institutions and seek private money. The academic star system, with the entrepreneur usually at the top, is grounded entirely on research, never on teaching. The latter still rules at "teach or perish" liberal arts colleges, but many of these are severely pressed for funds today.

Quarrels over curriculum, what and how much to teach, how and when, take place everywhere and under all conditions. In some places, to control a course is a matter of ego gratification, sometimes a substitute for a decent salary. Maybe a few quarrels would be more intelligently carried on if salaries were more equitable, but I doubt it. Some wag once said that academic quarrels are so vicious because the stakes are so small.

# 8

# Making a Campus: UCI 1

## 1.

As I entered my hotel late at night there was the smell of flowers. It was February of 1964, and I was in Newport Beach, California. On the next morning I was to be interviewed for the position of chairman (such people were not yet confused with a piece of furniture) at the campus of the University of California, Irvine, just being built. At that time, what is now the city of Irvine was a huge ranch mainly of orange groves stretching from near the ocean in the south to mountains in the north. Across the street from the buildings that were barely under construction a herd of buffalo grazed. The campus, designed by the well-known architect William Pereira, was to consist of a large circle containing a park with buildings on the perimeter and in spokes beyond. Nearby were the temporary offices of the architect, who was given to parking his Rolls-Royce squarely in the center of the lot for all to see, admire, and carefully maneuver around.

Pereira was an architect of large spaces and large ego. His buildings were all of uniform appearance with a few variations, deliberately futuristic for their time, but now dated. Later on, when I drove to work in the morning I would wonder fancifully whether they might have been folded up and removed overnight like some monstrous Hollywood B movie set. Indeed, shortly after the first ones were built and classes were in session, Hollywood descended, and *Planet of the Apes* was filmed there, using mainly the exterior of the humanities building, where my office was. For a couple of days we were invaded by acrobats dressed as monkeys, scaling the walls and scurrying about.

During construction, mistakes were, as we say, made. The consultant for the building that was planned to be used eventually by biological sciences was

146

UCI, circa 1964 (University of California Libraries, Special Collections and Archives).

a chemist. As far as I could tell no humanist was consulted about the humanities building. "I thought you people just read books," the first mathematics chairman said to me, demonstrating that he was a likely prospect for high academic office, which of course he later attained, but elsewhere. One of my small but cherished triumphs early on occurred during my first year at Irvine when, serving on the campus planning committee, I pointed out that on the plan before us a large pipe that came out underground from the library led absolutely nowhere. For the first time, my aborted training in civil engineering was put to work.

During the same trip to California I visited to be interviewed at the new campus in San Diego, two years advanced over Irvine but as yet without undergraduates. It was potentially sprawling and with no visible order. It had already become known for having attracted some Nobel Prize scientists, before whom I was paraded. Roy Harvey Pearce, the chairman of the literature department (it was to include the literatures of all languages), had brought a cabal of faculty from Ohio State, which had been suffering an internal disorder. His orientation, however, was really Johns Hopkins, where each professor was described as, for example, professor of early nineteenth-century English literature. This was to be my description. I responded with skepticism to this fixity, a retrogression to the ways of nineteenth-century Germany by way of Baltimore. I had never clearly fitted into that sort of classification and thought San Diego's contemporary use of it pretentious. In any case, San Diego opted out when it was learned that I was sought by Irvine. Later Pearce seemed to regard me as an upstart competitor, and our relations were edgy, though never unpleasant, as I had friends on his faculty. Years later, Pearce was, I think, startled when I gave a friendly and laudatory introduction for a lecture he presented as president of the Philological Association of the Pacific Coast. At least his face was an interesting study. By that time, I thought of the two of us as, in a way, together. We both knew what it was like to make a department.

Early on, Pearce coped with a problem I didn't have. His hands were full presiding over a department largely composed of people who thought in different languages, had different cultural and political backgrounds, and on the whole didn't understand each other very well. Things became particularly tense there when radical politicization began in the sixties. But Pearce was ahead as well as behind the times, for humanistic studies have since tended toward the interdisciplinary. Like English at Michigan State, his department was free of freshman composition. In addition, the foreign languages were taught in a department of linguistics. There were certainly some advantages in this, but my subsequent experiences have shown me that to mix the various literatures and languages in a single department creates merely a different set of tensions.

I do not believe that the higher administration at San Diego had made a decision to combine the literatures; it was probably Pearce's doing. No decision of that sort came down from above at Irvine. The campus was to begin with a college of arts and sciences and a college of engineering, both with deans. In the former there were to be five schools, each with subdeans of humanities, fine arts, biological science, physical science, and social science. Eventually there would be more units. This recognizable structure raised some problems from the beginning, compounded later. For example, mathematics was arbitrarily assigned to physical science (along with chemistry and physics). For two or three years Irvine was unable to find a dean for this school, which never became more than a fairly arbitrary collection of departments. But, of course, every plan of academic organization ever invented creates internal problems. Departments quickly become isolated. Where there are no departments everyone becomes isolated.

The School of Social Science at Irvine began with no departments, and the result was a disaster. The dean, a man who seemed always to think in large abstractions and possibly could think in no other way, was convinced

that the various social sciences could be brought under a highly abstract single rubric, which was analytical, mathematical, atemporal, opposed to area
studies (as they were then called), and in short reductive: social *science* with
a vengeance. But worse, it meant that the dean was supposedly in a direct
personal relation with each faculty member, there being no mediating level,
a sure formula for dictatorship. Internal disorganization followed: poor morale,
attempted defections to other schools, efforts to create separate programs
independent of the school, and so on. Eventually the school was divided into
departments, but only after the dean left the wreckage behind to become, of
all things, a professor of academic administration elsewhere.

Fine Arts took its own tack and emphasized performance, shutting out
almost entirely things like art history and criticism. The dean displayed a
deep dislike of such subjects, having felt himself and the performance orientation he favored looked down on in his past jobs. When it became clear that
there was pressure from the humanists to begin art history, his response was
half-hearted at best, indeed cold-hearted; the people appointed immediately
saw themselves as outsiders who belonged with the humanists. He had turned
the tables, and he had accomplished some things. The emphasis on performance brought immediate success on stage and some success in the studio arts.
Irvine productions were well done. But in time the humanistic side had to
be addressed, and the founding dean was not equipped emotionally and probably intellectually to do this. His style seemed to have grown from his work
as a director. He centralized authority in himself and personally controlled
the school's budget. Eventually this brought his downfall along with some
apparent irregularity over the appointment without consultation of a student
of his to a teaching position. Later they were married.

I have already implied that in various degrees the schools bore the imprint
of the personalities and views of their founding deans. This was certainly true
of Biological Sciences, which was fortunate in having an intelligent and inventive leader who molded the school in a new way and was unrelenting in his
efforts to obtain funding. Indeed, the vice-chancellor, irritated at his relent-
lessness, once characterized him to me as a crybaby. Personality was even
important by absence in Physical Sciences, which was really never more than
three unrelated departments. In the Humanities the situation was more complex, even though the organization of the school was conventional. At the
outset there were to be departments of history, English, philosophy, and a
single department of foreign languages. This last was eventually to be broken
up into linguistic units. We chairmen went our ways with little interference
or advice; at least I received little. We were of very different personalities and
notions of educational policy. Our recruiting efforts varied in results. The dean
had no particular plan to impose on anyone.

The most interesting, most intelligent, most opinionated and most cantankerous of the chairmen was the philosopher A. I. Melden, who brought from the University of Washington a reputation for being difficult. He recruited with great success a group of young analytical philosophers in the fashionable modern British tradition. The group was intellectually high-powered, their interests *au courant* but narrow. One aesthetician was eventually hired, but he was definitely on the department's margin. No one was interested in or conversant with the continental philosophers, who were regarded as caught in a dead end. At the same time continental philosophy was rapidly becoming important to literary scholars and historians. When I eventually became dean I was approached by a number of people from other departments and asked to bring pressure on Philosophy to hire someone who studied poststructuralists, deconstructionists, etc. After considerable persuasion the department agreed to interview some candidates. They were either found wanting or declared incomprehensible, which meant in this case that they were speaking nonsense. In the end, the department hired a young man who, it turned out, applied analytical techniques to continental texts at their expense. I had been fooled. In time, the department broadened its range and had better connections with literature. After I left Irvine, Jacques Derrida came for a period each year, and his presence could not be ignored, though Philosophy, I am told, did its best, and he functioned principally under the aegis of Comparative Literature.

History was another story. The first chairman, who seemed to me a man of little ability for the job and not much intellectual energy, made at the beginning what proved to be two fundamental mistakes, both of which stemmed from his recruiting. He appointed full professors all over fifty years old and other faculty all under thirty. In the late sixties these acts proved to be a disastrous. When I became dean I was forced to appoint someone from English to chair department meetings just to keep a semblance of order before violence escalated beyond the throwing of chairs. It had already reached that level. One of the young faculty, who visited me with complaints, suddenly crouched behind a desk in my office when he thought he heard the approach of a senior colleague.

The second mistake had to do with the range of scholarly accomplishment and competence in the senior faculty. Among the first four were a historian of the British navy, a historian of the Standard Oil Company of California, a scholar of middle Europe, and the dean himself, who studied British colonial history, mainly his native Australia. This seems to have left the bulk of standard history to the young, who quickly became politicized and Oedipal with regard to those they came to call "the old goats." In time, the department had to be reshaped, and that had to begin when I was dean and be continued by my successor.

At Michigan State I had already noticed that foreign languages when grouped in one department have problems, not entirely different from those encountered by the literature department at San Diego. The problem at Irvine was also that recruiting people to such a department was difficult. At the outset, most of the teaching would have to be of the language itself. Established scholars would not like doing that as part of their schedules, a sort of demotion. It also appears that the teachers of foreign languages take on the coloration of the cultures they teach about (or are ex-patriots from) and bring along certain likes and dislikes. Irvine began by putting together French, German, and Spanish, with dissension the probable consequence. After Classics and Russian were added, the department broke up somewhat earlier than planned. The professor who presided over this was left with Spanish, which was his subject. Even after the break-up, calm did not settle in. French, for example, had but two tenured faculty, two professors of some distinction who were married to each other. They turned out to be sources, or rather *a* source of irritation for the younger faculty, who thought them overbearing — *le deux*, they were called.

Meetings of the four chairmen with the dean were rarely cordial and often tense, particularly if A. I. Melden was in a combative or simply irascible mood. He was frequently at odds with the historian or the Spanish scholar, for both of whom he had unconcealed contempt. Often, I found myself in agreement with Melden, though troubled by his behavior. Sometimes, because he seemed to respect me, I could bring him around to my view prior to a meeting, though it was not easy if my view happened to agree with that of one of the others. I liked Melden, who was a good host and amusing when he discussed the other chairmen with comic disdain, one of his favorite words being "steeeewpid," well drawn-out.

I am sure that the dean found these meetings stressful and difficult to control. He was a genuinely good and genial person. He had not come to his position with any particular educational philosophy to put forward that might have enabled him to provide more firm if more controversial leadership, and I do not recall his uttering judgments about people I sent to him to be interviewed. His reputation at his previous institution, where he had inherited difficulties, was as a successful mediator, but the mix he allowed to be created at Irvine got the best of him at times.

The situation I came into as successor dean was one of vague disorder, perhaps in part a projection of my predecessor's own style, but he had managed to avoid problems that surfaced in the other schools. Humanities had not suffered under either a dictatorial, single-minded leader with an unworkable plan or a martinet. He had not shut out on principle one aspect of the school's potential range. Some things had been avoided and some opportunities missed. Change was expected from me.

Even before classes had begun the first vice-chancellor Ivan Hinderaker was appointed chancellor at Riverside, and Jack Peltason, the dean of Arts and Sciences, advanced to his position. The overall deanship he held was vacated, never to be filled, for at that point the subdeans of the schools saw an opportunity to increase their power in their fiefdoms and persuaded the chancellor to abolish the position. I was at the time, and still am, ambivalent about that decision, though it became an advantage for me in my work. On the one hand, a bureaucratic level in a still small organization was eliminated and freer rein was given to the deans and departments; the Irvine style of leadership had encouraged this, in any case. On the other hand, there was little oversight, no enunciation of policy, and much competition for funds that would have to be mediated by the vice-chancellor, who had enough already to do. In 1972, I assumed that position and found all this out at first hand.

## 2.

Irvine provided my first real experience of university administrators beyond what I had discovered at Texas. I had never met the dean at Cornell, and can't remember his name (if I ever actually knew it). I never saw the president. My one meeting with President Hannah at Michigan State I have previously mentioned. I knew the dean there, but not at all well. At Irvine it would be different. The chancellor, Daniel Aldrich, had been a soil scientist in the agricultural program at Riverside. He was a tall, vigorous man, a weights competitor in the Senior Olympics. In manner he was forceful and sometimes aggressive, a little distant with a touch of self-consciousness. I later learned that some of this was but appearance and that he was actually ill at ease with academics and perhaps others. His academic background had been closely involved with the land-grant college concept, which had connected agricultural colleges to regional farmers through agricultural agents. It was his idea to apply that land-grant spirit to an urban and suburban situation. The city of Irvine, which was to stretch north from the campus, seemed to him a good place to do this. It was to be the product of planning by the Irvine Company, originally in ranching and agriculture. Orange County was a rapidly growing area.

But Aldrich's idea did not seem to go beyond a vague notion, and he took no steps that I could see to bring it about. UCI's direction was developed by the leaders in the original faculty. I can think of nothing he did to further an academic plan as such except to give a relatively free rein to the founding deans. In my case, the responsibility in my field came without interference, for my dean acted much in the same way. The result of all this was that some deans managed to create strong programs or at least programs shaped to a particular purpose. Where the deans were not aggressive the chairmen took over and went their ways. The odd result was that UCI developed strong programs rather far from Aldrich's land-grant interests and far from his own scholarly competence. English and Philosophy were examples in the Humanities.

In time, this situation changed a little with the development of a program called Social Ecology, which provided, among other things, a refuge for some people from the narrowly conceived School of Social Science. In Social Ecology, courses addressing urban needs were taught. After a rough beginning, partly because of a decline in student interest in many places, Engineering came into prominence, and a medical school was developed. These things were brought about less by Aldrich than by external forces, although clearly he supported their development and his style allowed innovation.

I sometimes thought of Aldrich on occasion as a grown-up farm boy. There was an air of naiveté about him and little arrogance. He came on as aggressive, and he was very competitive, but he did not impose his will in intellectual matters. He tried to give support when it was needed. I learned only after I became vice-chancellor in 1972 that he could not bring himself to fire anyone, and I was obliged to do some overdue dirty work, if only to gain the faculty's respect. Aldrich was, on the whole, an optimist and wanted to give people the opportunity to succeed even as they were messing up. I recall that once when we were considering an appointment to a committee I said to him after a name had been suggested, "Well, you don't want to underestimate his incompetence." Aldrich for a moment thought I had said "competence" and nodded enthusiastically, then realized what I had actually said and broke into a large guffaw.

Both Ivan Hinderaker, the first vice-chancellor, and Jack Peltason, who soon left to be chancellor at Illinois, were political scientists. I believe they both, especially Peltason, correctly saw their positions as political. By this I mean that the model of administration they followed was that of politics rather than business. Peltason, a genial and intelligent man, was a mediating administrator and was successful at it, being chancellor at Illinois in a difficult period, proceeding to administer the American Council on Education, and returning to Irvine as chancellor when Aldrich retired. Later he was advanced to the presidency of the university. His was a distinguished career. I do not believe it was marked by an educational idea governing or standing silently behind his acts. Indeed, I do not think that he believed one should invoke and press such an idea. The aim was for things to proceed smoothly, for occasional squabbles to be settled diplomatically, and for educational ideas to rise out of the faculty. In the first year, I was assigned or volunteered (I do not remember which) to edit and write a good proportion of the first UCI catalogue. I recall Peltason remarking that he disliked vague high-sounding statements about education in university catalogues. I agreed, and the catalogue had no inspirational messages.

The campus went along rather smoothly with this leadership, its intellectual course not deliberately charted. Certainly, it was what the deans wanted, and it reflected what I think Peltason believed was best. Later, when I was at the University of Washington, another political scientist was president, with a similar attitude. The only difference was that he stated it explicitly, perhaps proving that such views (or lack of the same) contributed at least to the power of survival, for he held his position longer than any other Washington president, and the administration building was named for him when he retired.

It is very difficult for any administrator to press for a specific educational objective. There are stumbling blocks everywhere. Micromanaging is almost always a disaster, and stubborn single-mindedness when made apparent results in resistance and opposition. People can disagree rationally on educational policy. Middle-range administrators, of whom there are usually too many, protect their turf. Academics are mostly conservative on these matters, and many resist the unfamiliar out of vague fear combined with self-interest, often shortsighted. It is certainly more self-protective for an administrator to let educational ideas simmer up and to mediate differences. Because this is the way it is likely to be, it is extremely important that recruitment of faculty be done with care, competent people being superior to all the curricular ideas ever invented. However, it is also true that little attention in recruiting is given to whether at least some candidates would be capable of, for example, chairing a committee or serving as a department administrator, in situations where curricular decisions are actually made.

Still, I think some middle ground might be reached between a hands-on style and the role of broker of competing self-interests. Both Irvine and Washington seemed to suffer from lack of the former, but they may have gained from it, too.

# 3.

It may seem today that the carrot of sunny southern California would have been enough to attract prospective faculty to the new Irvine campus. But today is not 1964. At that time a number of things conspired against easy recruiting. Young faculty were profiting from the expansion of higher education everywhere. I doubt that I attempted to recruit any recent Ph.D. who did not have five or six institutions interested in making an offer. In the East I ran up against a certain prejudice against or ignorance of the West, amply depicted by the *New Yorker*'s well-known cartoon of the United States as understood by a New Yorker. Southern California was Hollywood superficiality and glitz. In some ways the reality was more distressing. In that first year, I spent much of my time searching for people I would want and were willing to come to a campus-to-be in politically and socially darkest Orange County. On the coast, at least, insulated from the ghettos inland, middle-of-the-road Republicans were thought to be dangerous leftists, the Rolls-Royce agency was one of the largest in the world, the PTA was considered part of a communist plot and was banned from the schools, and the owner and editor of the county's largest newspaper opposed public roads and fire departments, believing that they should be capitalistic enterprises. An early member of the UCI public relations staff told me he moved from that newspaper shortly after the editor came up silently behind him and whispered, "Save your money, young man." Older people displayed "Support Your Local Police" signs on their bumpers, and students took to displaying them in the hope that they wouldn't be stopped and harassed. The United States congressional representative for the area stood to the right of the John Birch Society, then in its heyday. Eventually he was disgraced in several ways at once, but much later his married daughter, teaching near Seattle, went him somewhat better by bedding her twelve-year-old student, with whom she had two children, and serving time for child rape. The nearby city of Newport Beach was flashy, vulgar and nouveau riche. Huge yachts that seldom left their moorages abounded.

On our arrival stock brokers and investment firms began to call us, ignorant of the meager financial powers of a college professor. No one knew that we all had spent our last cash on real estate we were sure we couldn't afford. On the other hand, many thought us dangerous commie leftists, and even the Irvine Company suffered a failure of nerve over the student activities of the late sixties.

For many of the prospective faculty, a new campus threatened peace of mind. Academics were as generally cautious then as they are today and conservative about everything except politics. No doubt many recoiled at having to help start a new campus from scratch. In truth, it was to be a big job. The University of California was and is a huge bureaucratic organization with the budget and population as big as that of some states. A small, new faculty would have to establish all the committees that a large campus had, complete with faculty representatives to their university-wide counterparts. There was a curriculum to create and its rules and regulations. Buildings were under construction, and campus planning continued. Departmental by-laws had to be created. There were students entering at every level, so classes appropriate to each had to be offered. Senior faculty would have to take on lower-division classes, at least for a while.

In the academic year 1964–1965 I traveled the country and recruited twelve faculty members of all ranks, some lecturers, and a few graduate students. I had learned that by a loosely applied formula each graduate student generated for the budget two and one half as many dollars as did an undergraduate. This struck me as ridiculous (at least in the humanities and social sciences), but I tried to turn it to advantage by starting graduate programs at once and recruiting students. This reminds me a little now of Lakeside's football recruitment in the thirties. Alas, the academic abilities of UCI's initial group of graduate students did not nearly match the athletic abilities of Lakeside's recruits, but we struggled along toward respectability. Fifteen years later, when I moved to the University of Washington, I found the UCI graduate students superior on the whole, perhaps because of the quality of the faculty, by then grown to some thirty.

What kind of a program ought students to enter in 1965? English study was different then. Despite the advances of the so-called New Criticism in the fifties, English study was almost entirely compartmentalized into periods and historically-oriented genre courses. The study of American literature, fighting its way into the curriculum, had done so with supporters thinking that in order to gain status it had to be even more conservative than the study of English literature. Study of literary criticism as a subject in itself was rather shapeless except for the traditional course on the history of the subject. Study of the history of the English language was tied loosely to that of old and medieval English.

In my initial interview for the Irvine job, which was conducted by a professor from Riverside and the vice-chancellor, Ivan Hinderaker, I proposed a department with three principal concerns: literary criticism (the term theory was only beginning to be used), creative writing, and comparative literary study. The last of these I proposed as an interdepartmental committee and offered to recruit a director. I proposed an undergraduate emphasis that a student could choose in creative writing and the first Master of Fine Arts in creative writing in the University of California. The literature curriculum was to grow out of a program of courses in the history of thinking about literature and seminars on various critical practices.

Comparative literature seemed to me in most places to be rather narrow. This is well expressed in a dream recounted to me about the wife of a Harvard graduate student about to take his general examinations. In the dream she answers the door to discover Professor Harry Levin, the head of Comparative Literature, and a colleague, both dressed in overalls and carrying tool boxes. Levin says, "We're here to compare the literature."

In the tradition of dissertations, comparative literature usually meant comparing a work in one language to one in another. As far as I was concerned any study that got across boundaries would do, including the relation of literature to other arts. Further, a program in comparative literature would provide an important connection to English. The Bible and Homer are not

English texts, yet they are indispensable for any student of Western literature. English departments teach the history of criticism, but most important critical thought before, say, 1680 and arguably after is not written in English. Comparative literature came to present an early problem at UCI, but not, I think, because of the views just uttered.

My experience at Cornell with *Epoch* and the writers attached to it influenced me heavily. Grown out of writers' interests, The New Criticism had been to a considerable extent a form of criticism different from the old literary history or the impressionist criticism emphasizing the response of the sophisticated reader. I hoped to bring close together the program in creative writing and one in criticism. This required the recruitment of a significant number of people without hostility or even indifference to such cooperation. That was easier said than done: I had some success, though in the passage of time it was fleeting. Still, it was worth doing, and the attitude of cooperation, perhaps mutual respect, or at least not hostility lasted for some time.

With this program in mind, I set out across the country to recruit faculty. My first appointment was James B. Hall, who was heading a successful creative writing program at Oregon. I had known Hall at Cornell. Although he had published poetry and three novels, his main reputation was as a short-story writer. His most successful work, published in a series of collections beginning with *15x3* (New Directions), are what he came in his last collection to call "Extreme Stories." They contain offbeat, weird characters and situations, like those in one of my favorites "The Freezer Bandit," which appeared in *Us He Devours* and again in *The Extreme Stories + 3*. Hall had a wild imagination belied by his occasionally Ohio farm-boy manner. Often, though, in conversation a vein of irony came through that was frequently lost on, sometimes at the expense of, the person he was talking to. You always had to listen to Hall very carefully to get it all. This made some people uneasy and even suspicious, uncertain of the veracity of what he had said. His letters, which I have kept, are full of sudden wit and fictive invention. As one has to do with any good writer, one must learn to read him.

Hall had earned a Ph.D. from Iowa, where he had been in the writing workshop and had studied literary criticism. Under his direction the MFA program at Irvine was begun at once. He had a picture of what such a program should be, based on his experiences at Iowa and Oregon. Many years later now, UCI's is one of the top programs in the country. In a fairly short time, however, he moved to be provost of a college oriented to the fine arts at UC Santa Cruz.

Hall acquainted me with the work of Donald Heiney, who directed Comparative Literature at Utah, and would be appointed to do the same at Irvine. He had published a book on modern Italian literature and its response to America, and he had also published two novels under the pseudonym of

MacDonald Harris. The first of these, *Private Demons,* deeply embarrassed him, and he was extremely reluctant even to let me see a copy of it, let alone present it along with my recommendation for his appointment. His second novel *Mortal Leap*, a far greater success, brought into play his experience in the U.S. Merchant Marine and strongly influenced me to appoint him, for among other things he could be a bridge between comparative literature and creative writing. Heiney went on to a distinguished career as a novelist, but his experience as director of the Comparative Literature Program was immensely frustrating from the beginning. The Department of Foreign Languages had other urgent priorities and hired no comparatists, but rather simply assigned some willing or perhaps unwilling souls from French, German, and Spanish to represent it. The meetings of this group turned out to display the worst characteristics of the United Nations. Heiney would report them to me in a state of severe agitation bordering on despair, punctuated by repeated offers or perhaps pleadings to resign. One day the dean came to my office to say that both he and Heiney had suffered enough and comparative literature was now to be part of my department. This reorganization persisted until 2004. By that time, I am told, the comparative literature people had bonded with each other, having found a suitable common enemy, their colleagues the English professors. As I understand it, they were free, after thirty-nine years, from the English yoke and could proceed to act with hostility once again toward one another. Heiney, himself, was a witty and intelligent man, neither aggressive nor unpleasant. He did, however, suffer from time to time from a feeling that he was being looked down on. This required some management at times. But his quirkiness, if that is what it was, attracted some devoted students, though his relations with them were usually, as far as I could tell, of a love-hate sort.

One of the most interesting lectures I heard at Irvine was Heiney's in a series we organized to present members of the department to the community. He gave a witty talk on why authors employed pseudonyms. Most of the audience was unaware that he employed one and was discussing himself. When he felt like it, he was a raconteur, but he detested large social gatherings and was uneasy in them unless he was able to hide himself center-stage by playing a role and launching a narrative of his own. It was usually entertaining and based on fact, as compared to Hall's, which one suspected were sometimes fictive or at the least artistically embellished. Heiney was, I think, mainly an autodidact, and like some others I have known he tended to lecture one on subjects one knew more about than he did.

Both Hall and Heiney were unusual people, unusually talented. Some might say that they were eccentric. Their writings are. I must confess that I have a liking for the eccentrics of what many think is an eccentric profession. I suspect that this may be genetic and I was helpless not to indulge it in recruiting faculty in 1964. I may have inherited it from my father, who as a prep school headmaster collected or in some cases inherited such people. Or perhaps it came from acclimatization at Hawken and Lakeside. If I were to do it all over again, I would not change. Some of my best appointments fit this profile, and my worst were those, usually urged by others, who were combinations of aggressiveness, ambition, and anxiety. Some of those latter turned out to be academically very successful, though they were, as we say today, "pieces of work."

I offer as further examples of the eccentric or, as Jim Hall might have said, extreme ones the following. First, Howard Babb. He was a big, rugged man whom Hall called the conscience of our department. He was the scourge of any meeting he attended, whether it was of the academic senate, the school, or the department. In the early years at least, he responded physically to any show of mendacity or sheer stupidity by loosening his tie, rising from his chair, and, with progressively reddening face, prowling the meeting room while others froze in silence. In those moments he seemed threatening to vent a Vesuvian rage. People outside the department were often shocked and intimidated by these performances, but inside it he was respected with affection. In a booming voice he would seek to put everyone straight, even as he knew sadly that with some of those present this would be an impossible task. However, there was absolutely nothing arrogant about him. He was, in fact, a man of humility. His conscience required that he make such attempts. Babb was rigorous in his attitude toward students, who found him a bit frightening before coming to respect his intellectual integrity and his sense of responsibility toward them.

In his office, Babb often peeled down to a T-shirt, letting off steam over the phone or in the act of writing, which for him was like a wrestling match. In this state he revealed a nautical tattoo on his arm, product of his Navy service in World War II. Asked what it was like to be tattooed (in the days before tattoos became trendy and common), he replied that there was nothing to it. You wake up and you're tattooed. Though he was a Harvard graduate, he was at Cornell in the Navy V-12 program during part of the war and played tackle on the football team. That year Cornell had the misfortune of playing against the great Army team of Blanchard and Davis. Asked what it was like to play against them, he said, "Hell, I don't know. I was flat on my ass the whole game!" I based a character in my novel *Home* in part upon him. The most admirable side of him, it being an academic novel, I had to play down. Babb succeeded me in 1969 as chairman and a few years later died of a heart attack in the surf at Corona Del Mar. The department was not the same after his death.

My second exhibit is John F. Adams (no relation). A medievalist, he was short and slight, with a blank face misinterpreted by coeds as expressing innocence. As a result they flocked to him in full devotion. This was the result of a demeanor non-threatening, considerable wit, and patience that on occasion flowed over into stubbornness. He was a naturalist who could wait quietly to let a small hawk land on his wrist and subsequently to domesticate it. However, as the spaces of Irvine grew more congested, he became restive and moved to eastern Washington and Washington State University. For him much that was medieval was funny, sexy, and scatological. I recall a public lecture he gave in which his ultimate argument was that in the lyric "Sumer is icumen in" the phrase "bucke verteth" should not be interpreted to mean that the buck snorts but that he farts. He backed his reading with a short discourse on the behavior of bucks in the forest during mating season.

Adams could at times make a radical suggestion as to how to proceed in a serious academic situation. In a meeting about a graduate student who was not very good and proved a trial to her teachers, we dithered unhappily and tried to rationalize what we were about to do. After this had gone on for a while, Adams proposed that we not choose the nastiness of termination, but that we consider acceleration toward the degree.

Adams was a country westerner. I had to intervene with the doggedly unpleasant campus police chief because of a license-plate mix-up involving Adams. Search of his car had produced a rare and valuable six-shooter, and the chief regarded it as a concealed weapon since it had been in the glove compartment. This was not my only intervention with the law over the behavior of faculty members during my administrative career, but it was the most vexing. After the matter had been resolved, the police would not return the weapon, and this produced high dudgeon in what had always seemed to be a mild-mannered man. I was barely successful in preventing Adams from storming the police department with I know not what artillery he still had at home. No doubt this event, unthinkable in eastern Washington, hastened Adams's removal to that state.

On the whole, in the first few years the department and its eccentrics got along pretty well, without internal squabbling. It was gratifying a few years later to hear Jim Hall's successor, the novelist Oakley Hall (no relation), say to me that he had never known a bunch of people he liked better.

## 4.

Not every academic generation makes significant changes in the way people teach or the structure of curriculum. In the modern history of my subject, literary criticism and theory, new ideas generated by a few lively minds come on the scene, are spread about, assimilated into college courses, and in time spawn a method. By the time the last occurs, a certain dullness sets in, usually first detected by students in their boredom or unrest. The method has by this time been adopted by the less imaginative faculty members trained in it. The changes that occur with new, or apparently new ideas (sometimes they are like re-inventions of the wheel), tend to bring new life for a while to literary study.

I was a student during the transition from the dominance of the old literary history on the one hand and critical impressionism on the other to the New Criticism. It arose in part as an intellectual accommodation of literary modernism. Creative writing was just getting a foothold, partly because the New Criticism was friendly to contemporary writing, was founded mainly by writer-critics, and was more writerly in approach than the practice of literary history, bibliography, or textual editing. As for critical impressionism, its pretension was to be a form of creative writing. For the most part, my teachers had not been New Critics, but some were not unfriendly to its approach.

By 1964, the New Criticism, with its close attention to the words and formal aspects of a text, had gained dominance across the country and done its best work. By virtue of theoretical inquiry that developed with it, there was a renewed interest in the history of criticism. In 1959, two major players in the politics of the New Criticism, W. K. Wimsatt and Cleanth Brooks, published their *Literary Criticism: A Short History*, which surveyed the subject from Plato to the contemporary critics whom they associated with "myth and archetype." This movement threatened the dominance of the New Critics. Wimsatt came to detest what grew out of it, but Brooks, who was partial to Yeats and his "mythical" book *A Vision*, was less hostile. The acknowledged leader of this change was Northrop Frye, and the dominating literary figure for several younger critics like myself was William Blake. The romantic poets, generally looked down on since T. S. Eliot's critical writings became influential, gained prominence, with Blake now a major if not *the* major poet of the period. Wimsatt, after criticizing Frye, released his invective on the new generation, apparently including me: "A generation of critics today, especially in America — the younger evangelists of Blake and of Yeats — is not likely to suffer from absentmindedness regarding the lovely colors of combustion, the fiery permanent discontent which may be generated by contemplating the gospel of contraries."

Sympathetic to the New Critics' close attention to words, but not to their generally reactionary politics, I sought a broader view of literature that had seemed to be potential in the writings of Giambattista Vico, Ernst Cassirer, Susanne K. Langer, Frye, and others. However, I had no interest in a cabal. In recruiting, I looked for a faculty with eclectic interests who would work in a curriculum accommodating different views. This could happen only through people, not a preconceived structure of courses. The curriculum, as the catalogue described it, would have to be flexible enough to embrace or at least accept change and a range of subjects. So, rather than designate courses in the usual way, for example, in fixed historical periods, I planned to have only broadly conceived rubrics that could include period study: studies in criticism, studies in literary history, literature and society, literature and psychology, and so forth. Under each of these titles could be offered whatever seemed at the time a valuable course. Literary history didn't have to be divided up artificially into centuries or half-centuries. A variety of critical approaches could be offered; connections to other disciplines would be possible. All this could be accomplished without submitting more than a skeletal program to the campus bureaucracy, where every course would have to be approved by the committee on educational policy. Establishing a new course would amount only to offering a section under one of the general titles above. As far as I know, the committee on educational policy has even today not caught on to this ruse. I am less sanguine about the results now than I was then. Out of control, it can be used as an excuse to avoid offering courses that students need the opportunity to take and to create courses whose only value could be the professor's personal interest in them, often political in one sense or another. An offshoot could be the use of the classroom overtly to further political or other views. I conclude this chapter with a brief account of an unfortunate example of the latter at Irvine. It has been a fairly common result, I am afraid, in some places where the approach was later adopted, but I still hold that on the whole the innovation was a good idea and politicization the result of forces other than curricular change. One advantage worth mentioning was that it tended to discourage establishment of courses "owned" by some professors and to encourage faculty to keep rethinking what they were doing. Today many people would argue that there is too much encouragement of this sort, and I suspect they are right.

The emphasis on "criticism" gradually changed everywhere to one on "theory." This was not just a semantic change. In those days it could be said that criticism included philosophical or theoretical speculation on the nature of literature. Today theory is rarely thought of as "literary theory," includes criticism, and is generated out of an ideological or political position. The department at Irvine began with an emphasis on criticism in the former sense, but at a time when the latter was just beginning to have its effect in America. The emphasis on criticism was deliberately intensified by the appointment to the faculty of Murray Krieger, who had written the first discussion of the New Criticism in *The New Apologists for Poetry* and had at Iowa and earlier Illinois, as I had at Michigan State, pushed for a stronger role of criticism and literary theory in the curriculum. He brought a reputation as a strong teacher and a competence in the whole range of literary theory probably unparalleled in our generation of scholars. He brought a high degree of intellectual intensity. The program eventually attracted graduate students nationwide, as did the Master of Fine Arts program in creative writing, deliberately kept small.

The nature of the department, however, was subtly and gradually changed after Krieger's appointment. He was a strong, aggressive professional, but his work did not cross the boundaries of the three programs as did that of some others. He wanted anxiously to be important and for his department to be important, to be known by important people in the profession, to know everyone and about everyone. He liked professorial hierarchy, though he would not admit it. He wanted academic stars at Irvine and paid little attention to the matters with which I have been concerned in this chapter. At the same time, he opposed nothing that I was doing, indeed always supported me. We were friends and had much in common intellectually, though not much in personality. I must admit to having been swayed to propose some appointments on his advice, putting aside my trepidations. These people were stars or potential stars. However, they were miserable colleagues and egos that required management. Luckily, in most cases their stardom generated offers elsewhere, and in time they left. As in most professions academic stars are often egocentric, rather paranoid, often chronically discontented, unpleasant to their colleagues, narrow in their interests, and with little concern for the fate of their institutions. Departments with a fair number of them often blow apart.

It turned out that over time creative writing grew to be somewhat isolated, its faculty limiting itself mainly to teaching writing workshops. As I have already recounted, after thirty-nine years Comparative Literature broke away to form its own department. The combination of English and Comparative Literature had been, in the politics of the campus, fortunate for the department, which, already strong, was now even more formidable; but it was unfortunate for literary and humanistic study generally, for it alienated the department from the other language units and earned the undying enmity of the chairman of foreign languages, who seemed to blame me for what had happened, though I was not in the least responsible. There was, however, little harm from this, for he did not like me anyway. Thus ended my first effort at what we call interdisciplinary study. It is a word I have come to dislike and would be just as happy to see disappear from among the current academic buzzwords. It is raised up today in support of much that is usually shallow sociobabble. You can hardly find an administration anywhere that does not mouth it at every opportunity.

# 5.

In the academic year 1968–1969, as it did in many places, trouble set in at UCI. It was nothing compared to what had been and was going on at

Berkeley or Santa Barbara, to say nothing of Kent State and elsewhere. Indeed, it had something of the quality of absurd comedy or even farce, but it was no fun for the faculty, with the exception of a few true enthusiasts who seemed for a while to convince themselves that they could make monumental changes in the life of the campus parallel to the great changes they imagined coming to the university as a whole, to the nation, and even to the firmament. They were too naïve and inexperienced to know the university as a great leviathan of bureaucracy with a life of its own almost impervious to change imposed from within or without. Even Ronald Reagan as governor experienced this inertia, though I doubt that he understood it.

In four years' time, an event occurred at UCI similar to what goes on every year at universities across the country, but it was the first time that it had happened at UCI. Some young faculty were promoted to the associate professorship and some were not reappointed. In the School of Humanities one person in history and two in English were let go. One of these had failed to complete his doctoral dissertation in the time required and had no grounds for complaint. The work of the person in history was judged inadequate for reasons unknown to me at the time. Probably neither of these cases alone would have brought about any significant student response. However, the third was a popular teacher in English who had developed a following. His subject was, more or less, literature and psychology in the twentieth century. Before his appointment at Irvine he had published two or three articles in the field, an unusual accomplishment at the time for a graduate student.

Some faculty members, perhaps many, found him abrasive and were suspicious of his teaching, which seemed to them, by the usual hearsay, skewed toward proselytizing, disdainful of the views of others, and less attentive to literature than to other matters. He seemed to appeal to students, who were impressed (his critics would say taken in) by his iconoclasm. A few of these students I knew, and some I respected. He had recently been invited to a major university to speak and be interviewed for a position, but nothing had come of it, in spite of his colleagues' devout wishes. The tenured faculty had for review his book-in-progress, which had almost nothing to do directly with literature and much to do with the views of a currently popular psychoanalyst. It proved to most of them that his interest was no longer literary and that his writing and powers of argument had declined since the time of his earlier publications. Some people, I think, regarded him as a real threat to fitness and order, others the sort of nuisance better done without. With both groups the idea of spending a career with him was distasteful. After much discussion behind closed doors, some of it expressing distress and anger, I could see that the vote would go substantially against him. I warned the department at that meeting that his popularity with at least one group of the students would cause unpleasant repercussions and we should be prepared for them. I felt that another year should pass before we made a decision on tenure and promotion. In my mind was the hope that he might be influenced to improve his relations with his colleagues and perhaps get some help in reshaping his manuscript. Those who deeply disliked him — and there were many — wanted action now and were frank enough to say that perhaps in another year he would have published enough that we wouldn't be able to get rid of him. They claimed that they had seen quantity triumph over quality too many times in the past. I was surprised to find the vote against him unanimous, and I came to realize that many of the other untenured faculty were at best ambivalent about him even if I discounted the normal anxiety at seeing a colleague denied tenure.

My conveyance to him of this information was not one of my successes. It said something to me that he was surprised and even dumbfounded at the department's decision. He had held me in high regard and asked me how I would have voted. For me to have said that I would have supported him would have set me against the unanimous vote of the department I had created, some members of which had implied that they could no longer tolerate his presence and might leave. I did not trust him not to make public any answer I might give and use it against the department with the students. I told him that I agreed with the department's judgment of his book in progress and that I would have voted with my colleagues. It was a painful moment for both of us, but his absolute surprise at the decision affirmed a general belief in his insensitivity. He had, I later learned from a student, bragged that he, with me, would revolutionize literary study at UCI (presumably according to his views), and now this fantasy had blown up in his face. It was another sign of a display of what had turned out to be an enormous ego that outstripped even his own sense of self-interest. To my suggestion that to protect himself he resign rather than be dismissed, he responded bitterly that I should fire him. I tried to explain to him the folly of this, but he would have none of it, thinking that I was trying only to protect the department. He declared that he had no respect for anyone associated with it. I responded that it was all the more reason to resign. I told him I would support him in a search for another position. But he now saw himself as a heroic martyr to reactionary power and would fight to have the decision overturned.

For a while after this event I thought I could have handled it differently. I might have told him of my regret that things had come to this, of my desire to stave off the decision. Or I might have declined to answer, saying that whatever I thought was now irrelevant. There was no way in the UC bureaucracy as things stood to turn around the department's decision. (Today formal appeal processes exist, usually on grounds of sexual or racial discrimination, but not then.) I could not seriously quarrel with the decision on the merits. I think it was naïve of me to hope that he might profit from a delay in the decision and reconsideration, but it turned out that I was right to have said no more to him than I had.

Some months after all of the hullabaloo died down, one of my untenured colleagues presented me with the first "book" of a Miltonic epic poem that, alas, never saw a second. It began gloriously as follows:

> Of startling gloom, of Pandemonium
> Built new upon the sultry Orange coast,
> Of dread Sheerego's terrible intrigue
> And howling fall, I dare, O Muse, to sing.
> He had been Angel call'd, with forehead broad
> And wisdom like a cloud around his head.
> The woolly sheep from Irvine's dusty hills
> Observ'd the cloud, forgot their grass, and throng'd,
> Wond'ring to hear Sheerego's horrid words:
> "O, nibblers on these tasteless hills. Blind mouths
> That scarce yourselves know how you're forc'd to feed!
> High Alreek hath devis'd deception foul
> To coax you out of thought. Behold, I come,
> A gleaming sword thrusts from my dreadful mouth
> To pierce the gloom [etc.]"

He made his dismissal known to students, and there followed a protest movement that was UCI's contribution to the student unrest of those days. The students seized on all three dismissals and declared them unfair. Certain faculty on the campus vaguely sympathized with those who were to lose their jobs. Others had been latent protesters against institutional and governmental power, and they were drawn in. A few were or promptly discovered that they were leftist radicals. Quickly, it seemed, a few people descended on Irvine to agitate, cause trouble, and do their parts preparing the coming revolution, to which this was to be but a preface. At about that time, I received my first death threat.

In truth, there was a bitter comedy, even farce, about the whole thing, the events paling by comparison to movements elsewhere. Things began with the occupation of a large room known as the Writing Center, directly across the hall from my office. It was used principally for readings, meetings, and occasionally classes. It contained a poetry library, a record collection and, a hi-fi player. A premonition led me to disarm the player, and that prevented even more din than the coming and going of students provided. I gained some satisfaction that they would be frustrated without the apparently necessary music at all times. The occupation, which went on for several days and had the quality of a carnival or what was then called a "happening," was peaceful. The self-appointed leaders held that there should be no damage done to what would be theirs when they took over the university. Mass meetings took place outside, with rousing speeches full of accusations and statements of contempt for anyone perceived to be in authority. Songs were composed and offered to ridicule and generally irritate the faculty. Political theater of a basely amateurish nature took place. Everything was blended conceptually together: the war in Vietnam, inertia at all levels of the university system, martyrdom of the three assistant professors, and irrelevance in general. Free speech, seen mainly as the release into the atmosphere of as much obscenity as possible, was extolled.

The administration had remained aloof, Chancellor Aldrich stating that he would not intervene unless I was to declare that classes and the academic process were being disturbed. His view was to let it go on until the students tired of it all. I, too, felt that acting too soon would be a mistake. The sit-in became a lie-in, with sleeping bags spread about, take-out food consumed, and olfactory conditions rapidly worsening. The chancellor's inaction led some in the department to believe that he might overrule their judgment. Others found their nerves frayed, and wanted me to intervene. I asked the chancellor to meet with us. Our aim was to express how seriously we took the matter, and I spoke at some length about the department, its value to the campus, and the unanimity of our decision. I strongly implied that the department would break up if he chose to override it. I pointed out that in the past departments made decisions about dismissals and they were not countermanded from above. The chancellor did not respond on this matter. On principle I had no complaint about a higher review taking place, but I felt that review in this case would be a slap at the department because it had never happened before and had never been part of the promotion process.

At a special meeting of the Academic Senate, which at that time was composed of the entire faculty, there was a motion offered to force a retroactive policy of Senate review of all personnel decisions. Much heated discussion ensued, and I spoke once more about the impropriety of imposing a new rule retroactively on a department that had deliberated seriously and responsibly in reaching its decision. We were near mêlée. The chairman, a physicist, lost control of the meeting, and students were allowed to speak. Murray Krieger, speaking from the floor, publicly resigned from the Senate (and never again attended a meeting) on the grounds that the Senate was overreaching its authority in its attempt to dictate to the department.

After adjournment, the chairman of the Senate came to my office to convince me that I should calm my department. I responded to him that he had the problem of calming the Senate, had failed miserably, and that if he couldn't manage a meeting he had no function and should resign. To my surprise he did so the next day. Although the chancellor attended the meeting, he did not speak, and we still did not know what he might do.

The students remained in the Writing Center, and I determined that it was time to bring the sit-in to an end. I entered the Writing Center the next day and had a polite, lengthy conversation with the students there. I outlined university and departmental policy and practice, and I answered questions. At the end, I declared that this all had gone on long enough, that I intended to hold my class in the Writing Center the next morning. If the place wasn't vacated I would inform the chancellor that my class had been disrupted. What he would do was not clear to me, but the students took my decision to mean that the police would be called in. Those who were red hot with anger urged resistance. For them the issue seemed to be larger than the fate of three assistant professors. However, my threat worked. Many of the students returned that evening to clean up the place. Thus ended the KBS movement, named after the initials of the three unfortunates. Cries of anger were uttered in the student newspaper, but for the most part the movement died quickly, and by autumn it was as if it had never happened.

There was an epilogue. On the next morning, when I held my class in the Writing Center, a middle-aged woman student known to some of the faculty for her oddity and, it was later learned, mentally ill, entered at the back of the room carrying a large bag. She took a seat, her hand in the bag by her side. I asked her to leave, and she refused, saying that she was protesting. I dismissed the class abruptly, asking everyone to leave at once. There was immediate compliance. Indeed, I have never seen a room emptied so quickly. She and I sat staring at each other, she with her hand still in the bag. I asked her what her complaint was, assuming it had to do with the recent events. She denied this but could not say what was bothering her. I told her that she had disrupted a class and if she did not leave the building I would call the campus police. She did not move. I stood up, moved toward the door, crossed the hall, and told my secretary to put in the call. Very soon two large officers appeared, entered the Writing Center, talked quietly with the woman for a while, and escorted her from the building. There had been only books in her bag. It turned out that that her protest had been about her grade on a paper she had submitted to John Adams. Even his patience had been exhausted by it, and he had given the paper a failing grade on the ground of its incoherence.

I called her husband that day, explained what had happened, and suggested that she badly needed help. He readily agreed and confessed that he had not been able to bring himself to commit her to an institution. I asked him if he would like me to attempt to arrange it through the campus physician. He was profuse in his thanks, and that was what I did. None of this, it turned out, had anything to do with the KBS movement.

Of the three assistant professors the two in English were indeed let go, but the chancellor went against the Department of History and retained the third person. Of the three he was almost certainly the worst teacher, a man, it turned out later, who had many disabling personal problems, probably including alcohol and drugs. History was already regarded as a problem department, and its weak chairman did little to convince the chancellor that he should support it. Thus a bone was thrown to the students and an oblique reprimand to the department. This may have gratified its younger faculty, but I doubt that it was understood by the senior members. The chancellor's decision was not only a mistake in judgment but also a politically inappropriate intervention. I do not know that anyone ever publicly offered this opinion. The assistant professor in question eventually became an embarrassment all around.

Several months later I had a call from a faculty member, whom I knew slightly, at the University of Nevada. He inquired about the man who had been the center of the whole matter. He clearly wanted to appoint him there. News of the events at UCI had traveled to Nevada, and people were jittery. I told this person that the man was bright, that he should have another chance, and that the events at UCI were over and done with. The Nevada department went ahead and proposed his appointment, but it went all the way to their Board of Regents, who rejected it on the grounds that he was a dangerous radical. Later I learned that during this period his wife had caught him in bed with an undergraduate and was divorcing him. When the academic year ended, I was told, he set out eastward with another female undergraduate who, regaining her wits, cut and ran before the journey ended. He became, in a new career, of all things, a marriage counselor in the East and as far as I know never held another permanent academic job. One day, many years later, I was surprised to see him as part of a panel on a national TV talk show. He was a psychologist talking about how all people had to take on responsibility for themselves and what they do.

> ...The bold Sheerego smil'd
> As praises swarm'd upon his trembling ears.
> The woolly tribe now huddl'd in his shade,
> A massy shape which darkly flung itself
> Across the hills. And as he 'gan to stride,
> A hulk of intellect, the sheep were quick
> To stay within the charmed gloom. Of sweet
> Community they sang, of freedom soon
> To be embrac'd, and unrepress'd desire.
> As when, because of Pharoah's stubborn crimes,
> A host of frogs, spawn'd from the Nile's mud,
> Sent loathsome noises through th' Egyptian night,
> So did these rebel songs croak through the air,
> Until they rose to that grim Irvine tower
> Where slumber'd, dreaming of irrelevance,
> And bibliographies too long to read
> (by which, 'twas fondly hoped, might be secur'd
> A nearer Seat to almighty Allreek's throne),
> The Senior Shepherds of the dusty hills.
>                    The End of Book I

The author of these words, the last lines of the sadly aborted poem the beginning of which I quoted earlier, was the late Albert O. Wlecke, author of
*Wordsworth and the Sublime,* a former student of mine at Michigan State and
one of the assistant professors I had recruited.

# 9

# Administrative Adventure:
# UCI 2

## 1.

It's not easy being dean. For an unusual reason, in my case becoming dean wasn't either. I had by now served five years as chairman of English and Comparative Literature and had settled back into teaching and scholarship with relief, just in time to rescue myself from a nearly terminal loss of competence in my scholarly fields. I knew, however, that the vice-chancellor, Roger Russell, thought it was time for a change in the humanities. The first dean had been on the job from the campus beginnings. He was encouraged, I think (though I do not know) to resign and was probably ready in any case. One evening Russell took me to dinner, offered me the deanship, indicated my salary, and asked for an answer. I was reluctant. How could I ever hold on to my literary subjects, complete the book I was working on, and, as we say, have a life? I knew that Russell wanted me to take the job. He had earlier queried me about the state of the humanities and what might be accomplished next.

So I thought I was in a relatively strong position to bring to an acceptable conclusion something I had not succeeded in accomplishing for my department. This involved making a successful foray against UC's bureaucracy. For six years my chief assistant had remained at the rank of secretary. She dealt with the largest department at Irvine, with the most faculty members, the most students, and with the largest array of courses. All the science departments had administrative assistants at higher salaries. The reason for this was that in order to hire or to promote to that rank the department's budget had

171

to reach a certain number of dollars. With expensive equipment and large research grants, even the smallest units in the sciences could surpass this. The question of the range and complexity of responsibility did not seem to be considered. It was clear to me that the department's secretary should be raised in rank. Unfortunately the vice-chancellor for business and finance, who had come from the U.S. Army, read the university's regulations as what we now call a strict constructionist and kept turning down my annual request.

I told Russell that I would accept the deanship if the secretary of the Department of English and Comparative Literature were raised in rank. This was not his territory, and his first effort to accomplish this failed, university regulations apparently having been read to him. Russell was a likeable man, with whom I had become friendly; but for someone in his position he was oddly timid. He called me and told me it couldn't be done. I said I would decline the deanship. He came over to my house to cajole me. I declined again. He perspired visibly and left. This was on a Sunday. On Monday I received a visit from the campus personnel officer. He informed me that the departmental secretary could be made an administrative assistant, but on a temporary basis. I realized this meant that if she should leave her position the new chairman would not be able to replace her at that rank. At this point I am afraid that I ceased being merely stubborn and became angry. I called Russell and informed him that the offer made was offensive, that I would not accept the position under that condition, and that perhaps he should reconsider appointing a dean who might behave as I did.

Another day passed. I have no idea what transpired, but finally I was called. The University of California all the way from Berkeley and in all its might bent its rule, and the position of my secretary, Betty Becker, was to become that of administrative assistant. I would like to say that such accomplishments as I had as dean ranked as high in personal satisfaction or even in difficulty, but they did not. A few years before, I had been offered a dean's position at the University of Washington by the then president Charles Odegaard. In the last chat we had before I turned it down, Odegaard mentioned something he wanted to get done. I offered the opinion that it would be very difficult to accomplish. He replied, "Everything is difficult!" He was right, and I knew it as he said it.

## 2.

Often in academic life it is the faculty, or some of it, that seems to be the problem for an administrator. This didn't turn out to be the case for me as dean. With a few exceptions my relations with the faculty were not bad. My stumbling blocks were budget and bureaucracy. When I was chairman,

Russell had reason to be irritated with me, but, as far as I know, never was, even when I ordered the telephone service to the humanities removed in protest against the budget allocation to the school, which was simply inadequate. My arguments for more funds were being met with dithering silence. Silence was to be my reply. The faculty was for a moment annoyed, of course, but I had consulted them and given my reasons and the bad alternatives. Of course, there was inconvenience all around, but after a few days incommunicado the humanities budget was increased and conversations resumed. I suppose the ploy would not be successful today because of personal cell phones.

On the whole, except for my occasional irritation at the vice-chancellor for business and finance and a few other people, I found the Irvine administration reasonable and for the most part pleasant to deal with. Indeed, the attitude was that if there was an idea we should consider it, and if we decided it was good the administration supported it. But though the University of California had many virtues, simplicity was not one of them. Because it was so big and because it was spread over nine campuses across the state it was an object of political interest in a way unparalleled elsewhere. My deanship coincided with the governorship of Ronald Reagan, who had run his campaign mainly against the University, the Berkeley free speech movement, Mario Savio, and all of the student unrest of the time. The man who had presided over the growth of the world's first multiuniversity was Clark Kerr, whom I came to know slightly and admire as a decent human being. In California the governor was not only on the board of regents of the University but also its chairman. Reagan had virtually promised to remove Kerr on the ground that he could not maintain campus discipline. This did not happen at the first meeting Reagan chaired. Kerr was asked by a television reporter as he left the meeting what the most important thing to occur at it was. He replied, "Adjournment."

At the next meeting Kerr went. We prepared for Reagan to savage the University budget. There were difficulties for the new campuses. Dan Aldrich returned from a regent's meeting and said to Diana, "We're going to have to educate a governor." He was remembering, with his usual optimism, that Pat Brown had not been friendly to the University at the beginning of his first term but came around to being a strong supporter. This didn't happen with Reagan, who did more harm to the University with his tongue, however, than with his bite. His attention strayed once he had arranged Kerr's symbolic firing.

During this period Aldrich asked me to go to a meeting of southern California deans of arts and sciences, there being no such dean at Irvine. The meeting reflected the universal budgeting anxieties of the time and was taken up principally by a rambling discussion of how best to reduce faculty size if that became necessary. For most of us the problem was to find a way to do so without violating rules of tenure and commitment to contracts. I recall

**UCI, 2000. (University of California Libraries, Special Collections and Archives.)**

that I met there William Gerberding, dean at the time at Occidental and later to become president of the University of Washington not long after I arrived in Seattle. We were both taken aback when after some general discussion the dean at California Lutheran said he didn't see what the problem was, you just fired people, claiming budgetary necessity. This represented a side or level of our profession that I had not experienced. I was reminded of a meeting of the regional Modern Language Association in Tulsa when I was still at Texas. A small group of us was griping among ourselves about the University when a professor from the University of Tulsa, who was apparently eavesdropping, remarked caustically, perhaps even angrily, that we folks were lucky. Try it where he was and we'd know!

**3.**

It is possible that if budgetary stress does not make it possible to decrease faculty size by getting rid of people one devoutly wishes would disappear on grounds of incompetence or general obnoxiousness, it may make people willing to consider curricular changes if it can be shown that there will be some benefit. Budget played a role in my successful effort to establish what came to be known at Irvine as the Humanities Core Course. It killed several birds with one stone. It increased enrollments in the Humanities and thus the Humanities budget. I was able to convince the dean of Biological Sciences that the course would be good for his students, who constituted the single largest group at Irvine. This was not difficult to do, since the dean, Howard Schneiderman, was humanistically oriented and was enthusiastic about the program from the beginning. Indeed, he was an enthusiast generally.

The idea was to combine the usual freshman composition course with a humanistic subject matter. A theme was to be chosen annually by faculty from the different departments. These people would share the teaching duties with the help of graduate teaching assistants, who would handle the writing assignments. In effect, what was usually two courses would be combined into one, for which double credit would be given. This plan was to deal with the perennial problem of what reading material to cook up artificially for the composition course and would greatly increase Humanities enrollments. There was the possibility that other schools on campus would adopt the program, though I do not know how this worked out.

The young Humanities faculty quickly welcomed this idea. It gave them a chance to cross departmental lines and learn from each other at a time when this was becoming popular. It was hoped that eventually many faculty would be involved, with people coming into the course and leaving as topics changed. One hoped that in this way the course would not become stultified in either method or subject matter.

However, there was a bureaucratic stumbling block. We had all forgotten that no School could stipulate more than a certain number of required course credits. The double credit course plus our universal foreign language requirement would exceed the number allowed. With trepidation I proposed that we drop the foreign language requirement if all departments in the School agreed to make it one of their own requirements. The Philosophy faculty was at first opposed, for they saw the problem as a way to get rid of a school requirement they did not like. The chairman of Foreign Languages was concerned that some departments might go back on their initial commitments. With cajoling, the Philosophy faculty became convinced that they had nothing to gain and perhaps something to lose if they opposed the idea. I assured the Foreign Languages chairman, who tended to oppose, on a principle not entirely clear to me, whatever I wanted to do, that no one would look kindly on a department that went back on its commitment. I had in this argument the advantage that enough people were willing to see him defeated on the matter. The core course was established and was enthusiastically taught. I do not know of its state today. I hope that it has continued, with changes over time to make it better, and I hope the foreign language requirement has remained universal in the School.

My other curricular innovation did not survive for long. It was actually developed when I was still chairman of English and Comparative Literature. It was an effort to engage older faculty (though the faculty at Irvine was young on average) in teaching freshmen in courses that combined their expertise with inquiry into something else related to it. For this program I had to call on people to offer courses that were in addition to their regular duties. To lighten the load the courses were to meet only once weekly, usually in the evening. Examples were "The Beast in Man" by a biologist," "The Problem of Pollution" by a chemist, "Ecology and Human Behavior" by a psychologist, "History and Tropical Diseases" by a biologist, and "Time" also by a biologist. Altogether twenty-four courses were offered in the first year. Several faculty became enthusiastically involved, including some of the most distinguished, but after a while the program died, partly because I could not find a successor willing or able to do the labor of recruiting faculty.

The problem of sustaining such innovations is usually that in a relatively short time the original faculty is worn out, loses interest, has other plans to turn to, or recognizes that continued commitment is not in their self-interest. The Humanities Core Course avoided this and thrived by deliberately changing personnel and topics. College Studies did not and eventually expired.

## 4.

Curricular changes, especially those suggested or initiated from above, are probably the most difficult of difficult academic things. Too many issues are involved: individual self-interest, departmental self-interest, educational and ideological attitudes, personalities, regulations, a general academic conservatism, and sometimes an opposite rush to the trendy. Deans have perhaps some success when they approach the matter obliquely, recruiting faculty, as Ransom did at Texas, or influencing recruitment. But there is always the danger that they will overstep into an area where they are not competent to judge. In only a few cases did I intervene; encourager to both recruiter and potential recruit was my role.

There was, of course, the case of Philosophy that I have already mentioned, where I undertook persuasion and met wily subterfuge, a technique that might be prescribed to departments when deans interfere. Perhaps my most vexing experience in such matters was with German. By now German was a department of its own. The chairman had been born in Germany in the Hitler era and, I suspect, sought in his life to live down as best he could his membership in the Hitler Youth. He proposed appointment of a young African American from a group of three candidates who had been interviewed. As I studied the qualifications of each, it became clear to me that the man was the weakest candidate. Others, I learned, agreed with me. At the time there was no African American on the Humanities faculty and only three or perhaps four in the whole of UCI. It was very difficult at the time to find qualified minority candidates, who were in great demand and, for that matter, not likely to want to live in Orange County. In German it was particularly difficult. The question for me was whether the appointment of this person would be anything more than a political statement and whether in the prescribed time he would be able to attain promotion on merit. Indeed, it would be extremely difficult to terminate him without what is by now familiar trouble. German was a very small department, and an additional appointment in the near future was unlikely. I decided to reject the department's recommendation.

Sometimes fortunate events come from unpleasant ones. Although I could not have anticipated it, the chairman resigned in protest. I had not been impressed by his work, and suddenly I had the opportunity to make a new appointment. It turned out to be a most fortunate one. The person who came in as a replacement was a fine scholar, succeeded me as dean, and later became vice-chancellor, performing quite successfully in all of these positions. Well, you may lose a few, but also you don't know when you may win.

Usually no one wins when a department nearly explodes, and anyone rushing in may suffer serious injury, either from direct attack, crossfire, or flying shrapnel. The wreckage usually is strewn about, and it takes years to clear the field. The Department of History was near explosion when I became dean, and it was clear that immediate action was called for. With no solution in my sight I asked the associate dean, James Calderwood, to chair the department's meetings. The group, in an unfortunate display of masochism, was prone to meeting too often, and the result was that its communal anger boiled up weekly. Some people might hold that letting it all hang out on a weekly basis is a good thing, but in this case it was most certainly not. Calderwood managed to keep order and move business along, mainly, I think, by assuming stolidly the facial expression of an Easter Island statue and punctuating his utterances with ironies perhaps puzzling to some of the participants. I do not know how many of his remarks may have descended to sarcasm, but if some did he was to be forgiven. We managed to recruit a new chairman from the outside who was able to maintain a successful if perilous balance between the "old goats," as they were (not affectionately) called and the "young Turks," some of whom had been reduced to an odd silliness by their experience and the temper of the times. In a relatively short time the department became a different place, and a few years later it was regarded as a considerable success, experts on Standard Oil having given way with symbolic correctness to experts on the Beatles, etc. (sarcasm).

Sometime during my tenure we began Russian. I had suggested, when I came to Irvine, that we should start an East Asian language program, but this was met with indifference. Even later there was no enthusiasm in spite of Irvine's location. Finally, years later, that department was created and immediately became successful. (Irvine now has a very large number of Asian-American students.) We looked instead for someone to begin teaching Russian. This proved not easy. We finally hired a multilingual man who, I came to understand, seemed to have no native language. This may have contributed to his perpetual anxiety, especially in the face of authority, which meant me. Any conversation I had with him brought sweat to his brow, no matter how genial I attempted to be. This was the most obvious expression of anxiety I had seen in a profession that generates it, even among many who are quite successful.

## 5.

I had been dean for a couple of years when Roger Russell accepted the top position in an Australian university. For reasons not entirely clear to me, I was chosen to succeed him. I had decided to put in five years as dean (if I was tolerated for that length of time) and return to full-time teaching. Ten years of administration would be quite enough. I did not seek the vice-chancellorship and did not welcome it. I recall walking down to the seashore in Laguna Beach with Murray Krieger and trying to talk out a decision. On the surface he was noncommittal, but I could tell that he wanted me to take the job. Murray liked to be near power and to think he was influential. He was, of course, in his aggressive way; but it was not all self-interest. We both knew that an alternative to me would not be a humanist. Indeed, though I did not know it at the time, I would be the highest-ranking humanist in the whole university. It was the possibility of bringing that perspective to the Irvine administration that in the end led me to accept the job. Eventually it would take me out of teaching for a time. As dean I had continued to teach a class each quarter. As vice-chancellor I attempted to do this, but in my last couple of quarters on the job I could not find the time or energy. Further, I was losing grip on the scholarship in my field at the very time when changes in literary criticism and theory were rapidly occurring. Luckily Dan Aldrich was willing for me to have two months in the summer free for scholarship — or nearly free.

## 6.

Aldrich was a man whom in my new job I came genuinely to like, though there was always some distance between us, generated, I think, by his unease with others. For me, his finest hour occurred shortly after I became vice-chancellor. It was what many would call a small matter, and I was the only person from UCI to witness it. The occasion was a large dinner meeting in a nearby hotel ballroom. Attending it were local friends of the campus, mostly business and professional men. The aim, of course, was to launch for UCI a support group of wealthy and influential citizens. The toastmaster offered a pep talk, then (as seems to have been a tradition in those parts) ordered the doors closed with no exit to anyone who did not produce a check or pledge of money. Dan rose up at once, took the podium, and countermanded the order, succeeding in doing it in a way that seemed not to offend, and implying that an educational institution just didn't operate in that way. The truth is that Dan hated to talk about money, and he was occasionally criticized for not exploiting the resources of the community; but the moment illustrated one of his greatest strengths, nevertheless.

Some of Dan's mistakes came early out of inexperience. At the outset, he had to make a number of non-faculty appointments, and some of these were mediocre. I had my own prejudices, but it seemed to be generally agreed that the public relations people were not very good, that his own chief assistant was not a success, and the campus police chief was just short of parody. Then there were the two other vice-chancellors — one for business and finance and the other for student affairs. Neither of them proved to be of more than limited competence, and the third student affairs officer, present when I assumed my job, was an irritation. His idea, among others, was that all remedial preparation ought to be under his direction. This included what was known in the university as "Subject A," a course for students who had not met the standard of the entrance examination in English composition. Subject A was taught by the English department. Among his innovations was one reported to me by a graduate student who worked on his staff for a time. It seemed that at a staff meeting everyone was provided with a poker chip which was to be tossed on the table whenever it was thought that anyone there was acting or saying something out of line. This included expressions of dissent, sarcasm, or improperly directed levity.

My first experience related to him was the most unpleasant though indirect. His wife asked to meet with me. She arrived carrying her young baby and proceeded to pour out a complaint against the man I had succeeded as dean, saying on the edge of tears that before her husband was hired she had been told that she could have a position in the French department. This had not materialized, and she hoped that I would set the matter right. I was surprised, being certain no such promise would have been made. I checked with the former dean, who declared emphatically and with uncharacteristic indignation that he had said only that she could apply for a position if one became available. It occurred to me that she, and almost certainly her husband, thought that this had been a cozy way of making a promise. It would have been in his character. When I asked the chairman of French about the whole thing, he declared that he knew nothing about the matter and added emphatically, "No way!" I believe she was suffering from the already accomplished dislike her husband engendered. He never mentioned any of this to me. He might well have deliberately misled her. I know only that she got a position in a nearby community college, and eventually they divorced. He proceeded to nibble where he thought he could around the edges of the academic program. By now, faculty and deans were vigilant, and his efforts were merely an irritant about which there was, however, much fulmination until he left. Clearly he had been seeking another position, but honesty about him seemed to prevail when prospective employers made inquiries. Finally, what seemed to be an unspoken grassroots conspiracy gave him strong recommendations for the presidency of a consortium of eastern colleges. No one had asked for my evaluation, thank heaven.

The vice-chancellor for business and finance was a retired army officer and at times seemed to confuse his job with that of a colonel when he wasn't taking the lowest bids for elevators and such. In the Humanities Building I and others began walking the stairs, not just for our health. He was either not effective at prying money out of University Hall in Berkeley or he was stingy on principle, or both. The morale in his office was low, though comment about it had not reached the comic level of that in student affairs. I heard many veiled utterances from people on his staff. Dan Aldrich acted as if he were oblivious to all of this, but I think the truth was that he could not bear to fire anyone. It was either that or he thought that everyone should be given a chance to show he could do better and bring out the best in himself. Dan was a good New England Protestant Christian, once involved with the Moral Rearmament movement. I learned this because when he found out that my father had been headmaster at Lakeside he remarked that he had met a Lakeside headmaster, Veo Small, who I know had been an active participant in Moral Rearmament meetings. The truth was that Small had been a French and geometry teacher but never headmaster. My father had inherited him and would have been happy to see him fade away. He had already been known to claim in his travels that he was the headmaster. I told Dan this and he was silent and, I think, thoughtful.

# 7.

I learned that Dan's view of people could, however, sometimes be quite critical. On occasion he treated my predecessor Russell with contempt to his face and before others. My observation of this on a couple occasions led me to advise him that if he wanted my resignation — and at once — all he would have to do was treat me in the way I had seen him treat Russell. Silently he seemed to acknowledge his action and his feeling that Russell was timid and perhaps sycophantic with him. He deeply disliked that in people. He never treated me in that way, and I think he appreciated that I spoke forthrightly to him. Probably not many people did.

Dan introduced me as vice-chancellor to students at a large meeting, the reason for which I do not remember. It must have been a meeting asked for by minority students to air grievances. I do remember that there were several black students present, none of whom I had ever seen before and one of whom, in an effort to be as insulting as possible, called me a miserable person and followed by asking what I had ever done for them. I responded, "Not a damned thing, and as for the future, you'll have to wait and see." No one responded to this. Shortly after the meeting I had a visitation from two young men who called themselves officers of the Native American Association. They began by telling me that they liked what I had said. It was new for them to be talked to straight, and they thought that maybe they could trust me. After a long and cordial conversation they left with smiles and handshakes. I never saw either of them again, and someone in Student Affairs told me they were two of only a handful of Native Americans on campus and it wasn't certain that one of them was in fact an Indian. No black student, except one of my graduate advisees, ever came to see me. I think they had wanted to hear me fumble around, say something inanely condescending, or mawkishly defend my record. I had not obliged and did not prove what they already devoutly thought. This episode seemed to have put me on a good footing, especially after the so-called KBS movement three years before. One advantage that administrators have, if they survive, is that students do pass out of college, and thus the collective student memory is short. On the other hand, there is a tendency for each generation of them to reinvent the wheel.

## 8.

The vice-chancellor's responsibility is, among other things, budgetary, and recently Irvine had not been very successful getting funds out of University Hall. Dan Aldrich had a New Englander's distaste for seeking funds there. Our business and finance officer seemed not effective in Berkeley, returning from the annual effort there with little success. As a retired army officer, he did not regard his job as having a political component. I suppose he had always followed orders from above and allocated what he had been given. I was told that the universitywide budget officer was difficult to reason with, indeed a dragon guarding a hoard. I went to Berkeley with neither sword and shield nor chain armor but with various colored charts invented in meetings with my staff. I lectured wand in hand. Apparently this Merlinesque rather than St. Georgish approach was unique and interesting to the dragon, who turned out, at least on this occasion, to be genially withholding his firebreath. I can recall what only one of those charts depicted. It was a list of sixty academic positions put in priority. My lecture, complete with mystical if somewhat pagan gestures, was on how they would be allocated at Irvine and why they were needed. This chart I had developed through consultation with deans, and I had presented it at a meeting of the academic senate as part of a report on budget. This was the first time this kind of presentation had been made to the faculty. I don't know whether it has occurred since I left the job.

While at Berkeley I learned, in spite of his silent presence at my presentation, that the person who had a large and often decisive hand in the Irvine budget was a young man with a cubbyhole of an office down the hall. It turned out that he was a California graduate with a degree in drama. When his role suddenly became clear to me, I invited him to come down for a site visit. This offer seemed to startle him. It was apparently beyond his experience. He had never seen the campus for which he was doing the budget analysis. When I returned to Irvine I called up the dean of the School of Fine Arts and told him to show this man, when he came, every nook and cranny of the fine arts complex, complete with running commentary on all plans and needs. This appealed to the dean, who was a drama professor and was known for his performances in various venues. This happened, and I waited.

Dan Aldrich was astonished to receive notice that Irvine was to be allocated all sixty new positions for the following year, far and away the largest number it had ever received. Riding this wave of good fortune, I yet suppressed the urge to suggest that I be sent to Berkeley to propose the business and finance budget. It was probably just as well as luck is often fleeting.

My opening of the academic budget to faculty scrutiny was welcomed, and I received but one complaint about how funds were to be allocated, should we receive them. The truth is that, except for a few, faculty don't have a lot of patience with such matters, and any report one makes is likely to seem so abstract as to confound full understanding. Still, the illusion of knowledge, of being let in on what have been thought the mysterious workings of the inner court, seems always to have a salutary effect. Further, there is little if any danger in it, and openness and dissemination of information is by far the best for faculty morale. If consistently practiced it might somewhat reduce grousing and suspicion conducted in a state of ignorance, though the state of ignorance is not really reduced by very much.

The one complaint surprised me and made me realize that my lecture to the senate on the budget had not covered one topic important to this one person. He was the founder of the new Program in Social Ecology, which came nearer than anything else at Irvine to expressing Dan Aldrich's notion of creating a land-grant institution for urban and semi-urban areas on the model of those for agricultural regions. In my lecture I had neglected to say how I would allocate graduate student teaching assistants. Social Ecology quite reasonably wanted to attract graduate students and give them support. I hadn't allocated enough, or perhaps none (I can't remember) to that program. Indeed, I couldn't. I had to take care of serious needs in English composition, mathematics, and some of the sciences. For this I was privately berated. I bore the onslaught with as much stoicism as I could muster, given my immediate feeling that this man was an ungrateful ass. I had put myself on the line in an extraordinary way to support his program with new appointments. I had been somewhat surprised that no one had complained about this, and perhaps I would have fared better had someone done so publicly so I would be perceived as a vigorous defender of his interests. I must say that his behavior, though abrasive, was straightforward and honest, and he was doing an extraordinarily good job for his organization. I reminded myself of this under his hail of barbs.

I had already known that some faculty members will lie to you and betray confidences. I now understood that some would press even harder as a result of their good fortune. As a result an administrator is likely to act a part and learn the self-protection that a certain distance affords. Perhaps it is no matter, because as one rises up the chain of command one is treated as an object to be managed, devoid of the usual humanity.

# 9.

Dan Aldrich's dislike of having to fire anyone had left a series of inherited unpleasantnesses for me to confront. It was clear that if certain academic administrators were not removed much of the faculty known to me would be properly critical of my inaction as they were of Dan's. I was supposed to accomplish the job that Dan apparently shied away from, and for reasons many were ready to enumerate, the sooner that I acted the better. The academic profession is geared to upward promotion. It has become expected. Of course, an occasional hapless assistant professor fails to achieve tenure and is let go, but this occurs less often than one might think (and probably less often than it should). On the whole, no one in academe likes to see someone terminated, unless it is a losing football coach. When someone is let go, he or she is forgotten almost at once, as if something had never happened, unless, of course, the cause has been colorful enough to go into the folklore of the tribe.

The most obvious need was to dispose of the dean of the recently acquired School of Medicine. Its acquisition is part of the story. The California College of Medicine was founded in Los Angeles as an independent college of osteopathy. Eventually a full-fledged medical school, it was nevertheless on its last legs. As I understood at the time, a powerful state legislator was a graduate of the college and one of its strongest supporters. The University of California budget was, of course, always a political object, and it became clear that the president had better find a secure place for CCM, as it was called. Clark Kerr, still president at the time, either talked Dan Aldrich into taking the college on at UCI or ordered him to do it. There was a stormy faculty meeting at Irvine over this matter, but the decision to accept it was made, maybe already had been made.

Actually, it wasn't as bad as many of us had feared, in spite of the fact that we had inherited one of the lowest rated medical schools in the country. What came under control of UCI was only some property and buildings in Los Angeles, a dean, a dozen or so senior medical faculty, and, perhaps most awkward, a board of trustees. The property was disposed of and the funds dedicated to new buildings to be built on the UCI campus. Most of the faculty members either retired or resigned or were gradually submerged in a much larger staff recruited after the move. The board of trustees, luckily composed of quite senior men, was gradually eased with retirements into nonexistence. The dean, however, remained, and the situation had moved well beyond his powers to deal effectively with it. The most public evidence of this was his tendency to make speeches in the academic senate that unerringly turned even people in support of his view against whatever motion he was advocating. One of my colleagues, a close friend of mine, enjoyed consistently mispronouncing his name in my and perhaps everyone's presence. Dan Aldrich knew that the dean had to go, but it was I who finally had to induce him to resign. I think he was sentient enough to know that his time had come, though I am not sure of this. The dean had a certain opaqueness impossible to grope through. However, I like to think his knowledge made our conversation a little less painful than it might otherwise have been.

The new dean's first act to which I had to respond was the removal of the chairman of radiology. The dean came to me wanting to make certain that I supported him, correctly convinced that there would be an effort to go over his head. Sure enough, in a few hours I had a visit from the chairman, a genial personality, but according to the dean "dangerous" in his position of responsibility. I made clear to him that I supported the dean. At once, when the chairman had left me, I rushed to Dan Aldrich's office where the chairman was already seeking an appointment with a secretary. I barged past him.

Dan then heard my version of the dean's story, and the chairman was soon gone.

I had to commit a few other such unpleasant acts, and no complaints got back to me. On some occasions I was actually congratulated, an unusual experience for anyone in administration.

Medical school matters have a way of taking up a lot of administrative time. My initial charge was to bring what was still called the California College of Medicine into cooperation with the School of Biological Sciences. The latter was regarded as one of the best academic units at UCI. Easier said than done! The biologists regarded themselves as superior to the medical people and, at least at the beginning, wanted no part of them. The medical people, already suffering from an inferiority complex in their new surroundings, exhibited paranoia. I had to preside over any meeting arranged to foster unwilling curricular cooperation. There was no throwing of chairs, as there had been in the Department of History, but there was a good amount of grumpiness among intelligent people. I am not sure that the division was ever overcome, not during my tenure, at least. The fact, I am afraid, is that in academia the "pure" and the "applied" sciences usually don't work well together.

Part of the attempt to bring those schools into cooperation was to avoid costly duplication in a time when budgets were a serious problem. A perceptible danger was that some of the planned and even established (though barely established) academic programs would be eliminated by edict from Berkeley. It seems incredible today, but one of these was UCI's small School of Engineering, suffering from a dearth of students. Was there the possibility that, if we had to, we could "hide" it in some way until better times came? Surely such times would come, and for this reason elimination seemed no choice at all. My idea was that if worse appeared to be coming, but only then, we hide it as a department in the School of Physical Sciences, composed at the time of physics, chemistry, and mathematics. Unfortunately, like anything that is likely to fuel the apparently natural anxiety of academics, my idea got out in garbled form as an imminent event. I had to quell a disturbance mainly of my own making. This included having to listen to the engineering dean's tedious and repetitious lecturing explanation that engineering was a professional school and had quite different aims from those of the physical sciences. I was, of course, but an ignorant humanist not supposed to understand this. I could not convince the dean that the idea was but a last ditch plan if it became necessary and that it was not part of a plot in high places to get rid of engineering entirely. In the end, he was right about one thing: He seems to have assumed, perhaps without giving it much thought, that it is very difficult to get rid of anything in academe and there was no reason for alarm. He was right. Engineering survived as a school. As it turns out, he resigned some time later for reasons having nothing to do with this brief episode.

Eventually, we brought in a new dean, appointed with some trepidation by both Dan and myself. His time as dean was not much of a success, and he eventually went away.

# 10.

UCI was growing more rapidly than first planned. Administration of it was becoming more complicated. Dan still tried to run it as a small campus. There was some unrest in the ranks, though perhaps no more than the usual grousing when an administrator has been around a while and has committed a certain number of acts. I was not the only one on campus to think that Dan needed a true second in command, though I was not convinced that I should be that person. I was one of three vice-chancellors, though the one in charge when he was absent and the one most deeply involved in matters of policy. At a staff meeting I raised the issue, knowing well that my act would be regarded by many as a grab for more power. Dan received the notion with some positive feelings. A day later, I was surprised to read the minutes of the meeting kept by his dragonish assistant and find no mention of any of this. I was angry and let the dragon know it, gaining an enemy that probably had grown from a fundamental mutual dislike. That was the end of that and contributed to my decision to resign and return to teaching full time. It wasn't the thought that nothing would come of my idea; it was that the facts had been deliberately suppressed. How much Dan knew of this, whether he had paid any attention to the minutes or had simply forgotten, I do not know. My successor did become executive vice-chancellor. I had told him he needed to be.

I had other reasons to step away. I had put in ten years in administration, enough to have given it a good shot. I needed to get back to scholarship, then or probably never. I had found how difficult it was to find people to sustain what I had started. I had also begun to realize that I was in the midst of a major, worrisome, and wearying change in higher education. Universities have since become deeply involved with private industry as they had earlier with the federal government. Short-term practical objectives have become more important. High-level administrators have had to become involved in fund-raising to a degree unparalleled in earlier generations — and at the expense of internal concerns. Universities have become less and less places where the word, that is, the power and dignified use of language is highly valued. This is exhibited mainly in the decline of the humanities as part of what universities regard as central to the life of intellect. As UCI became larger, technical and professional schools gained the ascendancy. Parts of the campus were eventually sold off to accommodate so-called cooperative arrangements with technological companies. A huge science library devoted to retrieval systems now dwarfs the main library. UCI is not unique in any of this, though it is probably positioned where it is more susceptible to such trends. A liberal education, as we used to call it, reaches fewer and fewer students in any effective form. For someone like me, dedicated to that form of education in the arts and sciences, the choice was to join up in effect with these trends or to oppose them by stealthy struggle. The likelihood was that I would be one of the losers in a battle of attrition.

Also, I had no desire to rise higher in administration and, particularly, to become a fund-raiser. At about this time I was approached about a presidency, and it had been made clear to me in various subtle ways that in my position I should *want* advancement. I

The author, circa 1974, about to escape from Administration.

came to realize that powers above found this desire a convenient deterrent to a possibly irritating independence of mind. I do not mean that this was a conscious attitude. No, it was somehow woven into the fabric of administration. My successor, a man whom I liked and admired, observed that when he was considered for higher positions he was often not trusted. He was a distinguished biologist, and everyone knew he could quit when he wanted to. When I told Dan Aldrich I intended to quit he observed that he couldn't do that. He was too far removed now from his academic field.

Finally, though, I think it is the wearing away of one's identity that is most debilitating. The more public one becomes the less one is oneself.

My last act as vice-chancellor was to write to my successor a letter describing unfinished business, including my advice to seek the appointment of an executive vice-chancellor. This eventually occurred, and he occupied the position. Eventually, too, he resigned over, I think, disagreements with the chancellor.

## 11.

In *The Academic Tribes,* the first edition of which was published in 1976, I noted that former administrators, now no longer quite suspect, become committee persons. However, the distance from colleagues does not entirely disappear, or at least not for a while. This was my situation, except now I was not only treated with a certain deference but also called on for sage advice or action in the English department's behalf. Part of this expressed an attitude possibly best described as an academic syndrome: Let him take care of it, I don't have the time or, in the end, even the interest or, it might be said, the self-interest. In the first year out of administration I gave a series of public lectures that, with additions and revisions, became *The Academic Tribes*. In spite of the tendency of much writing on academe to become satire, my book had a serious undercurrent beneath its parody of an anthropological study directed toward academic life and culture. I enjoyed writing it and believe the "principles" and "antinomies" (*pace* Kant) offered there apply to this day, perhaps with more force than then.

Ten years is a long time to be an administrator if one intends to return full-time to the classroom and to literary scholarship. I had taught regularly until the last year, but keeping up with the reading in my fields was impossible. Indeed, keeping up with it full-time would have been impossible. The amount of material published increased tremendously in that decade (and we hadn't seen anything yet). I recall Northrop Frye saying to me in jest, but with his usual straight face, that there should be a brief moratorium on scholarly publishing — about five hundred years, he thought. During the decade major changes occurred, illustrating the fact that everything was speeding up.

From sometime around 1968 I had begun to write the book that finally became *Philosophy of the Literary Symbolic*, frustrated by my other duties and subject to the swift changes brought about principally by the movement known as Deconstruction. The book took a long time to write, suffered radical surgeries, endured some rejections, and did not come out until 1983. I haven't read it through since. Its reviews at the time were mixed, depending, I suppose, on where the reviewer stood on the theoretical issues of the day. I had taken a line independent of the fashions at work, and I paid for it. Brents Stirling's reminder of many years before came to my mind: "Don't buck the Greenlaw trust." Greenlaw at that time was the most powerful scholar of Edmund Spenser.

My book on Joyce Cary, which came out at about the same time, was more of a success though it sold less, limited to the readers of a novelist no longer popular. It had begun as a long article that I attempted to put into *Philosophy*, but it didn't fit. The book became a labor of love as against the albatross that *Philosophy* turned out to be. I still return with pleasure to Cary's trilogies. They are full of insight into character and seem to me wise books. In preparation for a new project I recently reread my book. It's pretty good, maybe my best.

## 12.

Murray Krieger and I had always talked together about developments in literary criticism and theory. In the seventies we spoke more and more about what seemed then a chaotic scene of discourse about literature. At that time, theory still meant something like *literary* theory, that is, a discourse devoted to inquiry into the nature of imaginative literature, both its external and internal relations. Literary theory was not very often the deliberate application of social thought or some ideological position to the reading of texts. When I had published my anthology *Critical Theory Since Plato* (first edition 1972), I was still able to treat critical theory, as addressed to literature, and in a sense different from critical theory as professed by the German social theorists of the Frankfurt School. Because of the success of my book, now in its third edition, I am stuck with its title, but I would probably now title it "Literary Thought Since Plato."

Krieger and I viewed the scene of the seventies — deconstruction, feminism, social thought, etc.— and decided that a new school, modeled somewhat on the old Kenyon School of English (later the Indiana School of Letters), would be a good idea. The Kenyon School disseminated the so-called New Criticism and its surrounding conflicts. We saw what we would found as a place not committed to one philosophy or method but rather to the hearing of the variety of stances that had grown up at the time, sometimes in conflict and sometimes merely logically different. The times seemed to require a forum of that kind. We hoped to make the School relatively independent of institutional control, though it would be housed on the Irvine campus. I approached the National Endowment for the Humanities for initial support, proposing a summer session of five or six weeks for young college faculty and advanced graduate students. The rationale was in part that with the expansion of higher education many young faculty were relatively isolated in small institutions and could profit from time spent in conversation with well-known scholars and other young people. The idea was to invite five or six distinguished scholars, not all necessarily literary, who would teach seminars on advertised subjects pertaining to contemporary literary thought and/or its relation to other intellectual disciplines and developments.

My first experience with Washington bureaucracy was interesting. Our project, it turned out, did not fit into any of the categories the NEH had constructed for grants, and each type of grant seemed to have its own administrator. I was passed from one person to another, some of whom knew nothing of the application. Finally it settled squarely between two people, both of whom either did or did not want to deal with it. Returning to my hotel room in frustration, I telephoned the NEH director Ronald Berman, a professor at UC San Diego whom I had only briefly met previously in California. I did not know how I would be received, for the chairman of literature Roy Harvey Pearce had in the immediate past seemed to regard the UCI department as a competitor. Berman expressed surprise at my vehemence about bureaucracy and asked me to come to his office the next morning. There, in my presence, he settled the jurisdictional dispute to the satisfaction of no one but me. However, I was able to come away with support for three years, and The School of Criticism and Theory was born.

But UCI, too, had its bureaucracy. There was an office for housing, one for food, one for allocation of office and classroom space, one for cleaning up after the academic year had ended, and perhaps others I do not recall. All of this we fought through. Krieger and I created a governing body of Senior Fellows that included a number of scholars, among them Geoffrey Hartman, Edward Said, Ralph Freedman, Hayden White, Leonard Meyer, and René Girard. M. H. Abrams and Northrop Frye were honorary members. Krieger and I were co-directors. We recruited from this group and from outside it the first summer's faculty.

We had to find housing for these academic luminaries. Then came the prima-donnish demands. Over the first few years, one person required a grand piano, another the *New York Times* (no western edition then), another certain foods. One even wanted the walls of his rented house painted afresh to please him and his academic spouse. Most wanted rental cars. One of the rented houses was flooded under unknown circumstances. A visiting scholar from England showed up for dinner resplendent in a karate suit with colorful sash. Another brought what may have been her young paramour with her and expected that he would be able to attend seminars free of any charge. On the first night a poor dinner was provided. A young UCI faculty member, later well-known elsewhere for difficulty, sulked because he had not been introduced at the dinner with appropriate pomp. Later in the evening I received a frantic phone call from a young woman from India who reported that the window curtains in her dormitory room had been taken away and she was open to the view of all. I rescued her, and she spent the night at our house while I attempted to discover what had happened. Some campus office had decreed that all dormitory curtains be cleaned at the end of Spring Quarter, and someone had begun with her room. Frightened though she was, she was equally astonished that I had come to rescue her myself and did not have a driver at my command. On the whole, though, things went fairly well. Krieger, having never fought administrative fires, was more agitated than I by these various events.

When NEH resources ran out, UCI supported the program; but then a phase of budgetary hard times set in, and that support ceased. We looked around for help and landed at Northwestern University. It appeared anxious to buy prestige, which we were apparently regarded as able to supply. In

Evanston in the first summer there, I remember mainly the stifling heat. Diana and I hauled our mattress into the living room of our apartment every night, it being the one room moderately cooler than the others by virtue of a slight breeze. To escape the heat, Diana spent much time driving around in an air-conditioned car. On a train back from Chicago one afternoon one of our students declared, "I'm poached."

Krieger and I now saw the school as properly peripatetic. Northwestern had been hospitable, but after a few sessions there, a new director moved the school to Dartmouth. Today the school is at Cornell, which has taken it over as its own in ways we had resisted. Certainly we did not expect or want the school to last as long as it has. We thought of it as something that could perform a service at a certain intellectual moment. Today, things that had emerged from the chaos of the seventies have either died out or become institutions of a kind themselves. The school no longer has the purpose we imagined, and its interests have been extended, on the whole, away from literature. All of the original members of the board of senior fellows are either retired or dead. I became an honorary senior fellow, but I play no role in the school's business. Developing it was an interesting experience, albeit a continuing, sometimes depressing education in academic attitudes and behavior.

## 13.

Aside from the School of Criticism and Theory my academic life went on relatively quietly. I was teaching among friends the subjects I had known best and I was catching up with them. When the University of Washington approached me about coming there to replace my dissertation director E. E. Bostetter, who had died, it seemed that it might be time for a change. A philosopher whom Diana and I had known at Texas claimed that one should move every seven years. I was in my thirteenth year at UCI. It turned out that if I were to move in 1977 my tenure anywhere would have averaged six years. Not a good reason to move. However, the Northwest was attractive. Our families were there. We had, of course, spent summer time when we could at Harstine Island on my mother's property. We now had a small house there. UCI had been a splendid adventure that I was lucky to have experienced, but Southern California had already become a vast wasteland of identical shopping centers connected by clogged freeways. At UCI, I was never liberated from being regarded as a former high administrator. The department was also changing, a sign being the appointment of someone quite different from the sort I would have recruited. Gradually, after I left, the department, desirous of what I will call star power, changed its identity. It began to thrive on a national reputation driven by the presence of well-known academics, some of whom spent only a fraction of the year in residence: Jacques Derrida, Wolfgang Iser, various visiting poets.

In June of 1977, I was asked to give the commencement address at UCI. Later it was printed in the alumni magazine. Here is what I said:

It is obligatory to begin a commencement address with an illustrative joke. My joke was supplied to me in its original form by the father of a graduating senior. I have corrupted it, added to it, and quite changed it in order to illustrate the principle that 1) the prime requisite for the bachelor's degree is stamina and moderate speed afoot, and 2) the rewards are odd.

A young B. A. cannot find a job and finally is hired to paint the yellow line down a highway. His test is to paint a 500-yard stretch. He is given a brush and a bucket of paint by his foreman, who leaves him to do the job, remarking that no college boy had ever applied for this job, that he doubted he could paint a straight line, and so forth. The young man paints the 500-yard line in record time. The foreman is impressed and hires him. On the next day he must paint a line a mile long. The foreman remains pleased at his speed but is puzzled that it has taken him twice as long to do the second 500 yards, four times as long to do the third, and so on. Still, he has worked faster than any of his predecessors. The foreman is suspicious by nature and asks for an explanation. The young man, breathing hard, replies that it's quite natural. With every 500 yards he got farther away from the bucket.

The foreman hires an M. A. to replace the B. A. The M. A. contracts for a B. A. to carry his bucket, but consequently makes less money while increasing the speed of the operation. A Ph. D. comes along and observes this and writes an essay about it for a learned journal, for which he gets no pay. This is known as life in the real world.

Most of you have just painted a 180-credit yellow line marred only by a few wavy stretches. It has been a long-distance race. And it isn't merely, or perhaps even mostly, intelligence that has brought you to this point. It's stamina, endurance. It's a commodity that is more rare than you think. It's a commodity that, incidentally, most of your parents have been exhibiting for some time now, and often with respect to you! You've also had some luck, and so have they — in you. No one accomplishes much alone; we are all involved in each other and thus accumulate debts.

I want to speak briefly to you, then to your families, and then to my faculty colleagues.

One, to the seniors: You belong to a generation assaulted more relentlessly by words than any in history. You are witnesses to noise. It is everywhere, growing in volume, and trying to sell you something, whether that something be an underarm deodorant or a politician's tax plan. The techniques have reached unparalleled sophistication. Among age groups you belong to a majority, so that it is specifically at you that the techniques are directed. You are the first generation actually to wear advertising slogans on your shirts. All previous generations would have required payment for that. No farmer I have ever heard of allowed a Mail Pouch Tobacco sign to be painted on his barn for free. You are collaborators in your own torment. You are subjected to and cooperate in oscillations of style the speed of which has been unknown before to man. If you want to be *au courant* you must run as fast as you can — to stay in the same place. You belong, indeed, to a period of cultural decadence that has been signaled for some time by our writers and artists. You *need* that stamina you have developed here — and more. Keep in shape.

It is part of the mythology of decadence that a university's principle role is to serve *you* and to provide *you* with a vocation. Or rather, the term "vocation" itself has undergone a change toward decadence. In its earlier forms it meant a calling, not a calling from the inner desire to feed and clothe oneself or to rise in the social scale, but a calling from God to exercise some special function, especially of a spiritual nature. By the same token "profession" has become decadent as a word. It once meant a declaration, a public avowal; this means that one didn't join a profession but professed something, declared a faith. The university has perhaps lost sight of these early meanings, but not entirely. The university has not been here merely for *you* or any particular gratification of *your* desires, as worthy as they may have been. Neither is it here for the faculty or for your families, or for the state. It is here to *profess* a vision of culture better than any we have had or probably can have. And it ought to provide you with a true vocation involving a vision of your own that you wish to profess for the sake of everything that lives.

One necessary element of that preparation in an age like ours is to offer you the negative power of skepticism before the ubiquitous hype, the subtle hype directed at you and perhaps now so habitual that you don't notice. That skepticism is the necessary other side of the desire to know the truth. I do not know how well we have done that job. I sometimes fear not very well. Clearly an effective skepticism must not be cynical. Matthew Arnold thought that the best positive education against cynicism and despair was *to know the best that has been thought and said in the world.* This involved for him an historical outlook, a sense of our intimate connection with the past, of our identifying ourselves with all men and women who have lived. For some time now, education has not paid much attention to that perspective. Nor has the culture: we abandon our cities for newer former pastures that have become suburbs sodden with presentness. Our immediate past we store in alien retirement communities, where it is allowed to rot and to which our older people choose to go in order to escape whatever it is their culture is saying to them. From what I can tell, the word "history" isn't a word much used in primary or secondary education today. There has been in relatively high academic places an effort to debunk even the idea of great books of the past.

Certainly the set of breadth requirements you have recently met at UCI pays little attention to questions of intellectual heritage but is the result of political compromise between academic power groups. So with respect to this matter I'm not certain what you have learned. If you have managed it, you have done so for yourselves. But I do know that you have proved your drive and stamina. So it is not too late. Find out about the past. Develop your taste. Don't let CBS, NBC, or ABC get your mind. It's more of a challenge than you think. Just try to work your way through the tons of junk, to say nothing of the noise, in a music store to find the great music. Just try to find a piece of clothing in the stores catering to your age group that doesn't make you look like something out of Ringling Brothers rather than Brooks Brothers. Just try to find the serious book you hear about in what passes for a bookstore today. The least success in any of this you will cherish.

Remember, too, that there were people here who tried to help you — some people you probably never even saw. UCI was put here as part of the effort to build community, and that takes time and luck. You have been part of it as it struggles to be more than it is today. I hope that in the years ahead you will look on its struggles and successes with affection. There have been people here who have worked hard for you, who have found a vocation and professed it.

Two, to your families: You have put up with a lot. This ritual is *not* your last test of endurance. You will worry over your children as long as you breathe, but more silently. Some of you have seen your children take unexpected turns in their years here. Perhaps my experience as an advisor will be of interest to you. I have often seen students who come here set on some particular goal only to discover it was the wrong one. Sometimes it has been the parents' goal. This is not entirely bad: better some goal than total innocence. What is unfortunate is to observe the struggle in that young mind when there is not enough openness in the minds of his or her loved ones. Of course it works the other way, too. Parents can err with too much openness.

My point is that perhaps the achievement you are honoring is not quite the one you expected or even at one time hoped for. I assure you that it *is* an achievement, probably the right achievement, and one made by independent effort. Men and women have many ways of fulfilling themselves and the needs of the culture. Parents learn that there is always more to learn every day. One piece of knowledge is the necessity for everyone, including their children, to make their worlds for themselves. With help, yes, and guidance, but at different times different sorts.

Third: to my colleagues. Each year at this time we scatter to regenerate ourselves and return in the fall enthusiastic for the new academic year. We belong to perhaps the most cyclical of professions. It is an axiom that matters of great pith and moment should, in academe, be allowed to rest in the months of May and June, when the academic soul is frayed and tired, and remain dormant until October. Now is not the time for exhortation, but I cannot resist saying again to you that the system of requirements at UCI is unfortunately not based on the assumption that students should study the best that has been thought and said in the world but on the assumption that the campus is a supermarket, and that somehow to stipulate our aims clearly is an assault on student freedom. My view is that education is a means by which the most important kind of freedom — imaginative power — is given the means to develop itself. This necessarily requires that certain freedoms have to be abrogated in order that this power may be developed. The Academic Senate has made efforts to review its requirements, but they have come to nothing as yet. It is time to act.

A final word to those of you graduating: Some of you were probably confused by our strange ways when you came here and have only recently learned to manage your small corner of this place. Now you pass on to another confusing scene. I have news for you. It's always going to be like that. Education doesn't dispel confusion but teaches you, I hope, to rise to appreciation of the ever greater levels of it. Gradually you become less surprised at being surprised, and somewhere along the line you realize that the surprise is the source of life and joy.

I don't know whether there has been change in the breadth requirements at UCI. I somehow doubt it. I'd probably not bother to mention that matter today. But the rest, it seems to me, could remain about the same.

# Excursus: It's a Bum's Game

As I look back at the previous chapter, it appears to me to be an account of a series of firefights such as any administrator might tell about. Still, for that very reason it gives some idea of what it is like to lead the life of an academic administrator, though not of the highest rank. Perhaps there is imbedded in it some cautionary advice. If there is not or it is not readily detectable, this excursus properly follows to clean up.

The words of the title of this excursus — those of the late textual scholar Fredson Bowers describing an academic career — sum up the business of administration fairly well. However, one type of administrator manages to evade this description. I'll call him or her the survivor. This is the person who recognizes the first principle of academic administration as set forth in *The Academic Tribes* and is not particularly bothered by it: "No one has the complete power to do any given thing." Or, there are the words of Charles Odegaard, a very successful president of the University of Washington, "Everything is difficult." If the president is not inclined to chafe against this reality or at least stolidly appears not to, he survives, unless something beyond control (frequently in the Department of Intercollegiate Athletics) occurs. The survivor manages to ride the waves of academic discontent, staying out of education's way and making as sure as he or she can that academic decisions are made elsewhere and carried out with a minimum of interference. Occasionally the president may suffer a lapse of judgment and run something of direct educational significance up the flagpole. If it flaps too much or is a red flag he retreats and appoints a committee, which duly pulls it down. Then things go on as before. Sometimes such efforts are driven by a budget crisis and involve attempting to sever something from the academic body politic. But it is more difficult to get rid of something than to start something. When something dies in academic life it is usually by inertia or internal terminal illness.

The survivor paddles through troubled waters wearing a life vest; the doer runs risks. The danger comes from all directions: from faculty members protecting their various self-interests and expressing short-term views, from administrative underlings ambitious to do *their* things, from a cautious board of regents and, in the case of state universities, a legislature with entirely different interests. Harry Ransom at Texas was a doer until he was apparently told to cease and desist. John Silber was a doer as a dean at Texas and president at Boston University. By Machiavellian handling of the board of trustees he even managed to be unretired to a new position as chancellor. Charles Odegaard was a doer by force of personality and the ability, without giving too much offense, to lecture people on the history and purpose of universities. He also managed to be a survivor.

Dan Aldrich was a survivor by looking the part of a chancellor, projecting an attitude of optimism in all directions, and never irritating University Hall in Berkeley. Jack Peltason was a survivor by means of shrewdness in academic politics and treating his position as a political one. Bill Gerberding, though of different personality, was the same. Both Peltason and Gerberding came from the discipline of political science. As far as I know none of the three initiated or carried out an educational or intellectual idea. They were brokers or mediators, or cautious stewards.

Vice-chancellors and deans each have their own kinds of difficulty to deal with and each their advantages. Deans remain relatively close to the faculty, though apart. They may still in some cases be regarded as knowable human beings. They may hold on to fundamental human nature even though they imagine it ebbing away with every act they perform. They recognize, if sentient (I have known a few deans who did not seem to be), their growing abstraction by the change in behavior toward them even of old friends. They seem to require manipulation by stealth or, if not that, by a sycophancy that can turn suddenly into hatred.

The vice-chancellor (or vice-president or provost) is more abstracted, in the faculty's and even his own eyes, from real life. He is thought to lose touch even as he comes into touch with all the crises of the institution, which he must manage in the frequent absence of the chancellor and sometimes when the chancellor is present. His advantage in this, if one can really call it one, is that he is no longer expected to be entirely human, and if he perpetuates acts that seem grounded on the law of the Medes and the Persians no one is surprised, least of all those against whom it is alleged that they have been committed. Unfortunately for him, he does remain, in spite of all accusations to the contrary, a human being with feelings of regret when the alleged outrages for which he is deemed responsible have occurred. Sometimes such acts have actually been devoutly desired by much of the faculty, who would have criticized him if he had not done them. In such cases he is not inhuman enough. It's a bum's game, all right.

# 10

# In the Pacific Northwest

**1.**

In the summer of 1969, relieved to be free of the chairmanship after five years and ready to let off steam after the irritations of a tough academic year, I began to construct a small house on my mother's property on Harstine Island in southern Puget Sound. When she had bought the place in 1955, Harstine was regarded as rather remote; it did not have very much population, perhaps fifty families. Except for a small one at a marina to the north, there was no store. Once there had been a grade school, but no longer. My mother's property consisted of two hundred feet of waterfront and about an acre of land that included part of a forest of old fir, hemlock, and cedar. Across the water there was a splendid view of Mt. Rainier, Mt. Adams, and (until its top was blown off) Mt. St. Helens. In 1955 and for several years thereafter, the property could be reached only by an eight-car ferry, which ran after six P.M. only on Saturday. Disembarking, one was faced with about seven miles of gravel and dirt roads. These were sometimes barely passable in spots. In places there was but one lane with occasional clearings on the sides. These could be occupied in case one met another car. Deer were plentiful, and one had to be careful not to hit them (this is still true). If you had an emergency that required you to leave the island at night you went to the ferry ramp (there was no dock) and rang a large bell formerly belonging to the vacated schoolhouse, and this was supposed to summon the ferry captain and his one helper, who would take you across to the mainland for a modest fee.

With heroic determination and perseverance, my mother succeeded in getting workers to come the inconvenient distance from Shelton, the nearest town, and a small house was framed up. That summer I helped complete the interior. I had no experience with building or carpentry and learned on the job.

In 1969, I was to learn much more, still by trial and error. In my mother's library was a book she had obtained a decade before: *How to Build Your Dream House for $3500*. The writer of that book had a genius displayed by no writer of computer handbooks known to me. He left out no steps in the process of building, anticipated all one's queries, and explained his terms. The book was out of date with respect to some matters, but in every case its suggested methods were superior to those that had taken their place. I literally interpreted this bible and followed it chapter and verse all the way from preparing concrete for the support pilings to the finishing of the interior walls. Construction occupied three summers. I had the help of my two sons, fourteen and thirteen when we began. Their feats of daring on ladder and scaffolding were sometimes breathtaking, and their work was invaluable. By September of 1969, when we had to return to California, we had framed up the house on a slope facing the water. The house towered two stories in the back and three on the water side. Walking around above was a bit scary at first, but we got used to it the higher we built. In that first summer, we failed to construct the roof before we had to return to California. That work was, as we say today, outsourced, and the spaces intended for windows were boarded up for the winter.

Point Wilson, where my mother's property was located, was discovered by a friend of hers, the writer and Northwest journalist and historian Murray Morgan. He had ventured on to the island to visit a friend and promptly became lost. Wandering down to the beach at Point Wilson, he found an old one-room shack supported precariously by wood pilings under which the tide came and went. It is said that this shack was once the cabin of a barge. It was a splendid evening when Murray reached the shore, and he saw Mt. Rainier in clear view and was much impressed. It turned out that the property was for sale, and he and his wife Rosa bought it complete with fir and madrona forest.

Nearby, his friends Otto and Phyllis Goldschmid bought a cabin. Otto, a chemist at the Rayonier Lumber Company research laboratory in Shelton, had escaped Germany with his mother in the dark days of the early forties. They had walked across Europe together. For several years before her death she could be seen just as tenaciously gathering blackberries and huckleberries on the island. Some years after Murray's discovery, the Goldschmid cabin was bisected by a huge falling fir tree and was replaced by a larger house of pleasant design. My mother bought her property not far away because on a visit to the Morgans she too was captivated by the stunning view of the mountains and water.

## 2.

Murray Morgan liked to sit on his deck over the water and converse at length with friends or neighbors who might come along the beach. It would be wrong to say he held court there, because there wasn't an imperial bone in his body. He was a wonderful conversationalist and raconteur. He and Rosa had been to many places, and he had had a career in journalism that began with the editorship of the student newspaper at the University of Washington in 1937. He had been nearly removed from that position for publishing an article on venereal disease in the student body. Many years later, he abruptly quit a job as head of journalism at the University of Puget Sound when one of his students was prevented by higher administration from publishing an article complaining about the rise of the cost of a cup of coffee on campus. Although he worked at one time or another for *Time*, the old *New York Herald Tribune*, and CBS, he was, by his own admission, never comfortable in such organizations and preferred free-lance work. For some years he had a news and commentary program on a Tacoma radio station. *The Seattle Times* commented that he offered "opinions that probably are not shared by most of the bankers of the world." He also probed the ample seamy side of Tacoma politics and crime, the two things not being far apart in those days. He was once severely criticized for using the word "whorehouse" on the air.

Murray's stories of Tacoma politics were fascinating, but I remember best his account of tending a drawbridge on the Puyallup River. It seemed that the job was something of a sinecure allowing time to write, since the bridge was very rarely ever raised. One evening, however, he heard a boat whistle and promptly raised the bridge. After what seemed an appropriate length of time, he lowered it again. After a while he heard yet another whistle but saw no boat on the river in either direction. Shortly the whistle was repeated. Still nothing. Then, after a while, a man climbed up the stairs to the tender's tower. He opened the door and shouted in anger, "Get your goddamned bridge off my boat."

In a newspaper article about Murray, he was quoted talking about the plan for a bridge to Harstine Island. He reported that without the ferry's late Saturday night crossing, one of the islanders complained, "How will guests know to go home?" Before the bridge was built another person had said, "You almost can't get here from anywhere." Murray liked it that way and furthermore resisted any modernization whatever, including electricity and plumbing in his and Rosa's cabin. He extended this attitude to the cutting down of trees, no matter how dangerous. The privy remains to this day, complete with signs pilfered from who knows where and donated by friends or having mysteriously appeared on the wall: "Unload on this side." "Park here at your own risk." Murray's many friends, including my mother, the Goldschmids, Eugene and Dorothy Elliott, and Wilmott Ragsdale had built cabins nearby, all with electricity, septic systems, and running water.

It is said that during World War II when Murray was stationed on the Alaskan island of Attu, far out in the Aleutian chain, the commanding officer befriended him and asked him if there was anyone he'd like to have for company in that desolate place. Murray suggested his friend Eugene Elliott, and, lo and behold, poor Eugene, innocent of this plot, appeared there one day. Murray had in this way managed to obtain a chess opponent for the remainder of the war. Eugene had been in drama at the University of Washington and wrote a book on the history of vaudeville in Seattle. Later he took a Ph.D. degree in art history at the Sorbonne. In between, he taught me senior English at Lakeside. He reported about the Attu experience that the wind blew ferociously and continually and Murray, who had terrible coordination, would fall down several times as he proceeded from the radio Quonset to the mess hall. Eugene would dutifully help him up only to have to help him up again.

If Murray left his deck it was to tramp down the beach to pick mussels. Usually he was accompanied by one of the big dogs he had rescued from the pound: Kiska, Sitka, Nootka, and others. For a while he had a small poodle whom he named Balzac because he looked like the Rodin statue. There was also Balzac's sidekick Wilmott (shortened to Mottie), who was named for his friend Wilmott Ragsdale, also a journalist, who had become our neighbor, as well as his, on Harstine.

Ragsdale began construction of what first became an A-frame but grew in all directions in random shape, even on to the beach. Somehow Rags, which was what he was called by everyone, managed to involve all the neighbors in the original enterprise, even Murray, who was in serious danger even one rung up a ladder. Over about fifty years Rags added to his house, usually on sudden impulse. Rob Garratt, his friend from the University of Puget Sound, where Rags taught a course after his retirement, tells of being in the A-frame when Rags suddenly seized a chain saw and cut a huge hole in the wall, declaring that it would be a good idea to add a bedroom. I asked him once if he had plans for more building. He replied that he had no plans; his philosophy of carpentry was to do something and then see where it led. A neighbor, the psychoanalyst and writer Allen Wheelis came by to visit one of Rags's building projects. At Rags's invitation he climbed a ladder to inspect the work, endeavored to steady himself by grasping the frame of a wall only to have the whole wall collapse around him. Luckily he was on a ladder leading to a space for a door and the falling studs missed him.

Not long after, I came by, and was greeted by Rags's son-in-law, the writer Peter Stark, with the words, "Welcome to the far dark side of carpentry." I recall later peering at the vertical supports for Rags's deck, which

**Wilmott Ragsdale and Murray Morgan on the Morgans' porch, Harstine Island, 1960s.**

protruded from the A-frame toward the beach below, and I saw that most of them dangled free, no longer reaching the ground. Eventually this was fixed, but not by Rags, thank heaven.

Rags had had a varied career. He had tried prize fighting, worked in the oil fields, and sailed on merchant ships. He became a war correspondent and was on the U.S.S. Texas during the Normandy landing. He worked for *Time* and *Newsweek*, published some poems in *Poetry*, taught journalism at Grinnell College until he was dismissed for having an affair with a professor of dance whom he later married. Moving to the University of Wisconsin in Madison, he became a much revered teacher and won a coveted award there for teaching. Former students and other friends, whom he gathered wherever he went, would show up at Harstine. When well into his nineties he swam for twenty minutes each summer evening in the frigid waters of Puget Sound. At various times he taught abroad: Cairo, Bangkok, and elsewhere, prompting Murray to wonder whether he might be employed by the CIA. Rags declared that he was not but added that of course he wouldn't admit it if he was. At ninety-four he traveled to Mozambique to visit his daughter and son-in-law, who were temporarily there, returning via stops in Paris, London, and New York, where he and his family had for years rented a small apartment under ancient rent controls. A year later he traveled to Antarctica. Asked why he went, he answered, "Oh, oh, the penguins, you know."

**The Adams houses on Harstine Island in the 1970s.**

Having lived in England during the war, he seemed to have known every-one, though he never bragged about this. Someone would come up in con-versation, and he'd have a remembrance. In spite of his wide acquaintance throughout the world and his unfailing friendliness, he was a loner and eva-sive when he was asked where he was going next or even about what he was next going to do. Two wives, I presume, had enough of this and separated from him, though he kept in touch with both, and they subsequently visited Harstine. Murray Morgan is gone now, but Rags still lives at Harstine and Tacoma and continues to travel, though not, I think, engage in spontaneous carpentry, which is left to his children.

## 3.

By 1977, the prospect of occasional weekends and extended summers at Harstine appealed to us. That and emancipation from the freeway culture and Orange County politics figured in our decision to move north. It is also pos-sible that I had grown a little tired of UCI. I may have known by then too much about its inner workings. Too, UCI seemed to me to have become a bit like the crude *nouveau riche* culture that surrounded it. An appointment the English department had just made led me to believe that a corner had been turned and other values were to become dominant. It had been an exciting thirteen years, and I valued most of my colleagues; but things were changing. It was not going to be the department I had founded very much longer. My involvement with the workings of an institution would never again be what it was there. Indeed, at the University of Washington, where I had taken my graduate degrees, I was to become an outsider. I came to learn that most people there seemed to think they were, too.

For well over twenty years, back to my student days, Robert B. Heilman had presided over the English department. The tenure of his immediate successor was short and apparently unsuccessful. When I arrived the chair was Donna Gerstenberger, a hard-bitten veteran of the university's politics, which were very different from UCI's. My first telling experience of the department came upon my election to its executive committee, the by-laws of which had been written in apparent terror of the future just prior to the coming of Heilman in 1948 and had been deliberately made to curb the chairman's power. At the committee's meetings I was astonished at the members' irrational distrust of almost everything and everyone. They were suspicious of the upper administration and seemed to be wary even of Gerstenberger, who had been one of them for some time. She seemed to me a straight shooter and, I think, proved to be that. It finally dawned on me that the general attitude was probably the result of Heilman's long tenure as chairman and an eventual universal hatred of him among all but a few veteran professors whom, it was thought, he had favored. Several people expressed resentment at every opportunity, but now it was displaced to anyone in authority. Many of these people had failed to measure up to Heilman's ambitions for the department and his standards. Some had paid dearly for it in salary over the years. Much of that resentment came from a group of associate professors who seemed to be stalled in rank. There was almost universal rejection of anything suggesting change, though there was also dissatisfaction with the state of things in the present. An aura of fear and suspicion characterized not just the response to matters taken up in meetings. Anything from the dean or provost was regarded as a provocation.

Disgusted by this general unpleasantness, though others seemed either not to recognize it or had become acclimated to it, I went to Gerstenberger and asked to be taken off the executive committee, declaring that I found the meetings intolerable, progress being stymied at every moment. She craftily challenged me not to be, as she said, a "quitter" (implying correctly that many in the department had become such). It was just the right thing to say, and I left her office with nothing changed.

In time, I came to see that most people in the department worked in isolation. The department was large and was perhaps divided into cliques of which I knew nothing. Little social life occurred among the members, or at least I did not detect any. People seemed to retreat from campus into some part of Seattle society.

One autumn a departmental retreat was planned. I had not heard anyone speak about a general sense of alienation, not until that retreat. At one session it was gradually voiced. I myself finally spoke, expressing that I, too, felt isolated. This clearly astounded many, who assumed that I was among a small elite in the know, content with my relatively large salary and other suspected advantages. In other words, I was regarded as a member of a sort of royalty in the Heilman tradition. It is probable that the malcontents simply assumed that what they were experiencing was common in academia. The senior faculty member who had briefly been chairman followed my observations with an assertion in no uncertain terms that the isolation I had described was just fine with him. Perhaps after his short tenure as chair it was a relief.

This meeting seemed to clear the air a bit. I was thanked by several young faculty for speaking out about what they were too timid to mention, and with good reason. Their behavior seemed to have become a tradition. Diana and I were in the homes of senior colleagues of that time only twice, as far as I can remember. My friendships turned out to be confined to some younger members of the faculty.

I had come from UCI at the same salary I had there, turning down Irvine's effort to keep me by raising it. There my salary was not the department's highest, but at Washington it was. This did not prevent a colleague from complaining to the chair who succeeded Gerstenberger that my salary was "obscene." This came, of course, from one of the "deadwood" associate professors who had somehow achieved tenure with almost no scholarship to his credit. In exasperation the chair, who quite gleefully told me this, answered when this person compared his salary to mine that I was worth every penny more than he was.

In truth, Washington salaries were shockingly low. In truth, the University of California seemed to lose as much money annually in the wastebaskets as Washington had in its budget, and the budget was never subjected even to the most cursory faculty review. Suspicion of the administration's stewardship flowed down into suspicion of one's colleagues. There was no fixed scale for academic salaries. This was in sharp contrast to the situation in the University of California. Even senior faculty were never consulted about such matters. Chairs and the dean had full authority over the allocation of salary money and everything else.

Washington, as in the past when these processes were established, surely needed to pinch pennies. Power was collected at the top. Apparently the administration came to like it that way. It ensured control. It made possible administration efforts to respond without consultation to competing offers and to allocate money for retention of a favored few. However, for morale it was and still is a disaster. It breeds anxiety and a complex of inferiority. It leads to irrational acts; the result of one happened to work to my personal advantage. I only infer this, but it seems that a rumor got started that I was about to return to UCI. Before I knew it, I was granted a substantial (for Washington) raise, and an offer was made to reduce my course schedule or, as we call it, course load. Along with this came the remark that it was hoped I would now stay. Well, by this time I knew how the game was played at Washington. The only faculty bargaining chip was an outside offer. If you didn't have one you would fall behind and probably never catch up. The result over time was that some full professors made no more than the highest paid assistant professors.

An argument could have been made that some deserved no more. If that was the case they should never have achieved tenure. But once they had, it was terrible for morale that they were deliberately kept back. I accepted the raise, my salary becoming even more "obscene," and even the decrease in course load. By that time I was directing something like sixteen doctoral dissertations and serving as a reader of several others. Some tenured professors had no graduate students working with them, and some may never have had even one. Among the English faculty there seemed to be a culture that actually opposed scholarly activity or, at least, publication. One cadre of faculty played cards frequently in one of the offices, dominated by a publishing scholar who decried publication and seemed to have entranced his colleagues into inactivity.

At UCI I had set up outside the department's office a display case for recent faculty publications. When I suggested this at Washington it was rejected out of hand as elitist and offensive, apparently to those who didn't publish. A display case was finally put up a couple of years later by a young faculty member who had gotten into a position of limited authority. I think he just went ahead and did it, perhaps raiding the department equipment budget or spending his own money for it. Once it was up, there was no movement to take it down. Perhaps the dissenters hadn't noticed it, for the dominating temper seemed to be aloof disinterest masking here and there deep anger.

The curious organization of the College of Arts and Sciences probably contributed to a sense of isolation. When the College was divided into subunits, the Departments of History and of Philosophy chose to go to the Division of Social Sciences. This left English alone in the Humanities with Comparative Literature, the foreign languages and Linguistics. All university organizations are, of course, irrational and usually behind the times in their irrationality; this arrangement probably said something: that those two departments saw an advantage in being defined away from the Humanities. It was odd because Philosophy at Washington was more open to humanistically oriented thought than the one at UCI. I still don't know about History's decision, but History has always straddled the line between the social sciences and the humanities. However, the later creation of a program in the comparative history of ideas suggested that some of the historians knew what they wanted. This program was put into the Humanities.

## 4.

In Ireland, as I have recounted, a saying often heard was, "Ah, you can't do that in this country." I was subjected to various equivalents of it more than once at Washington, even from Gerstenberger. As an associate dean she had been affected or perhaps infected by the virus. This expressed a different attitude from that I had become used to at UCI. I came to challenge it with one or two small successes and some major failures.

For some reason, the graduate sequence in the history of literary criticism that had been of great value to me as a student had become moribund — this in a period of great interest around the country in criticism and theory. I got the courses started again, mainly by offering to teach them myself. Gerstenberger was not against such changes; rather, she seemed to take the view that they had to be accomplished by stealth. At my suggestion she initiated a discussion of the system of doctoral examinations. It had been a long time since any changes had occurred. The discussion was carried on in a committee of her choosing, and a change was successfully sneaked through the department meeting before serious opposition could be rallied. The new plan, modeled in part on the one I had instituted at UCI (though no one knew this), made a place for criticism and theory, genre study, and special topics in a system that had been based entirely on historical periods.

The new system was liked by most of the faculty, but not all, especially the medievalists, who feared that their courses would suffer a drop in enrollment. There eventually were drawbacks. Trendy ideological commitments began to influence choices of special topics and courses taught. Graduate students in increasing numbers chose to be examined in the most recent literature and theoretical discourse, not always literary. However, the fear expressed by the medievalists that no one would take their courses was not fulfilled. On the whole, the change was a wake-up call to a department still mired in the decadence that followed the heyday of the New Criticism. The department's energy had seemed to be bottled up, or was it a continued fear of change, a suspicion that nefarious hidden agendas were emanating from some ectoplasmic administrative power?

Several years after the changes mentioned above had been installed, it became clear that the department had lost faculty positions, and yet more students wanted to take its courses. The department would not have an increase in personnel except in part-time lecturers. At the same time the teaching load of each faculty member had declined. A colleague and I put together an analysis and a plan designed to enable us to offer small classes if the department created some large lecture courses. The proposal with a budget analysis was offered for discussion. Part of our argument was that to present the plan to the administration would put the department in a better position at least to retain the number of faculty it still had.

I should not have been surprised that as a whole the English faculty did not want to hear an analysis of its situation. Some persisted in arguing that the plan threatened the small classes that they now taught, in spite of the fact that it was designed to save them, and in spite of greater student demand and no increase in faculty size, and in spite of the fact that these classes were growing larger every year and were now no longer really small. Nothing came of any of this, and the department muddled along on its usual *ad hoc* basis. It was reported to me by a friendly colleague that a relatively new young faculty member had said to her in exasperation or perhaps wonder, "Why don't they listen to him?"

Now retired, I have recently learned that a similar analysis has been made in great detail by the colleague with whom I did the previous one. Some simply refused to believe its results, one of which, incidentally, was that students sought courses in which literary texts were actually taught, often in historical periods, and that the department did not need to give or expend so much of its energy on so-called cultural studies. Further, it was determined that the average teaching load per faculty member had declined.

After my analytical efforts had failed, I limited my participation in departmental politics and did what seemed to be the natural Washington thing: hoe one's own garden in the best of all possible worlds. But not quite, because there seemed to be an opportunity beyond the department to change what had long been regarded as an irrational system, that which governed undergraduate requirements for so-called "breadth." My commencement address at UCI, as the reader has seen, had ended with a complaint about the situation there. Washington's system was no better, perhaps worse because more complicated, and still founded on departmental self-interest. Breadth requirements are supposed to help broaden the education of students by forcing them to take courses beyond the confines of their majors. There is good reason to conclude that lists of acceptable courses to fulfill the requirement are almost always the result of a spoils system in which by tacit agreement departmental self-interests are protected. In the Washington system there was a smorgasbord of available courses from which students could choose, no effort to establish intellectual connections between courses or to make certain courses appropriate for students not majoring in the subject.

My idea was to collect in small groups or in some cases encourage establishment of courses that were deliberately related to each other. I went to President Gerberding hoping to enlist his support for this effort. It quickly became clear to me that he was not interested or deliberately uninterested. He was not going to get involved in a purely academic matter, probably on principle. I was not able to determine whether he thought the breadth requirement was a problem as it stood, whether he assumed that his support would be counterproductive, or whether he disliked the whole idea.

I went to the dean of the College of Arts and Sciences, who was somewhat more friendly to the idea but without any inclination to endorse it. I took a proposal to the academic senate, for I needed an exemption from the breadth requirement as it now stood. This would be a new program that would compete with it. My request squeaked through. Some senators opposed it, predicting doom. In the end they were right, but for the wrong reasons. The director of the college honors program, thinking erroneously that I was invading his territory, wrote me a letter vowing enmity and combat to the end. I traveled through the faculty trying (sometimes successfully) to enlist people to teach new courses or, in a new setting, acceptable old ones. I tried to interest those with reputations as good teachers.

The program began modestly with some success. At one point, it looked as if it might eventually replace the smorgasbord. Because the program seemed to me to be to the advantage of the university in attracting students, I traveled to about thirty high schools that sent the majority of students to Washington and spoke to seniors thinking of attending. High school teachers were frequently puzzled when I appeared, and I was turned away from some schools, especially if my request to come was routed to principals. In the schools the general view of the university seemed to be that it was a big factory, just what my program was designed to fight. After a few years, I relinquished my responsibility for the program. Over time, it suffered a slow decline, and then one year it disappeared without a whimper.

Why? There were several reasons. Washington is a big university. Many of its programs are unwieldy. Mine depended on the cooperation of departments, but there was not enough in it to appeal to their self-interests, and some departments seemed strongly opposed to it. The university is a publish-or-perish institution. Commitment to a liberal education is not high on the faculty's list of concerns, and in any case there is little if any agreement on what such an education should look like, perhaps far less than, say, thirty years ago. Finally, growing and sustaining such a program is exhausting for a director. Subsequent directors did not have as much academic prestige as I had and the modicum of persuasive power that went with it.

There was, however, a good side to the effort. Many courses were established and survived the program itself. In time, there was a move to identify courses in the smorgasbord list that could be linked together and recommended as groups. Students could decide to follow these suggestions as they chose. I do not know how this has worked out. If it has worked it is perhaps the best that can happen in a monster university.

The lesson the university imposed here was the one I had heard in the Department of English: "Oh, you can't do that here."

## 5.

It seemed that the university was in a perpetual budget crisis. At one point President Gerberding considered eliminating some departments to save money. A list of departments scheduled for demolition was developed. I do not know who advised the president about this. There was, of course, an immediate outcry from those faculty whose oxen were about to be gored and silence from most of the rest. It was finally agreed to create faculty committees to review each case. I found myself sitting on a committee to review the decision to eliminate the Department of Near Eastern Languages and Literatures. From the beginning it seemed to me preposterous beyond comical that the department was on the list, considering the contemporary situation, to say nothing of world history. True enough, the department was small, generally (though by no means entirely) undistinguished, and without many students. If those were the only grounds for judgment, perhaps it would have to go. Apparently whoever made up the list thought those were the only grounds, though it was difficult to believe that bureaucratic stupidity had reached such a level.

Hearings were held. It turned out that the Jackson School of International Studies had a stake in the matter, and the chair of the committee was from the School. We soon learned that if the near eastern languages were not taught the school would lose substantial federal support. No mention was made by its representative that the study of near eastern culture and literature was important. To the surprise of the administration there was a great outcry from the local community of people of near eastern descent. They attended the hearings in force, not afraid to show their approval or disapproval of what was said. Their presence was impressive though it perhaps did not have to be influential after representatives of the Jackson School had spoken about money.

It is not often that in such matters the community beyond the campus causes such a stir. Usually the issue is a losing football team or a scandal in the athletic department. Not long ago, the athletics director attempted to eliminate swimming as an intercollegiate sport. The waves this kicked up, and the splashing about, caused the director to seek dry land within a week.

In the course of the hearings, I spoke vehemently about the subject matter the department taught and delivered a homily on bureaucratic stupidity. From even before the day that the decision not to eliminate the department finally came down, I and the others on the committee were treated as heroic saviors, invited to events and parties at faculty homes, and made much of.

Several other small, and perhaps less well defended, departments were on the chopping block. In the end, however, I think only one or two were eliminated. I cannot imagine that any significant amount of money was saved, and I know that a lot of faculty time was expended. It is possible, though I think not, that the real point of these reviews was to jostle departments and the dean to do something to improve them and their states. This actually happened in Near Eastern, and it is now far better off. But on the whole, this exercise once again proved only that it is even more difficult to get rid of something in academia than to make something new. The process involved in neither is easy. As Charles Odegaard had said to me, "Everything is difficult."

# 6.

Teaching at Washington was both a pleasure and a challenge. It was a pleasure because many of the undergraduates were good, serious, and amiable students. In the West, with a few exceptions, the leading institutions had long been public ones, and many good students attended them. No university west of Minneapolis and north of Berkeley competed with the University of Washington. The challenge in the classroom was to keep the best students interested and still reach the others who formed the usual mass of mediocrity.

But you never know. Some students who received a C from me later told me my class was among the best they had experienced. I had the help of Blake, Wordsworth, Coleridge, Byron, Shelley, and Keats. The main problem was to make things interesting after their collision with Blake, who seemed always to stimulate them while at the same time causing considerable anxiety. Bostetter used to say that you climbed the hill of Blake, descended into the valley of Wordsworth, then climbed the mountain of Coleridge. No pleasure dome that. In the second quarter of work, you climbed the hill of Byron, descended into the cavern of Shelley, and negotiated the hill of Keats. That was about right. The hills tested the undergraduates' mettle. The valleys did not generate the same degree of anxious attention, or, as in Shelley, they turned out to be thickets, not glades.

Teaching graduate students was different. On the whole, Washington did not often attract top students. There was not much opportunity for them to get financial support, especially in the first year; and those who did were thrust into teaching a relatively heavy load. Sometimes those who enrolled were eccentrics or autodidacts or both, unable to get into certain other institutions. They had gone their own ways as undergraduates or were unique for some other reason. A good many had to conquer difficulties in order to attend. The most satisfying of these students for me was a woman who one day showed up at my office unannounced. She was seeking admission to graduate study but had been turned down with the admonition that her Humanities M.A. from the University of Chicago was not appropriate. I was astonished, visited the graduate office, and got her admitted. But there was another difficulty. She was teaching full time at a Tacoma high school. On most days she could take only those classes that were offered after 3 P.M. I scheduled my seminars for 3:30 and asked some others occasionally to do the same. She would sometimes arrive a little late because of the freeway traffic. She gave brilliant reports, completed all the requirements in a time that shamed most students, and eventually published a book on Joyce's *Finnegans Wake* shortly after taking a university teaching position.

One never knew who would turn up to study romantic poetry or Yeats or Joyce or the history of criticism. I assumed blithely in my own autodidactic way that these subjects were in the main stream of literary study. But when I came to Washington no one seemed to be teaching them, or rarely. The decadent phase of the New Criticism had persisted in Seattle even into the days of Deconstruction. The New Critical prejudice against the romantic poets with its denigration of Shelley, dismissal of Byron, and confusion about what to do with Blake seemed to have influenced graduate students away from the whole field. Yeats was an anomaly, a holdover from romanticism, and the history of criticism was hardly taught at all. It was like being in a time warp. Luckily there were a few other newcomers sympathetic to these subjects. Charles Altieri had just returned to Washington from a short stay at Buffalo. Leroy Searle came from Rochester. Raimonda Modiano was an assistant professor who alone since Bostetter's death bravely held up the banner of romanticism. Gradually as an informal group we began to attract students, and we were often chosen by students to sit on their examination committees. After a while, it seemed that we constituted a department within a department. We were all quite different from each other, but we respected each other. I sensed in my students the presence of the others, from whom they had learned important and interesting things and, more than that, an enthusiasm for critical inquiry. For me, the presence of the others made professional life at Washington tolerable.

All of this lasted for a while. Altieri eventually departed for Berkeley and was never adequately replaced or replaced at all. Then came the rise of feminist agitation and the fashion eventually to be called cultural studies. Neither of these seemed to take a fortunate tack. The problem, I think, was the quality of the people who first embraced them. Ideological aggressiveness grew and became manifest in departmental meetings. I was told by a graduate student that the feminist director of graduate studies warned her away from me, apparently on the grounds that my courses would not further her feminist understanding and I was thus irrelevant. I recall about this time having lunch with a faculty friend who really was and had been for some time in one of the main lines of cultural studies, the one connected with the Frankfurt School of social thought. I observed to him that it was too bad that he had to be leagued with people so intellectually inferior to him. For a moment he was taken aback, but then he nodded slightly and said he knew what I meant. After a while he left.

Any ideologically driven movement generates its fanaticisms and idiocies, and it usually breaks up into competing sects as Protestantism did. Such movements are eventually caricatured. What they protest against is also caricatured. Soon, to outsiders there seem to be two camps, both of which are strongly fictional, the extremes being taken for general truth. I am reminded of a meeting a few of us had with Lynne Cheney, then director of the National Endowment for the Humanities. Her illusions about what was going on in English education were preposterous. She asked us why we were no longer teaching Shakespeare. We taught Shakespeare to full classes every quarter, but our response did not shake her conviction. Later, I was told that she thought I and my colleague Ernst Behler, a distinguished scholar of German literature, must be communists.

The problem of politicization was also a problem of leadership. The dean's office and that of the chair of English after Gerstenberger were occupied by pleasant leaders who never had much control of things. They seemed to be influenced by the last person in their offices. It became imperative before an important meeting to be that last person. Recruiting of faculty took two tacks, both in my view disastrous. First, there was the vague effort to recruit specialists in rhetoric and English composition, not the history of thought about rhetoric but rather the method of teaching that subject. Now, it is true that English departments thrive, or rather survive, on teaching composition, often with limited success but much expenditure of effort. However, it has never been shown to me that students profit from its having been specialized into a teaching and research field. Further, it has not been shown that the field attracts strong intellects. Perhaps the rest of the university thinks that expository writing is naturally best taught as a skill like taking apart a Chevy. Perhaps it is even just as well that it does think that. In present circumstances the illusion keeps graduate students in English at work for pay and seems to convince administrators that the department needs some support, along with the notion that English somehow teaches, as we say in catalogs, what it is to be human. My experience, however, tells me that competence in writing

comes with literary experience, and that teaching writing without challenging literary subject matter that began in about grade three reduces to exercises in comparative futility what is organized by specialists and taught mainly
by graduate students. Over time, the expository writing group became the
largest single pressure group in the department. The only real way to deal
with the problem of the writing of college students would be through massive pressure brought by universities and colleges on secondary education. I
note recently some discussion of the need to develop more communication
between higher and secondary education. Over the years I argued for this on
numerous occasions to numerous people, but without success.

Second, departmental recruiting turned to cultural studies. W. H. Auden
once offered his admonition, "Thou shalt not commit a social science," long
before cultural studies entered the curriculum of literature and language
departments. It is now, alas, too late to carve that commandment in the foyer
of the department office. One can say, of course, that what some call escapes
from teaching literature have always been present along with attacks on poetry
going back at least to Plato. English didn't begin as literary study. It was language study, and things like *Beowulf* were documents that enabled study of
the history of the language. Biographical scholarship about writers has always
been possible, though the usual argument for it seems circular to me. Why
are we interested more in the life of an author than in the author's works, if
he or she is mainly important for the works? Of course, within limits biographical information may help one to understand details of a work, and biography has its own interest. Writers are sometimes interesting simply as
personalities and often for nonliterary activities or their involvement in the
issues of their day. But little of this is central to a reader's literary experience.
Nor is pure impressionistic criticism of the kinds written by Walter Pater, Ana-
tole France, and Oscar Wilde, or that of much reviewing.

Then there are dominating ideological interests, principally political,
and those seem to claim capture of the high moral ground. Cultural and feminist studies, among others, belong here. They might be called soft forms of
social science. As did the New Criticism in its own way, cultural studies
spawned a shifting canon of essential works, many not literary in the traditional sense. Students used to come to me to complain that all of their courses
required the same books, the most ubiquitous of which seemed at the time
to be *The Color Purple*. A feminist canon developed, or perhaps more than
one, depending on what kind of a feminist was setting it out. The New Critics insisted on the canonization of John Donne, but not, I think, because of
his politics, morality, or religion. In cultural studies, canonization seems to
be driven ideologically. Marx, Freud, Nietzsche and later Foucault had their
days. Writers of books of social thought — Baudrillard and Bourdieu — are
more recent examples. Some of these are intelligent people who are simply

awful writers: Judith Butler and Gayatri Spivack come to mind. Interesting things are in the books of these people, sometimes deeply buried in jargon and syntactical thickets. Many seem to employ literary texts, when they employ them at all, as either whipping boys or support for their social agendas without much respect for the subtleties of their literary character.

The undergraduates whom I taught late in my career at Washington came to be less and less capable of reading literary texts. It was not just that Chaucer and by then Shakespeare seemed more and more to be writing in a foreign language. It was the result of less familiarity with technique, with forms and genres, and with literary conventions generally. I learned that these students sensed they were missing something.

Recently, I am told, in the department's study of enrollments it was discovered that the courses in cultural studies were under-enrolled by comparison to the literary period courses. I wonder why.

There were other problems. Departmental meetings became progressively more mean-spirited and, on occasion, chaotic. Pressure groups intent on self-protection and occasionally self-aggrandizement emerged. Early in my career, the creative writing teachers tended to align themselves with New Critical trends, insisted on their traditional opposition to the administrative hand that was feeding them, and maintained their usual suspicion of all things orderly. Now, however, they constituted the academically conservative element in the department, regarding writing as an art. Medievalists and others professing the earlier historical periods hunkered down to protect their diminishing turf. The feminist-lesbian contingent banded together with those advocating or won over to cultural studies and sought to control recruiting decisions both of faculty and graduate students.

At meetings, emotional displays ranging from pathos to undisguised anger occasionally occurred. Willingness to grant intellectual rights to those having a point of view other than one's own disappeared. Perhaps it was time to consider breaking up the department into the groups that seemed to have formed. Then perhaps it would come to be understood that views could be logically independent instead of always at odds. Perhaps every issue would not be one of power.

As for what went on in some of the classrooms, I am not competent to say. My only so-called knowledge came from students and, over the years, former students who liked to entertain me with their reports, some lurid, some comical, and some both. My old colleague at Michigan State, Herbert Weisinger, used to say that if the public and the legislature knew what we really did that would be the end of it. And we were all behaving pretty well in those days!

But the break up of English would in the end solve nothing, because, as I have suggested, like Protestantism the new units would create their own inner disagreements. English has always been a collection of different intellectual interests, some of which have come and gone, others of which have changed gradually. There is nothing neat about the humanities, and intellectual disagreement is inevitable along with different interests and how one views one's field. Nevertheless, many disagreements are grounded on thirst for power or a sort of paranoia. The fundamental question has to be whether there is real scholarship being done, not corrupted by hectoring and prejudice.

At about this time, I asked the dean to transfer me full-time to the Department of Comparative Literature, where I already had a joint appointment. The English department meetings had become increasingly repulsive, though I had tried to keep relatively decent, if distant, relations with my colleagues. That did not seem to matter much. You were what you were thought to be in the eyes of those pushing agendas, and I was apparently suspect.

I was not, of course, a trained comparatist, but the graduate program in theory and criticism was properly comparative, and I had been devoting quite a bit of my time to directing it and teaching in it. While I was in charge, it kept its literary emphasis, the central courses being the history of criticism back to Plato. Still, there was a power struggle between English and Comparative Literature over control (and the naming) of the historical courses. English took the position that these courses should be cross-listed in both departments or English would teach its own. So the history of theory and criticism, which is composed mainly of writings by continental European writers remained to some extent an English colony. After I retired, the program, like the School of Criticism and Theory that Murray Krieger and I founded, became less literary in orientation, and it eventually died of faculty indifference. The young faculty even turned the historical sequence into courses in which they rode their own hobbyhorses. Their own training had become more specialized. Someone else would have to revive the sequence, as I had when I arrived in 1977.

# 7.

Comparative Literature was a rest camp after English, as relaxing as was Michigan State after Texas. The reasons were several and are worth thought for anyone interested in the woes of academe. Comparative Literature has no "service" courses that it is compelled to offer. It is free of teaching foreign languages or English composition or basic science courses that should have been passed through in high school. No faculty member finds any of that on the teaching schedule, except for people with joint appointments. In this respect it is similar to English at Michigan State, where composition was taught in another department. As a result one of the most vexing problems, source of much difficulty, is absent. In addition to this, most of the faculty in Comparative Literature, having joint appointments, have offices with other departments. Faculty members see each other infrequently, usually only to confer with the chair or to attend meetings. The chair wisely kept formal departmental meetings to a minimum. There was little time to develop and cherish animosities. People were relatively tolerant of those they hardly knew. Further, there was not much business to transact and little marking of personal territories. I do not recall at meetings any unpleasantness or, for that matter, much debate. Competence in the chair helped, of course.

During this period UCI actually did make efforts to bring me back there. The dean at Washington generously made it possible for me to return to UCI for one quarter each year. This seemed a pleasant idea, and Diana and I spent the next five winter quarters in a rented apartment in Irvine. After that, the arrangement became somewhat disruptive. During the periods I was there it was interesting to me to compare the Irvine graduate students to the ones at Washington. By this time literary theory had been pretty well replaced by theory in the larger sense leading to cultural studies. However, Krieger had managed to continue the emphasis on the history of literary theory, and I rejoined him in this effort. By then UCI had developed a national reputation in both theoretical discourse and creative writing, but in the latter the emphasis had become more professionalized and different from Jim Hall's emphasis on a more general literary education along with the so-called writing workshops. Students were specializing in poetry or the novel or short fiction. As a whole the creative writing program had become rather more isolated from the rest of the department. New people had given a new shape to graduate study. J. Hillis Miller had come from Yale, Wolfgang Iser from Constanz, and Jacques Derrida for short periods in winter or spring. The competition for entry into both programs was more intense. I sensed a considerable rise in the communal anxiety level, approaching that I had known on the east coast. Students held their cards close to their vests. They were competitive. They became upset if one criticized their prose styles or made suggestions. This may have been caused by an anxious drive to be at least as *au courant* as they thought the next person was. They were perhaps trying to absorb the vexing style of quite a bit of contemporary theoretical writing. Perhaps it was unconscious osmosis. Unfortunately, to me it had the look of parody.

I was not convinced that on the whole the students were any better than those in Seattle. Their style was different, and they were harder for me to get to know. I also learned that the UCI department's success in placing their graduate students in jobs was no better, and perhaps worse, than Washington's. The Washington students I knew may have had, on average, farther to go on arrival, but they seemed to catch up at the tape. UCI's students appeared to have been cut out of a mold; at Washington you never knew what would turn up.

UCI, like Washington, was becoming more technologically oriented. Private corporations began to appear on university land. The medical school grew larger. The new science library, from its place on a rise, seemed to dwarf the original main library. Irvine's public relations reflected more and more the *nouveau riche* culture of Newport Beach. The Department of English and Comparative Literature, once one of the most powerful on campus, increased its national reputation, but its influence in high places locally seemed to be diminishing as UCI grew. I sensed some isolation and insulation, also anxiety about national standing. The academic stars the department had attracted — Miller, Iser, and Derrida — were good scholars and conscientious teachers; but I sensed that the department now had two tiers. Then those at the top all retired.

## 8.

After five years, I desired to return to Washington full time, but the third of my salary was already committed for the next academic year. It so happened that the Department of Romance Languages and Literature was in a turmoil that seemed to have beset it in ten-year intervals in the past. The dean discussed the matter with me; I cannot recall how it came up. I offered to become acting chair for a year if he could find the salary to relieve me of my annual trip to California. The dean was fed up with the department, saw no way to invest more funds in it, and welcomed the possibility that someone from the outside might bring a degree of order. I put on what I regarded as a white hat and my pistols and entered into the chaos. A good number of the faculty saw the hat as black.

The mathematics and history departments at UCI were nothing compared to what I found. Even the dean did not know all of the story that I would unfold to him in our subsequent conversations. To begin with, it is possible that there is something fundamentally flawed with a department that puts together French, Italian, Spanish, and Portuguese. The old notion of romance languages as a glue holding together different nationalities and cultures has a certain sentimental attractiveness. But it hasn't worked well for decades, at least at Washington. The French regarded the Spanish as paranoid, the Spanish regarded the French as arrogant, and the Italians and Portuguese held on with their fingernails.

The recent history was as follows: Sometime in the eighties, with the department lacking effective leadership, the former dean, desperate to change things for the better, engineered through the College Council, a body elected to give him advice, the promotion and commission in the field, as it were, of a young assistant professor of French. He was an ebullient fellow, but without much in the way of publications to boost his reputation and power. As the new chair he was allowed to make some appointments in French and seemed generally to have brought about a semblance of order. As time went on, however, the Spanish people became restive and finally openly rebellious. Then he made the serious error that caused his undoing. He appointed to a lectureship in French a young woman with whom he was having an affair. This was made far worse by having himself signed the appointment papers. Because of his relation to her, this was against university regulations. Proper behavior would have been to present the papers unsigned to the dean. In addition it appears that he had consulted no one in the department about the appointment. Enemies saw their chance. Someone in the department found his or her way into the personnel files, secured the signed papers, and leaked copies to the student newspaper, *The University of Washington Daily*. To have invaded confidential personnel files, let alone given some of the contents to anyone, is in a state institution a felony. *The Daily* put on its front page a story about the affair and the appointment together with a photograph of the couple walking on campus.

With but two exceptions, the Spanish group turned against the chair, complaining now of his arrogance, his denigration of them, and his general demeanor. On the whole, the French faculty, most of whom he had appointed, were loyal to him, though they were dismayed about what had happened. They were not loath to look down on and criticize the Spanish.

At the same time, a young woman faculty member who taught both French and Spanish was being reviewed for tenure. The French opposed her; the Spanish supported her. Over my year with the department her case festered through a decision not to promote, an appeal process that failed, and finally her threat of legal action, the last of which came into fruition after I had left the department. This woman was both a victim and in some ways implicated in the troubles by increasingly angry behavior as she saw what was likely to happen to her.

When I was appointed acting chair, I was introduced by the dean at a meeting of the department. The response was that of confusion and, in some cases, anger, brought on perhaps by a sense of communal humiliation. My first effort to deal with the situation was to interview everyone at some length. Clearly the department was in deep trouble. Part of the reason for this had to be laid at the feet of administration. The department was underfunded and overworked. The response of the administration seemed to have been that the department was not very good, troublesome in trivial ways, and, as things got worse, deserving of punishment. I had to overcome an attitude of anger and impatience in the dean himself. Anyone looking at the department's budget would immediately be shocked at the low salaries, even by standards prevailing in the Humanities. Further, even inside the department some salaries were oddly low by comparison to others. Spanish had but one full professor, whose salary was about the equivalent of that of a beginning associate professor in English. Others of lesser rank were making more than he. In French the most distinguished scholar was poorly paid, and the chair, who had never risen beyond the associate professorship he probably hadn't deserved to attain at the time, had somehow a nest feathered far better than that of anyone else. He had never published the manuscript he was supposed to have finished when he was promoted.

There seemed to be little sense of purpose in the department. Some members were supposedly engaged in scholarly projects that probably should not have been begun. A sort of cabal of three assistant Spanish professors — I came to call them the three caballeros — of quite different backgrounds and interests seemed to be held together by their concerted efforts to torment a young woman who was the major publishing scholar in Spanish. They engaged in disgusting sexism behind her back and occasionally to her face. The oldest associate professor, a Cervantes scholar of the old school, allied himself with the French along with her and earned the enmity of the three. The linguists in the department seemed detached and universally unhappy. The French group was complicated by the presence of the chair's paramour and a husband and wife duo, the husband being one of those people who manages to get on the wrong side of every issue (if one could grasp exactly where he stood and why). He seemed obsessed with professional status at the expense of common sense. His demeanor was interpreted as arrogance by many of his colleagues.

The interviews and subsequent conversations I had sometimes struck me as worthy of Lewis Carroll, and I was tempted to identify some of the faculty with characters from Wonderland. The chair, now replaced by me, had suffered a lot, though he was in part responsible for his own undoing. He had come to adopt an "off with their heads" attitude. Some of the heads were indeed already a bit off. One of the first things I learned was that the female support staff in my office were subject to verbal abuse, mainly from female faculty. The one exception was an African American woman who was apparently too formidable to mess with. When I heard about the abuse of the staff, I told her not to stand for it. She replied simply, "I don't." Then she said she had never seen anyone on campus work as hard as I did. I suppose this was mainly because I found myself in the office talking to people almost all of the time.

I suppose that many academics, should they ever read this book, would at this point want to claim that all of this was nothing compared to situations *they* had experienced or learned about. The host of academic novels, including my own trilogy, probably attests to this. Still, this one had its unusual confluence of oddities. Not the least of these was the appearance, almost the certainty, that a felony had been committed. The dean and the administration seemed to want to ignore this and did not pursue efforts to discover the culprit. *The Daily* lost interest once the chair was replaced. No one from the paper ever interviewed me. I came to have a pretty good idea of who the purloiner of the appointment papers was, though no one was talking. Oh, they talked about everything and everybody, not that.

Was there any solution to this mess? Band-Aids would not suffice. One solution would have been to infuse the department with new personnel and find ways to encourage attrition. These things the dean was either unable or unwilling to do. New positions were scarce, and one of my problems was that he was fed up, angry, and not willing to expend funds on a dysfunctional headache-inducing unit. I argued with him; he had become part of the problem, for the attitude that these people deserved punishment was going to make matters no better and probably worse. I got nowhere.

A possible way to improve the situation was to split the department up, separating the warring factions of French and Spanish. Of course, the two groups were not fully divided in this way, but separation would lessen tensions. This was opposed by some, particularly the young woman up for either promotion or dismissal. She quite accurately thought that if the Spanish faculty was not included in the vote on her promotion she would not survive. Hired enthusiastically by the former chair, she was now strongly opposed to him and he to her. A few other faculty members sided with her against separation. These were all in Spanish, the group most opposed to the arrogance of the French.

Once I had proposed to the dean the break up of the department, he discovered that it would not be so easy. It would mean creating two new departments, and that had to be approved by the statewide body that oversaw higher education. Timidity ruled. In a time of scarcity of funds, no one was prepared to propose something that appeared to cost more money. So it was all done surreptitiously. The Department of Romance Languages and Literature was to be divided into two parts, and each would manage its own affairs. No one in Olympia had to know. In the process the linguists attached to the department were shipped off to the Department of Linguistics and seemed content to be going there. All of this left many problems unsolved. No one in French was suitable to be chair, and finally a historian was dragooned from the Department of History. In Spanish the one, underpaid full professor was appointed. He had been visibly angry with me when I was made interim chair, but now it was as if I had been a lifelong friend. The young woman up for promotion in French was denied tenure and never spoke to me again. The senior faculty of French had been determined to get rid of her, and I was regarded as complicit in the conspiracy. Most of the others, now dispersed to their new places were cordial, some with a not unwelcome distance. Some I never saw again, including the person I suspected of the felony.

On the whole, there was an air of relief. The woman who was denigrated and harassed by the three caballeros eventually became chair of Spanish, but after a term she fled, as I had, to Comparative Literature, prompting some wag to remark that Comparative Literature was the current haven for fugitives as some nations were during World War II.

After about nine months in Romance Languages, and after many conferences with the dean and with the faculty, mad hatters and all, I returned to my teaching. The rest of the years in Comparative Literature went by without any foolish forays into the wilds of UW administration. All quiet on the Western Front. Except what I heard from my friends in English.

# 11

# Books and Other Things

**1.**

During my years of administration at Irvine, I had attempted to keep up with my scholarship and writing, but with every season it became more difficult. Time, exhaustion at the end of the day, and the inability to read enough and reflect got the best of my work. The adjustment back was not easy, for there was much catching up to do. I had been working on two books, one a novel that would eventually become *Many Pretty Toys* and the other *Philosophy of the Literary Symbolic*. The latter went through many stages, encountered a few hostile readers for presses, and was not published until 1983. As I look back on it, I realize that it did not fall in line with fashionable movements of the time. It looks better to me now, despite certain faults. By 1983 I had been six years at Washington. Revision and rethinking had reduced the book from some 600 pages to 465. Cutting across the grain of deconstruction, though not unfriendly to it, it reflected my interest in a tradition of thought about language and poetry traceable back to Giambattista Vico and through to Ernst Cassirer with the strong influence of Blake. It offered, I suppose, a "constructive" view of the poetic. Though it sold pretty well after it found a publisher, it didn't speak the fashionable language of the time. It seemed to some to take up issues out of the main-stream and was generally ignored, except for a few favorable and at least one arrogantly negative review. It is perhaps more timely today than twenty years ago. Certainly it is my most ambitious book.

Something happily unexpected grew out of my work on it. I had written a chapter on the novelist Joyce Cary's theory of art, but finally it had no place in the book. It was too long and was more or less a digression. I wanted to salvage it, and found myself deeply involved with his two trilogies, which I think have been underrated by critics. I went to Oxford to consult Cary's papers at the Bodleian Library and there met Winifred Davin, who had been Cary's friend and was his literary executor. Both of us felt that Cary deserved a better critical reception. My book *Joyce Cary's Trilogies: Pursuit of the Particular Real* (also 1983) was well received. The study was important to me, for Cary's methods influenced my own subsequent novels, in which I let characters speak for themselves. Some critics did not like this about Cary, arguing that in his trilogies his own voice was never heard and his own views were ambiguous. This struck me as a superficial complaint based on a mistaken view of how fiction performs.

*Many Pretty Toys* (1999) was my third novel, after *The Horses of Instruction* (1968) and *The Truth About Dragons* (1970), the latter of which I wrote in a burst of enthusiasm in about six weeks. It is about a Welsh dragon guarding a hoard in hills above Santa Barbara. I was inspired by attitudes I was seeing in students at the time. My narrator dragon is the last of his line, a solitary aesthete, learned in ancient Welsh dragon poetry. I never enjoyed writing more. *Many Pretty Toys* became the second of my *Academic Trilogy*. I realized when *Home*, the third, was completed that I had been writing a thematic fiction of academic life in the second half of the twentieth century. It has not been popular to write fiction on academic life with honest detachment (or perhaps Kantian disinterest). The tendency has been to fall into parody, farce, or ill-natured attack. My novels have some of all that, but they mean to be serious while not being solemn and didactic. *Home*, which has in it a history professor studying an anarchist commune that flourished in the Pacific Northwest circa nineteen hundred, sold less than was even respectable, though I think it was timely. It may have had one or two short reviews. I was, therefore, very pleased to read Elaine Showalter's *Faculty Towers* on academic novels and to discover that she ends her book with a very favorable account of it. For a former teacher of freshman composition, that's a position of emphasis!

In the late 1980s and early '90s I returned to my old interest in Yeats and now had the time to write two books, *The Book of Yeats's Poems* (1990) and *The Book of Yeats's Vision* (1995). I produced these in conjunction with seminars on Yeats and was in the debt of lively discussions with Washington graduate students. In my next-to-last year of teaching, I returned to Yeats but had only a few students. I was forced to realize that for them it was all long ago, in another country, and their connection to Yeats was almost dead. This contrasted to my experience in what turned out to be my last course, one on Blake, who continued to draw a lot of interest. I believe it was Robert Graves who said that literary criticism was Oedipal, but rather than wanting to kill the father sought to finish off the grandfather. My generation and its teachers picked away at the carcass of Victorianism. Yeats was now a literary grandfather and would have to wait for a while before he became the venerable ancestor. Joyce Cary is in a similar state today, and there have been efforts to bury James Joyce as well — a tough resistant old bird. Lady Gregory has been helped a bit by feminism and won't go into the ground. Come to think of it, my *Philosophy of the Literary Symbolic* suffered not a grandfatherly fate, but was victimized by the fashion of "relevance," always with us and part of the cyclical history of literary taste.

## 2.

During my time at Washington, I made the acquaintance of a colleague Ching-Hsien Wang, who under the name of Yang Mu was one of Taiwan's foremost poets. He held appointments both at Washington and the Hong Kong University of Science and Technology, later as a dean at a university in Taiwan, and even later in the Academia Sinica there. Diana and I visited these institutions and the National University of Taiwan on three different occasions, and I either gave lectures or participated in conferences. One series of my lectures was published bilingually in Taiwan. It turned out that I had something of a reputation in China and Taiwan because my anthology *Critical Theory Since Plato* had been pirated there for years.

On one occasion a former student teaching at the National University took us for a visit to an institution north of Taipei where he had been an undergraduate. When we arrived I was greeted and immediately ushered into a lecture hall where were assembled well over one hundred students and faculty. It was clear that without any prior warning or any indication of what I should say I was to address them. Introduced as an authority on Yeats, I decided desperately and on the spot to talk about Yeats and Eliot, remembering Eliot's declaration that he was a classicist in literature, a royalist in politics, and an Anglican in religion. That made for a clear contrast with Yeats, and under a huge portrait of Sun Yat-Sen I was able to improvise on the subject for the nearly an hour. Polite and prolonged applause followed. I had no idea what the ability of most of the audience to understand spoken English was, or Yeats and Eliot, for that matter; and I never found out. In my lectures in Taiwan I was never able to grasp whether I had conveyed anything with success. There was always, however, quiet attention. On a couple of occasions I answered questions, but they were asked by faculty, and as in the United States these questions were designed to show off the asker's knowledge, though I think they were also acts of good manners meant to show their interest.

Afterwards Diana and I were whisked away to a restaurant where, with a large number of students and faculty, Karaoke performed by some of them, we sampled eighteen courses before it was declared that the chef should bring no more. It turned out that he was a graduate of the university, unable to suppress his bountiful hospitality.

## 3.

We were by the late eighties still adding to our house at Harstine Island. There is something about building that, though hard physical labor, is greatly satisfying. There are, of course, mistakes and frustrations. At Harstine in the early stages I managed to do the reverse of making a boat in the basement by ordering a spiral staircase that I *thought* would be screwed through the front door. Wrong. I had neglected to consider the bracket that was to support a beam. Luckily I was able to take out temporarily a large window that gave the stairway entry. But even with well laid plans gone astray at times, one can be elated by the results. One warning, however: watch carefully the doings of friends who offer help. The day's work of one friend of mine had to be completely dismantled. My mother's methods with her house, carried out often by me under strict observation, were the opposite of Wilmott Ragsdale's freestyle. She approached everything with care, drawing detailed plans that included the placement of the furniture she intended to use. Her house was compact with all space utilized. She continued to her death to imagine an improvement here, an addition there, and woe to the workmen who would try to cut a corner.

In looking at my academic career I see that I liked making things and had less interest in sustaining them. The best known character whom Joyce Cary invented, the eccentric painter Gulley Jimson in *The Horse's Mouth*, declared that he liked beginning paintings, making the first stroke on a pristine canvas. However, from that moment the problems begin to appear. Every act narrows the range of possibilities until, as W. H. Auden remarked, the work is never finished, just abandoned.

My experience has been a little different in that once I established something and got it running for a time, surely with more patience than Jimson had, I thought it proper to leave it to others. I have always thought that no one should stay long in charge of anything. When one has put one's ideas into something it is nearly time for someone with new ones to come along. Unfortunately new ideas in academia are not abundant, and people with the energy to establish them are rare and often not in the right position.

What one has built, one sometimes cannot any longer recognize, but that may be all right if the foundation was solid enough yet capable of flexibility, not Wilmott Ragsdale's posts hanging in the air. The English department at

UCI was, I think, well established. Perhaps today it is one I would find alien, perhaps not. Whether the fittest ideas survive or eventually decay into a useless dotage is always a question. As I write, only one of the several faculty members I recruited over a five-year period remains. The study of English, which has always been many studies grouped together for academic convenience if not for ideological reasons, some from time to time at the center or at the periphery, changes in time and may even thrive best on crisis and disagreement as long as some modicum of decency and collegiality remains. If one is going to build, one must learn to welcome the changes that come after. It is a lesson learned by another Cary character, the reactionary Thomas Wilcher in the fine novel *To Be a Pilgrim*.

In looking at the books I have written or edited, I think I always took them up in order to learn something or how to do something. I know I wrote my first novel because I was teaching about literature without the experience of having tried to produce it. In my critical and scholarly work I often strove to do something different or independent. I have always tried to use a minimum of critical jargon. It's possible that I was deluded and merely thought I was in the main line of something or other. Writing on an early nineteenth century writer and a modern was not something much done when I wrote my first book *Blake and Yeats: The Contrary Vision* (1955). Blake was an outsider, and early on I didn't realize it. Yeats was not properly a modernist, but for me they *were* the main line. In college I was puzzled that Blake was often avoided both by those who taught the romantic period and by professors of eighteenth century literature. Art historians didn't know what to do with him either. An exception among literary scholars was my teacher at Washington E. E. Bostetter, who taught Blake with Wordsworth and Coleridge, but there was no chapter on Blake in his *Romantic Ventriloquists*. The New Critics, powerful at the time, had no patience with the romantic poets, connecting them with the Wordsworthian "egotistical sublime," as Keats characterized Wordsworth's work. Shelley was periodically beaten up, and Eliot's notion of the extinguishing of the personality held the day.

But my mother had read to me before lights out Shakespeare, Blake, Rossetti, Hardy, and Yeats, among others, and by osmosis I assumed the existence of a line of not unromantic poets that for me *was* the main line. With the exception of Shakespeare, of course, there was something of the outsider in each, and even the Shakespeare I knew — sonnets and the songs from his plays — were not the basis of his critical reputation at the time. Romantic modernism, as I came to think of it, had Blake as its precursor and Yeats as its main poet. The line went beyond Blake to Rossetti and later included Theodore Roethke, whom I would see in Parrington Hall at Washington. Once you began looking around you found Blake in a lot of places, and he even began to turn up in painters like Stanley Spencer. On the whole, however, for most of my teachers Blake was an eccentric who didn't fit, even for some a madman, a painter who couldn't paint, a writer of obscure, disorganized epics, a strange character who as a child saw God in a tree.

Mainly because of the study of Blake by Northrop Frye, the situation with regard to Blake changed, and others of my generation began to see Blake as a very important writer. Still, through my whole later career Blake was a mysterious figure to many college teachers, his long poems being difficult to read and hard to deal with, much as Joyce's *Finnegans Wake* was avoided for a long time. I came finally to teach a graduate course on *Finnegans Wake*, in which Blake's four zoas are given a friendly parody, as is Yeats's *A Vision*, on which I published a book in 1995. Yeats's book had tried the patience of even friendly critics, except for Cleanth Brooks, who reviewed it when it came out and had a pretty good idea of what it was all about.

## 4.

Of the critical books I have written, I am fondest of *Joyce Cary's Trilogies*. It also reflects my tendency, deliberate in this case, to write about things I thought good and important but not in the main line of academic interest. Cary had a certain vogue in the fifties but soon faded from public perception in spite of a few book-length studies of his works. He was, however, not taken up seriously by well-known critics. I had not read Cary until Diana suggested in about 1950 that I should look at *The Horse's Mouth*, partly because its main character was a follower of William Blake, and Blake was my main interest at the time and obviously had been Cary's at one point in his career.

The title of *Blake and Yeats: The Contrary Vision* reflected both a difference *between* the two writers and a difference they had *from* many others — a contrast and a parallel. My book on Blake's shorter poems followed, and many years later the two books on Yeats. In between I had tried to solidify on the theoretical side the line that it seemed to me characterized them, and I stretched an attitude toward language back to Vico and forward to Cassirer and Frye in my unfashionable *Philosophy of the Literary Symbolic*, which spoke a critical language apart from that of poststructuralism. My years in administration had delayed it, and my engagement with contemporary criticism had to be reestablished.

I notice that I picked another unpopular author to write about in the Bucknell series on Irish writers. I chose Augusta Gregory, overshadowed in the Abbey Theater by Synge and Yeats but nevertheless an accomplished playwright, not just of curtain-raising comedies, all well-made, but also serious drama, such as her *Grania*, a play with only two characters. When Lady Gregory told Yeats about this, he replied, "They must have had a lot to talk about."

My *Lady Gregory*, a small book of just over one hundred pages, was the cleanest piece of writing the editor at Bucknell said she had seen. She made no changes or corrections to the manuscript.

Among my edited works, *Critical Theory Since Plato*, going to a third edition thirty years after its first appearance, took the most effort, and had some influence. I recall that its early competitors included nothing from Kant or Cassirer, among others. I must admit that the third edition was a trial to produce, even though I added my colleague Leroy Searle to the editorship. In truth, I found little in the two previous decades of criticism and theory that I admired. I suppose that at a certain age one begins to see that either the critical wheel is being reinvented or that scholars are departing from what one had thought is the fundamental purpose of criticism. I leaned on Searle for his opinions about inclusions for the last two decades. However, I am not sure that he was very happy with some of them, himself. We reminded ourselves that our book was historical in intent, not polemical. There was by this time a new post-postmodernist decadence, similar to that which followed after the New Criticism and can be detected in earlier periods after major influential accomplishments. In any case the history of criticism and theory can probably best be seen as a history of errors.

My experience with publishers has been mixed. In recent decades the changes in ownership of publishing houses has been swift. I went through four different firms from the time I signed a contract for editing a collection of essays to publication. There is good luck and bad luck. The director at Florida State, Jeanne Ruppert, was a piece of good luck, and I published four books there before the Florida system centered everything in Gainesville. With Jeanne, not wishing to move from Tallahassee, gone, I cut my ties with that press. Bad luck tormented one of my novels, my editor dying while a manuscript was still on his desk, and the successors not liking it at all. The worst fate is to have a book published with no or very little advertisement, a fate not unusual for university press books.

## 5.

My "other career," sporadic with vast stretches of inactivity, has been the writing of poetry and fiction. In thinking about my four novels, lines from Byron come to mind:

> Nothing so difficult as a beginning
> In poesy, unless perhaps the end.

Middles aren't so easy either. My endings are better than my beginnings. Perhaps it is because I always began like Ragsdale, not knowing where I would

The author in 2001 at Home, Washington, scene of his 2002 novel.

end, and the ending came as the result of a narrowing of possibilities, the process that Gulley Jimson hated.

Sometime in 2005, one of my former students, Kirby Olson, now a professor in the State University of New York system, interviewed me in the hope that he would publish the result somewhere. There was no luck with the full interview, but a much shortened version eventually did come out. Because in the interview I discuss my trilogy of academic novels, the whole interview follows here. As the interview goes along, it meanders into my views of the academy as I see it today. As such it performs a bridge to Chapter 12, which attempts to look ahead, always a dangerous undertaking, especially if one hopes one is wrong.

OLSON: Your trilogy of novels is set in the years 1957–58, 1970–71, and 1990 respectively, or thereabouts. Are they thematically different from each other, and why?

ADAMS: I didn't intend to write a trilogy when I wrote *The Horses of Instruction* (1971). The idea came many years later when I reflected on change and what *Horses* by that time seemed mainly to be about. I think it marked the appearance of the academic entrepreneur, whose loyalty was to career and not institution and who later became ubiquitous even in the humanities.

One reviewer criticized me because there was very little about students in it. That was deliberate. The entrepreneurial administrator and the professors in my book were driven, certainly for the worse, by other interests. The novel is about how three young faculty members come to recoil at the actions of "the fastest dean in the West," who is captive to his own dreams of glory.

By the time of the Vietnam period, the entrepreneurial people were everywhere, but the focus now shifted to student unrest about the war and a generation of young faculty torn up by it. This is what one finds in *Many Pretty Toys* (2000), the hardest to write because the most ambitious, partly because it tried to include friendly parodies of fashionable styles. This wasn't grasped by reviewers. The development of more recently dominant political moralism, as I call it, is central to the third novel *Home* (2002). The young professors of *Horses* are now on the edge of retirement. Another generation is pursuing different interests. Many humanities departments are in turmoil. I think it was Mark Schorer who said that the academic profession is a parody of a lost original. My novels have satirical moments, of course, but they try to be serious about academic life.

OLSON: In *Home*, a female professor is to be hired into an English department. The hiring is almost entirely political in that various members of the department see the woman to be hired as a potential ally or enemy in the department's battles for power. Do you think this has always been the case?

ADAMS: Yes, in one sense; no, in another. There have always been struggles over hirings, and they have sometimes centered on power, or power relations, as we now say. But in most of my career the politics were mainly internal to the departments I was working in, and the behavior, except for an occasional weirdness was not usually so blatant. I can't remember until about a decade ago discussion of an appointment or promotion in which what I call political moralism was the issue. Of course, some people who regard everything as political will say it *was* an issue, but never discussed openly — a taboo; and some people on the right will say that in the days when there was so much agreement the matter didn't require discussion, and that in the great liberal conspiracy almost all humanities professors are now on the far left. I am reminded of a conversation my father, who was a prep school headmaster, had with the treasurer of his school's board of trustees, a ferocious boorjwarrior (Joyce Cary's coinage), who asked him why so many of his faculty were Democrats. This was during the Depression. My father laughed and replied that if their salaries were raised enough they'd become Republicans. As far as I know my father's thesis has never been proved or falsified. Recently, though, politics external to the academy have become blatantly internalized. They have clearly become an issue of morality and power for feminists and advocates of cultural studies. More up front, the discussions have become increasingly acrimonious, far more so than the mainly internal disputes I remember between the literary historians and the literary critics early in my career. They held some views in common about teaching and scholarship that transcended their differences.

OLSON: Let me put it differently. Your novels suggest a difference between your generation of scholars and its recent successors. Is it fair to say that yours viewed literature aesthetically while more recently the views have been ideological, that is to say, mainly political?

ADAMS: There are two things to answer in your question. First, the question of aesthetics against whatever is ranged against it. Aesthetics is historically identified back to Alexander Baumgarten with psychology and then in Kant with affect, that is, a certain kind of response supposedly not generated by reasoned argument. Strictly speaking, aesthetics for literary critics has not often been central to their work. When response to a text was central as in, say, I. A. Richards, it was based on a psychology quite different from Baumgarten's, and it opposed Kant's alleged notion of an aesthetic emotion. Since then, aesthetics has misleadingly become merely a general word for treating a poem as a work of art, whatever that may mean. In other words it's pretty much a useless term except when employed as an accusation of separation from life and all that. As a historian of criticism and theory I don't identify myself or my generation with it. Northrop Frye had already rejected it in 1957.

Second thing: As for generations, there are always differences. I was in college early in World War II and then again after it was over. I took my last graduate class in late 1950 or early 1951. My teachers were certainly not aestheticians in any sense that would be understood by a philosopher. I don't think many of them knew very much about philosophy, let alone aesthetics. Only one of my teachers, setting aside R. P. Blackmur, whom I knew but never had a full course from, could be described as a New Critic. That was Arnold Stein. The value of both of these men was that they could read and talk about texts in interesting, inventive ways. Indeed, Stein could do it nonstop while filling and lighting a pipe. It was not that they imposed a method on students. We observed what they did, what they said, how they did it and how they said it. But nothing was shoved down our throats. Blackmur became fed up when the New Criticism was turned by academics into a method. Nor did I have any idea of their politics. Critical movements have a tendency to end in stultification when interesting critical behavior and insights get translated into teaching methods, sometimes called approaches, that are taught to graduate students as the proper way to do things. Or rather, the impression is given that one should adopt a method, join up, as it were. There is something characteristic of American practicality and know-how about adoption and use of a method. You cash in on what is going around by making a book that emphasizes various current methods. My *Critical Theory Since Plato* deliberately avoids organizing texts according to methods and schools. I just put the selections in according to chronological order.

A method of some vague sort is what people identify with the New Criticism, but as a movement it was much larger than the methods of analysis that got worked into the ground later. Its innovators were vigorous and quite capable of disagreement with each other. Deconstruction went the same way, and what took over the word "theory" descended into boring ideological social analysis, sometimes, I'm afraid, in the form of bullying. Having been one of those who early advocated the study of literary criticism and its history and having edited an influential anthology, I suppose I must admit some responsibility for the present situation. On the other hand, I have never professed anyone's method. I have wanted my students to know what intelligent people have thought about literature. My late colleague Murray Krieger said that the most interesting critical theorists were those in whose work there is an apparently irresolvable contradiction. In other words, they generated thought rather than imposed it. All good criticism, intentionally or not, extends search. Another colleague said a student of mine complained that I was a terrible teacher because whenever she asked a question I asked one back. It was, in my opinion, an unintended compliment.

Method and political moralism are in my view two of the worst things to impose on students. I say this as someone who had been a graduate student during the infamous Canwell Committee hearings at the University of Washington when two of my teachers were suddenly fired for communist affiliations and a third accused with perjured evidence. I never heard any of them advocate a political position in class. The moralism came mainly from the right then. The recent political moralism, which has been limited pretty much to insistence on positions regarding race, gender, and class, can be regarded as an outgrowth of sixties militancy. It has taken on, particularly in the humanities, the characteristics of a displaced form of what is usually religious zealotry, complete with missionary work intent on conversion and secular soul-saving. Many have skepticism about such methods, which turn study, say, of literature, into the softest form of social science — a form with which most social scientists, I hope, would be embarrassed to identify themselves. Many faculty members timidly fail to stand up to the zealotry. The skeptics run the danger of being attacked as racists, male chauvinists, or elitists if they seek to reason about curriculum or what is appropriate or not in the classroom. The timid find it easier to acquiesce and thus appear to keep their political credentials.

The right seems to think that what is needed is more conservatives on faculties, extending the liberal notion of diversity to absurdity. I don't know where they are going to find them, at least very many of them. Extending my father's view, I'd say that when the right by its actions begins to value scholarship and teaching and the work of faculties, then there *might* be some change, but for other reasons I doubt it.

One product of the cultural zealotry I have mentioned is a view that literary theory began sometime in the sixties and there is no need for a student to study anything before that. Indeed, one view is that every student should be *made* to study contemporary theory, where, presumably, they can be indoctrinated. These ideas seem to me preposterous, perhaps offered out of ignorance or the desire to suppress dissent from Truth. Thus theory becomes the teaching of a certain political moralism. Some of the many problems with this are the repetitiveness of the message, the reduction of the meaning of literary texts, and the boredom that sets in among students. But the worst is the rejection of questioning, which is actually a betrayal of the spirit of the original sixties movement and could have been predicted. In fact, I saw it coming and said so. Today quite a few students are in revolt against all of

this. I suspect that the faculty who profess missionary secular religiosity will
eventually become departmental deadwood.

I am not opposed to method. Of course not. I am opposed to indoctrina-
tion. Everyone has some method at any given time, even the supporters
of the "schizophrenic" like Deleuze and Guattari. Everyone has a theory
of literature, though it may not ever have been enunciated and might not
be a very good one. I think Coleridge in his essays on the subject said what
needed to be said about it. He thought method was seeing the relations
among things and wholes implied in parts. What I particularly object to
is the *imposition* of a method as if it is a machine for use. Machines can't
change. Students in the humanities (and probably all students) need to know
that they must find their own ways. Cary's Gulley Jimson in *The Horse's
Mouth* misquotes Blake: "The Angel that presided at my birth/Said, 'Little
creature, born of joy and mirth/Go love without the help of anything on
earth.'" But there is help, and one can learn from the methods of great critics. However, there is no use turning the wheel in the mill of one's mind.
You pick up what you can from teachers and books, but you are facing new
things or old things that now inevitably look different. I've learned a lot
from Blake and invoke him from time to time. Some people who have read
me think I distort him for my own purposes. Well, that's fair enough. A
great Blakean, Northrop Frye, once said to me that disciples run as fast as
they can to stay in the same place. Good teaching and criticism should push
beyond discipleship.

In his delightful poem "The Lemmings: A Philosophical Poem," Donald
Stauffer observes, "After all reflective verse shouldn't give the answers./It
should merely set the questions moving like dancers." Teaching and criticism
may in the end be something like this, and Stauffer's "dance" may be a better
term than "dialogue" or "dialectic." I no longer like the word "theory." I
especially dislike the word "theorize" when it is used as a transitive verb
as if you were putting something through a mill or doing violence to it.
'Theory" used to mean, for me anyway, inquiry into the nature of literature
as itself a kind of nature. For Coleridge, the whole point of method was
inquiry.

OLSON: In *Antithetical Essays* you mention that your own schooling at Lakeside
School in Seattle was at its most memorable when it was weird and fun.
Looking back at my own schooling I'd have to say that the only time I paid
attention was when the teacher introduced something weird and funny. I
remember you reading some terrible poems by William McGonagall at the
end of your introduction to a critical theory course. What role should weirdness and fun have in higher education and specifically in English departments? What would you think of a totally surrealistic education in which
wonder was the principal subject?

ADAMS: Not much. I don't think I ever mentioned weirdness or fun, at least
those words. I did value a certain kind of eccentricity as perhaps valuable
in the rhetoric of teaching, mainly because most students have been brought
up to conform to certain attitudes and behavior as if they were nature itself.
They may profit from experiencing the eccentric, but that's not the same as

having a teacher who's a damned fool. I'll say this: I have always detested the emphasis on teaching methods and would be happy to see most courses in education abolished. Teaching methods are very dry in the abstract — what Blake called "fixities and definites." In learning to teach you observe teaching and then try to learn to observe yourself. But education at every level requires rigor and discipline, and the ability of the teacher to let you know why you are doing what you are doing. This doesn't at all dictate the absence of wonder and fun. For example, I have found that students can learn quite a bit from reading and discussing really bad poems. You can learn a lot from badness, and it's fun. The last chapter of a book I've recently finished called *The Offense of Poetry* (that's weird, I guess) is mainly concerned with McGonagall's trilogy of great bad poems about the bridge over the River Tay. Most people, I suppose would think of humor in education as an adjunct to proper seriousness, a sort of sugar coating to make the solemnity and righteousness go down. It's the other way around. Humor in the larger sense of comedy and its appreciation is the proper end, antithetical to the ways of the accuser. It's the only way to oppose and avoid fixity.

OLSON: What was the funniest moment you had in a college class as a teacher?

ADAMS: There have been many, but my favorite is a prolonged moment when at agricultural student tried to convince me in a quasi-Socratic way that Blake's poem "The Sick Rose" was about a certain kind of plant disease he had just studied. We were both serious (I had to be), but it must have been hilarious to others.

OLSON: What do you see as the prospects for the humanities over the next twenty years?

ADAMS: A man of my age shouldn't be asked such a question! I suppose I shouldn't answer. I might, like an old horse of instruction, take the usual fifty minutes. But here's a radically condensed response.

1. Humanists have unconscious enemies, but they are close to being their own worst enemies. There's a potential book in that sentence. There's no question that the academic power of humanists has been slipping away in academic institutions. There are fewer humanists in academic administration. I confess to guilt here again, since I left administration in part to avoid the march to a presidency. Universities grow more and more bureaucratic. Funding becomes more problematic, and universities turn to production of professionals and specialists, especially in the sciences, partly because they think their survival depends on it. All of this goes against what the humanities properly stand for, though for a long time humanists have aped the sciences in adopting standards for promotion, etc. I see all of this getting worse. If I were to write a fourth academic novel, this would be the subject (though, of course, novels don't have subjects).

2. If you consider the humanists' internal discord, which is more intense than I can remember, it is not surprising that administrators lose patience.

3. I have felt for some time that the humanities may not survive except in their roles as service departments, and someone at a university with an agricultural college once wisely said that when he heard service mentioned at meetings he knew someone was going to be screwed. Guess who? The

humanists need to reorganize, but with secular religiosity in sway and so much infighting a change right now might be worse rather than better.

4. It has always been difficult for humanists to explain the importance of the humanities for education and culture. It's like the history of the defense of poetry, which ever since Plato has been prisoner of the terms established by its enemies: humanistic education for citizenship, for moral uplift or the moral law, social change, and so on. Humanistic education should foster the particularizing power of poetry as well as the abstracting power of science, show the desirability of both, and recognize the absolute importance of continual inquiry. To make certain forms of action or belief or both the center of the humanities — no matter how morally or politically desirable they are — will not work for long. Poems have many things to say, perhaps endlessly. An ideologue has only one thing to say, and even the most noble of such statements tends to lose life in repetition. Poetry, I. A. Richards said, brings in the opposite. I don't think that is quite accurate, though it was a good try. It brings in a new perspective that neither of the sides in a going debate will like. The teaching of literature should bring out this antitheticality. Auden warned that one should not commit a social science. That isn't a universal commandment, but it should be for humanists.

OLSON: If you were starting out now would you go into this profession?

ADAMS: I certainly couldn't count on the good luck I've had, but yes. However, ignorance would be bliss.

# 12

# The Future; or, the Mother
# of All Excursuses

## 1.

There are occasional surprises for one recalling the past. On reflection things apparently long forgotten loom up. Surely, however, there are far greater perils in imagining the future, as I began to do near the end of the previous chapter. Even the present offers opportunities for misinterpretation through partial knowledge, bias, misunderstanding, or all of these. In this chapter, I take the risk of observing the present of the profession in which I have spent over half a century and considering its future. I remind readers of Blake's wise remark that prophets do not predict but say only that if things go on as they are the following is likely to happen.

I am going to concern myself not so much with old and new intellectual developments as with changes now going on and changes likely — changes motivated not entirely or even mainly by intellectual developments.

Current changes, often externally motivated, will deeply affect what and how scholars in the humanities study, what and how they teach, and the relative importance of teaching and research to their professional lives. I shall emphasize the professional lives professors lead and will lead and how that will affect what they are going to have to think about. ("Have" in both senses, because the changes we are experiencing not only dictate new subject matter but also vastly increase the amount of it.) Because the humanities are to a great extent dominated by literary study, my project requires attention to the history of thinking about literature, though it will have to be brief and superficial. That will lead to discussion of the present situation of the scholar in the academy and in society and the smaller societies to which the scholar belongs, for the practice of literary study and its fate is tied to both, and that relationship is subject to change as well as to the forces of tradition. Discussion of this matter will not be nearly as brief.

What I shall be trying throughout to show, at least by implication, is the present and future importance of these matters to the humanistic scholar's intellectual life. When I write of English studies, I refer to the study of literature written in English, not a national literature, not the language as such.

It has been widely acknowledged that literary studies fairly recently underwent significant (and for many, painful) changes — so significant that phrases like "culture wars" and "political correctness" became common, though they are now rather tarnished by public use. As a symptom of the discontent that this engendered, new scholarly organizations appeared to challenge the Modern Language Association of America. One of the early functions of these groups seems to have been to provide opportunities for public fulmination against the influence of structuralist and poststructuralist or postmodernist practices in literary scholarship (later principally known as "theory"). I won't review here the varieties of postmodernist thought and political movements that have been historically and sometimes ideologically intertwined with them. Postmodernism has been around long enough for one to recognize in a series of abstract notions its character and the objects of its attack, among the latter of which are the unified human subject, the transcendental signified, the motivated sign, all absolutes, metaphysics, humanism, and so on. It is well, however, to consider briefly the larger historical landscape from which this movement or, rather, congeries of movements emerged and to notice that they, including their generally deconstructive drive, are all at some level characterizable as political, either in motivation or in presumed result. It is no surprise that their heirs (sometimes oedipal) have been the so-called "New Historicism" and forms of "cultural studies." The claim raised in the 1960s that everything is political caused, at any rate, everything to seem political and, perhaps, everyone to want to be, though when everything becomes political the term itself dies of the disease of expansion. We have seen scholars take the opportunity this afforded to re-evaluate almost every famous writer and to discover as politically significant (for better or worse) writers forgotten or ignored by earlier generations with other interests (although it could be argued that there is really only one interest, the political either badly or properly pursued; thus a poem like Keats's "Ode to Autumn" has been read politically, a notion an earlier generation would have thought astonishing).

The speed with which all of this occurred (and the speed with which things academic changed) was breathtaking if one takes a reasonably long view, and we can expect the mills of academe to continue to grind ever more rapidly and finely as there is more and more to grind and there are more grinders to do it. The reasons for this, in addition to the growth of the population and greater access to higher education, are various and perhaps obvious to some, but it is worth collecting them together, thinking about them, and considering their interrelations. They are changing and will further change the profession of English and literary studies generally.

## 2.

First an historical preface to what will follow: As a beginning it is well to consider the historical conditions that strongly impinge on and frustrate the relations among the academic disciplines today. Anyone addressing what liberal scholarship and education ought to be must seriously consider the following: That we have passed through a "linguistic age"; that the distinctions between some academic disciplines, at least as represented by academic departments, have been blurred; that we have moved into an age of what I have called political moralism; and that the speed with which this has all happened and the uneasiness that the speed has engendered have been reflected in disputes over what books we should be studying and teaching and how we should study them.

Risking oversimplification, I am going to divide the history of Western thought into four ages or phases (the latter word may be better because the phases overlap): the ontological phase, the epistemological, the linguistic, and the politically moralistic. In the ontological phase, the principal question around which thoughtful discourse turned was the nature of Being. From before Plato all the way to the Renaissance, that question was paramount, whether the discourse was philosophical, theological, scientific, literary, or artistic. In Western literary thought, all through this long period the dominating term "mimesis" implied some truth the poet sought to imitate or represent. In the Renaissance, the question shifted and became an epistemological one, formulated in two great traditions, the empirical one of Bacon and Locke and the rationalistic one of Descartes. "How do we know?" was the question, and with it came the notion of the modern self and eventually the sort of subjectivity that produced a radically new note in literature: the poem as an act of self-expression or self-study, or, as it has been called, the inner made outer. In most minds, the objective world was the province of scientific constitution; the subjective world was left to poetry and art. But not for long, because subjectivity itself became objectified in such movements as Freud's, and even in the area of literary art there were efforts at objectification such as Zola's. One witnesses the last gasp and death knell of the epistemological phase in the famous utterance of Walter Pater at the close of *The Renaissance*:

Experience, already reduced to a group of impressions, is ringed round for each one of us by that thick wall of personality through which no real voice has ever pierced on its way to us, or from us to that which we can only conjecture to be without. Every one of those impressions is the impression of the individual in his isolation, each mind keeping as a solitary prisoner its own dream of a world.

Already a new phase had begun, and it is no surprise that Pater's book had an air of loss and nostalgia about it. The new phase was one of the hegemony of language. Its first stirrings can be detected in Locke's remarks on language, followed by the work of the syncretic mythographers of the eighteenth century, the search for the origin of language, and the hope that the discovery would unlock the mysteries of Man. One sees the further development of this movement from Rousseau through Herder to Humboldt, thence finally to the structuralist linguistics of Saussure, the opposed philosophies of Cassirer and Heidegger, Wittgenstein, the symbolic logicians, the analytic and ordinary language philosophers, structuralism, and finally deconstruction. The question of knowledge, which was Descartes' question and still Kant's question, and even Husserl's question, had been replaced by what was regarded as a prior though not necessarily more important one. If all knowledge was mediated by symbols, did not the question of the nature of language have to precede the question of the nature of knowledge or the knowledge of nature? Gradually almost everything came to be seen on the model of linguistic structure. After Saussure's formulation of language as an autonomous system of signs, that which was signified by a sign came to be seen as yet another signifier. Language rolled out in a differential chain of infinite length from which there was no escape into a nature apart from the symbols that structured it. Language was not principally a tool for knowing something prior to it, or a means of self-expression. It defined human beings. Rather than Man speaking language, language, as Heidegger remarked, spoke Man: "Wall-to-wall language" as Edward Said put it, deploring this prison-house view. Soon, as we know, everything was seen on this model: fashion (Barthes), mythology (Lévi-Strauss), the unconscious (Lacan), and so on. Banished was the old epistemological self or subject — caught up, transformed, and now merely a construct of forces intertwined in these differential chains, which implied no origin, center, or first principle.

The linguistic model was amazingly revealing — and powerful; and its ubiquity influenced our sense of the intellectual disciplines. Thus my second point: what the anthropologist Clifford Geertz in an *American Scholar* essay of 1980 called "blurred genres." He expanded the term "genre" from its literary meaning to make it refer to academic disciplines and other categories of research and thought. But the literary suggestiveness of the term was present not by chance. Geertz argued that the traditional boundaries of the disciplines were being blurred. This is a fact that we have been observing ever since and everywhere in academic life. Some of the scientific departments and research groups flourishing today were unheard of even when Geertz wrote. Departments cross the division between the natural sciences and social sciences, between social sciences and the humanities. Humanists now often give their principal allegiances to "centers" and interdepartmental committees, frequently theoretical in intent. These units are often fledgling disciplines. At the same time, French professors still occasionally complain that professors in English have been teaching texts by French writers, philosophers, and psychoanalysts. Old-line philosophers still occasionally deplore the appearance of philosophical texts in French, German, Spanish, English and comparative literature classes or declare that certain philosophers like Jacques Derrida, who discussed philosophical texts as if they were literary texts, were not philosophers at all. But the trend has been otherwise. A few years ago I picked up a book entitled *A Poetics for Social Scientists* and another about parallels between chaos theory in physics and contemporary literary theory.

The reasons for all this having happened are many and varied. The main one is the influence of forces from the phase of the hegemony of language, though there has been little acknowledgement of that fact at any level of the educational establishment. The old distinctions were being blurred, nevertheless. A simple example is what happened to the venerable opposition between prose fiction and history that Aristotle spent a significant paragraph on in *Poetics*. The work of Hayden White argued that any writer of history is governed by a master-trope, and this trope affects, maybe controls, the way he (all White's examples were works by men) produces his story. We came so far along this route that the term "literature" was itself blurred and in some camps was dispensed with entirely, since on this model and others like it all texts are literary texts; that is, sodden with tropes and narrative devices. Of course, when everything became literature it was just as easy to say that there was no literature, only writing. What began in structuralism as a system of differences produced a monolith. No longer did language point to a prior ontological or epistemological problem. Such problems were viewed as a product of language, and the term "language" soon became a ground for new intellectual communities, pacts, and treaties.

Geertz unashamedly called things he studied (for example cockfights) "texts," as if they were written. He then argued, "the properties connecting texts with one another, that put them, ontologically anyway, on the same level, are coming to seem as important in characterizing them as those dividing them." Geertz claimed that the value of the treatment of everything as a text was that it "trains attention on precisely this phenomenon: on how the inscription of action is brought about, what its vehicles are and how they work, and on what the fixation of meaning from the flow of events — history from what happened, thought from thinking, culture from behavior — implies for social interpretation." Literary study seemed to have triumphed methodologically here, having invaded the social sciences. But in a profound sense literature seemed to have disappeared or become greatly impoverished, its study transformed into an activity with precisely the ends Geertz mentioned, in which questions of artistic value were rendered irrelevant or at best deferred.

Actually this was the result of a process that began in the eighteenth century (or earlier) and has accelerated rapidly in recent times. Literary study, in addition to historical and philological scholarship, divided into two distinctly different branches: I shall name them, for convenience, the moralistic and the artistic. As the linguistic phase waned, both tended to disappear into the prior problem of interpretation or hermeneutics — to the extent that one could seldom find anyone in a literature department who was interested in artistic evaluation (or the traditional kind of moralism, for that matter) or even called himself or herself a critic. Nearly everyone became a theorist. My anthologies *Critical Theory Since Plato* and *Critical Theory Since 1965* (with Leroy Searle) construed critical theory as *literary* theory: that is, the study of what literature has seemed to be, what it seems to be, how it is made, what it does. The other definition of "critical theory" really belongs to social thought. It was formulated by the Frankfurt School, generally grounded on Marxism. One of the ironies of recent intellectual history is that, as Marxism became almost universally discredited in practice, it reasserted itself in various quasi-forms at the end of the linguistic phase, partly as a result of the generation of students of the 1960s gaining, with age but possibly not wisdom, positions of power in the academy. The resurgence of materialism, now "cultural" materialism, and the suspicion of structuralism and some aspects of deconstruction as new forms of idealism constituted one sign of another period of transition.

## 3.

One of the reasons that the work of Michel Foucault became so fashionable, in addition to the power and scope of his writings, was that he went beneath and behind language, transforming the linguistic model of a system of differences into one of relations of power (all the time, for this reason, declaring he was *not* a structuralist). His notion of power made it somewhat ectoplasmic, but he did emphasize something the social theorists thought they understood, or at least wanted to understand better. Foucault was himself a figure within a transition from a period that concentrated on language as a model system to one that concentrated on power and therefore politics. It was perhaps in the phenomenon of the so-called New Historicism that, after Foucault, the matter of power became most prominent. Now all was no longer language; it was politics, and the paradigm was the pattern of power circulation. One aspect of this shift was a return to value-judgments with respect to "texts" (not "literature"), but judgments of historical and contemporary interest made entirely on political grounds, where the political grounds were themselves based on a series of secular moral imperatives ungrounded on now discredited "Truth." If the phase of epistemology signaled its demise in Pater's melancholy *reductio* to solipsism and the age of linguistics in the concept of "wall-to-wall language," the phase of political moralism ran the risk of reducing all issues to the questions: Who is to hold power, and: In whose interest?

One of the chief dangers to liberal education in this kind of phase is reduction, not to a common denominator (which would be dangerous enough because of the common denominator's tendency to trivialize), but to domination of a single question in all discourse, no matter how urgent that question seems to be. For a number of reasons, I was skeptical about a phase of political moralism having the power to persist in this crude form for very long in intellectual life. A modern poet remarked that people cannot stand too much reality; it is likely that people will not stand for too much politics or, at least, a situation in which politics is the defining term and shape of everything from Washington, D.C., to every person's bedroom. In the classroom, politics can tend to take the form of the moralistic homily delivered by a stern, not to say single-minded or (less charitably) fanatical zealot. Another reason is that, being reductive, it misses or suppresses many things.

**4.**

One aspect of recent uneasiness has been quarrels over the so-called canon of great literary works. In the summer of 1988, I published an article on literary canons. I remarked then that literary canons are mostly the product of the invocation of power criteria but that the wholesale embrace of power criteria in canon-formation is dangerous and always has been because it tends to minimize healthy opposition and impoverish the potentiality of the canon as a means of intellectual liberation. Another point I made was that the literary canon has not been so static as many of its defenders and enemies would like to believe.

In periods of transition we become much more concerned about the notion of a canon. The recent uneasiness has been exacerbated by the acceleration of change. It took about 2,400 years for the phase of ontology to wind down, 400 for the phase of epistemology, and about 200 for the phase of language. The present age is likely to be much, much shorter; not so short as the 15 minutes that Andy Warhol predicted for the fame of each one of us, but progressively shorter based on the model I have described. In any case, the expression of uneasiness has some similarity to the radical literary and political discourse circa 1800 and an earlier time of debate about what should and should not be included in the Bible. Generally, of course, the pressure has been to bring works by women, minorities, and so-called third-world writers into the canon.

Those of us who over the past couple of decades have read such depressing journals as the *Chronicle of Higher Education* received outlandish reports of strife at Stanford and Harvard and read letters by people who climbed the barricades to defend the presence in the curriculum of books they had not opened since college or to attack books they may or may not have read at all. Canons have always changed; all things change faster now. There are more books to decide about and more parts of the world where writers are recording their thoughts and experiences in English. There are new matters of import unknown to past writers. The real question should not have been whether the canon should change; it should have been how does it change, whether there will be a canon at all in the sense in which it is discussed, and the implications for literary education. If the notion of a canon does survive, we will have to assume that the canon is constantly expanding, and that somehow scholarship and criticism must adjust to this fact. It will, however, be necessary to view skeptically wholesale attacks on canonization that consider virtually any canon reprehensibly representative of a bankrupt Western intellectual tradition that is declared to be phallogocentric, patriarchal, sexist, racist, perhaps vivisectionist, either for or against abortion, homophobic, or heterophobic, and generally against what is right — or left. After all, it is the Western tradition, including its capacity to change, its discovery of certain ideals of freedom, and its stumbling on the virtues of debate and dialectic that keeps reminding us that there is always a social agenda. Against other traditions one might examine, this is a unique and fairly admirable accomplishment for some 2,600 years of work.

# 5.

The phase of political moralism came, not surprisingly, in the midst of a cultural revolution profoundly transforming the way most people work and live. The revolution has been technological or technologically driven more than it has been political, though, of course, it has created political action and perhaps will create a new politics. As we all know, scholars have not been exempt from these effects. The production of books and articles is involved with computers from the first act of scholarship, the first written word to publication and distribution. Communication among scholars worldwide is common and nearly instantaneous. The availability of materials in electronic facsimile has grown rapidly. One can view all of Blake's designs with a series of clicks. Bibliographies, concordances, and catalogues are increasingly available. Along with all this comes a large amount of ephemera and trivia in the form of people expressing themselves on subjects they know little about.

This revolution has inevitably affected the kind of work done in English studies. With the new technology there has been a renewed interest in textual scholarship after decades during which that activity took third place to theoretical discourse and historical study. What used to take nearly a lifetime — a concordance, for example — can now be quickly accomplished. Textual scholarship has also flourished because of the vast progressive increase in the number of books published in a variety of forms, providing a virtually endless supply of materials to edit. This phenomenon occurred, along with feminism and the study of popular culture, at about the time that scholars, most not very venturous, were beginning to despair about what there was left to turn their attention to.

The revolution in book production has been called merely a first step toward the obsolescence of the book as we have known it and the advent of the electronic book, which, it is thought by many, will change reading habits. Actually these habits have already changed. Teachers of English have always struggled to develop in students the capacity to read, even when reading was one of the few domestic recreations. Now they face a body of students brought up on a barrage of visual and aural stimuli unknown to previous generations, with no end of new stimuli in sight. These students are certainly as intelligent as those of previous generations and perhaps in certain ways better informed, but many lack experience in written expression and in reading relatively complex texts, mainly because they have less experience with them and their orientation is not toward them. Not too long ago I taught a course in the history of literary theory and criticism to advanced undergraduates, a good number of whom were majoring in the new discipline of cinema studies. It became clear to me, after a puzzling couple of weeks, that these students thought differently from those I had been teaching and that they were fairly sophisticated visually and could "read" a film, but they were nearly helpless dealing with the written words of Plato, Aristotle, et al., or expressing their insights successfully. More and more students are likely to be in this state, confirming the view that "text" is no longer necessarily written or even verbal.

What will be the long-term effect on literary study? It is possible that it will become a small part of the curriculum, occupying a role like that of present-day classics departments. If this occurs, literature professors will have been complicit in its academic decline. It is they who allowed and for the most part encouraged the division in English departments between the teaching of literature and that of expository writing, succumbing to the short-term utilitarianism of the university at large. No one has ever shown that the separation of the teaching of writing from the teaching of literacy produces the desired results, whatever they are thought properly to be. The division was an easy way to turn the chores of reading many papers over to exploited underlings and graduate students, and administrations found the savings attractive. Once the separation occurred, and on the heels of a shortage of jobs teaching literature, there was spawned a group of specialists in so-called "rhetoric" with sketchy training in literature.

But let us assume that literary study will survive in some form. It is certain that there will be a greater emphasis on visuality and orality. The book, whether Gutenbergian or electronic, will be regarded as a composite of visual forms and words. This is, of course, not entirely new. In the nineteenth century many literary books were artistically illustrated, and, of course, there were the medieval manuscripts, now themselves works of art. Many of us identify the original illustrations to *Alice in Wonderland* and *Through the Looking Glass* as integral to the texts and are offended by later attempts to replace the engravings with new pictures. The Oz books of Frank L. Baum or those of Wanda Ga'g seem proper only if the original drawings are present. These are, of course, children's books, but the same could be said to apply to the novels of Dickens, Thackeray, and others. The study of design and verbal text has become fashionable, appealing to those scholars who have grown up in the early age of the electronic book. I think this trend will be seen to have begun in the late twentieth century with work on Blake, the interest in Blake not being limited to the flower children of the 1960s. This was not a bad beginning, because the relation of Blake's designs to his text is more than that of illustration, at least in its usual sense. We can expect the creation by poets and artists, often working together, of a great variety of such relationships. Generally, scholarly work in this area has been accomplished by literary scholars and not by art historians. This is not likely to change very rapidly, if at all; but literary scholars will have to become more sophisticated about design.

In the midst of all this, the storage of books as we know them will become even more of a problem than it already was some thirty years ago when I was put on a committee in the University of California to figure out what to do about it. There will have to be electronic storage on a large scale with, one hopes, everything at one's fingertips. But there will be so much of it that one might imagine a period of nostalgia for a manageable canon of great works and some criteria for their inclusion. Indeed, college libraries have in some cases simply gotten rid of many books as if they were thinning a herd.

Almost certainly, the plethora of material will continue to blur the distinction between works of so-called popular culture and those of so-called high culture. There will be a twilight struggle between those who find only "culture studies" worthwhile and others who want to separate out "great art."

The sheer amount of material to deal with will be more manageable under a high degree of abstraction, amenable to categorization by political or other content, and this will favor the cultural approach at the expense of artistic analysis. Nevertheless, artistic analysis will persist and even flourish, partly under the impetus of composite books.

For literary study, the fundamental danger of the electronic advances (of which we have seen just the beginning) will be, as it has been for so long, the utilitarian drive of institutions; and now the vast amount of material will require ever more efficient ways to process it. What easier way than a judgment of immediate usefulness, whether political, psychological, or escapist? This has always been the bane of some professors in the humanities, and they have had to create notions of long-term value not often convincing to their colleagues in engineering, medicine, and business. The university as a whole finds it often easier to surrender to the utilitarian while yet uttering traditional phrases about the value of liberal education; but more of this later.

## 6.

We all know that as a result of technological developments the world has shrunk astonishingly and political change now occurs very rapidly. The rise of a new generation of Luddites, demonstrating in places as far apart as Geneva and Seattle, has been only one symptom of this phenomenon and its attendant anxieties. On the profession of English these developments have had an important influence, and the results will continue to be experienced. English literature in most parts of the world is no longer just the literature of England. It is an international literature. A student studying the English language in Taiwan is going to study and speak American English and read primarily, at least among the moderns, American writers, or those whose English exists as the result of a now dead British colonialism. But even beyond this, and perhaps to some extent because of it and the tremendous growth of what is available to read, the notion of a national literature, which will no doubt persist partly because there has to be some way to divide up the field, will become less dominant and the notion of a world literature more forthcoming. Even for students of traditional English literature, beginning with *Beowulf*, it has always made sense to read translations of the fundamental literary influences — Hesiod, Homer, and the Bible — even though curricular requirements have tended to ignore these texts. The curriculum in the history of literary criticism and theory has, by contrast, not been tied very often to nationalism, it being almost impossible to treat the subject without Plato and Aristotle at its beginnings and a host of Europeans later on. It has also been held that critical and theoretical texts can be translated more accurately (whatever that means) than can poems, plays, and novels. This is a dubious proposition, however, and the notion of an international critical tradition is more likely the reason critical texts have been taught in translation without much complaint.

On the other hand, the Bible, being for many people a holy book, has presented a terrible problem for teachers, who have had to avoid as much as possible discussion of the single most important literary influence in the West. It is doubtful that this situation will change where it would most count. Nevertheless, globalization will offer the opportunity for some change with respect to the literary study of holy books. It will also make translated texts seem more legitimate while at the same time increasing attention to the whole problem and act of translation. With this should come greater recognition that translation is an activity acceptable for professional advancement, a legitimate form of literary scholarship. This will be especially true in the U.S.A., the size and isolation of which from other languages (except Spanish) make the U.S. citizen not very good at foreign languages.

Globalization will be a major factor contributing to the current breaking down of boundaries sustained by academic departments. I suspect that so-called humanities centers were originally formed as paranoid parallels to scientific research organizations on the principle that what is good for the goose is likely to be okay for the ugly duckling. Their main function seems to have become the fostering of activities that do not easily fit inside departmental boundaries. The rise of theory played a major role here, but even though theory waned as a fashion, globalization will hasten the movement of the liveliest parts of literary study out of departments as we now know them. English departments will survive, there having to be some way of organizing the bureaucratic university, universities being slow to change in any case. But English departments may continue to exist mainly as centers for language teaching, composition (increasingly remedial), and creative writing — unless these functions themselves are separately departmentalized.

Finally, it will be widely recognized in critical and theoretical practice that there are many more literary traditions than just that founded in ancient Greece. The first stirrings of this occurred with translations of Chinese critical texts. At the same time, there developed among Chinese, Taiwanese, Japanese, and Indian students an enormous interest in Western thought about literature. It may well be that fairly soon Eastern critical and theoretical texts will be assimilated into the canon of the history of criticism and theory as Westerners see it. The results of this will be puzzling and interesting enough to occupy Western comparatists and theorists for some time. The need for more translation of Eastern texts will become obvious, and there will be a shortage of people competent to do the job well or even at all.

# 7.

Anyone with any sense and experience of universities in the U.S.A. knows that they are simply too large to be managed efficiently, let alone to control the educational process in any reasonable way. Since the Second World War and especially since the advent of the Cold War, they have been fuelled and enlarged by federal funding in the sciences; this created an insatiable appetite for growth along with more and more scientific research, which in turn generated more dollars for growth. With collapse of the Cold War and consequent relaxation of federal interest in funding science in the name of national defense, business moved in to fill the gap, but with a different agenda. Business communities, usually high-tech, appeared on the borders of campuses and in some cases even on university land in joint ventures with scientific faculties. This was greeted with enthusiasm by state legislators, who have always believed with Calvin Coolidge that the business of America is business, and have learned that if business supports university research, state taxes will not have to do so. Indeed, at my university the state provides only about 16 percent of the annual expenses and tuition only about 12 percent. Since institutions of higher education are periodically viewed with suspicion by the public — in part because of the behavior of the liberal arts faculty — all of this is convenient and perhaps necessary. But university administrators need to be alert to possible adverse results. And faculty should not be loath to encourage vigilance.

Both the federal government and business have had a utilitarian influence on large campuses that has marginalized the influence of the humanities, though a certain amount of "overhead" charged to the federal government has over the years found its way even into humanities departments and both the government and business have made connections between the university and society at large that were unknown to past generations. The trend with business will likely continue and increase in intensity. There is a major threat from this development that most faculty members do not seem to pay much attention to. It has come with the realization by business that one of the substantially uninvaded sources of potential profit is the entire world of education from kindergarten through graduate school. This camel's nose is already under the tent. It is now well-known that profit-making companies, some calling themselves colleges and universities, some accredited, are offering degrees in professional training in business, education, some aspects of the medical profession, and so forth. Forays have been made into primary and secondary education, particularly since the federal government has become everything from diffident to hostile toward public education, where it has not been simply incompetent.

Here, the danger to the humanities is obviously the tendency toward a passion for short-term utilitarianism that will outdo all the dangers I have mentioned to this point. The trend will be, with the best intentions, anti-humanistic. There is virtually no attention to humanistic disciplines in the for-profit professional programs, and there is likely to be a similar lessening of interest in them in secondary education.

It is quite possible that these developments will change the whole nature of education in America, and in radical ways: from the subjects emphasized to the subjects actually taught. In higher education, the profit-motive (along with the survival motive for some institutions) is likely to bring tenure to an end, possibly academic ranks and the forms of security that go with these things. The academic year, as we know it, will likely change. Less importance will be accorded scholarship by humanists; their ranks will diminish; and they will be entirely occupied with teaching more and more students. Control, such as it is, by faculty over curriculum, will disappear, and decisions about organization and introduction of new courses and programs, as well as the discontinuation of some not pulling sufficient economic weight, will be made from heights more remote than they now are and with no faculty review. Perhaps those faculty members most opposed to unionization will reluctantly organize. The future of all public education and probably the character of private colleges and universities will be in the balance.

## 8.

The humanities scholar is in what could become a crisis. Most of this section is devoted to the present situation of the humanities scholar in the institution and in society at large, and it contains a good bit of comment on what the scholar will have to become if the humanities, clearly marginalized as a result of these developments, are to be an influential part of the university or even survive under these conditions.

Let me begin with the incursion of the term "research" into the vocabulary of humanities scholars. It is in part a by-product of the influence of the federal government already mentioned, which, along with the enormous increase in the academic population, dramatically changed the nature, conventions, and mores of academe as a result of the domination of the sciences since the Second World War. "Scholar" is a term that has become almost solely the denotation of a good undergraduate. The developments from this have not been all bad. The huge overhead helped sustain some kind of balance. The National Endowment for the Humanities, a mixed blessing, I think, but probably a needed one, would never have been created if there had not already been a National Science Foundation (and if it had not been realized that the N. E. H. would never be a big item of public expense). The humanities follow upon and respond to the sciences in contemporary life, and this may be their proper role. It is certain to be their future role. How best to play it becomes the issue.

But to adopt, where possible, the language of scientific professionals has been a bad strategy. The term "research" tends to separate the activity it denotes from teaching. The term "scholar," with its implication of "student," tends not to. In any case, the academic scholar, whether we call that person researcher or not, has relations with or belongs not just to society but to numerous societies. It is in these societies that the humanities scholar is going to have to learn to move more successfully and be more visible. This presents an important difficulty, because the scholar is in certain ways properly apart by virtue of scholarly stance.

Something needs to be said here about a few of these societies, and, at the expense of sounding like the young Stephen Dedalus, I shall name some of them. The academic department, other academic units, the college and/or university, the local community, the state, nation, and the world and humankind. In addition to these, and belonging to and overlapping them, are the academic world, the community of scholars worldwide, and the various academic disciplines. There are also more abstract or amorphous notions of societies in the humanities scholar's mind, such as the world of letters. They all call for their own allegiances. Finally, there is the society composed of students, to which the scholar-teacher both does and does not belong. Unfortunately, or perhaps fortunately if one believes that a degree of conflict prevents stultification, these different societies produce opposing views of and demands on the scholar. Though some scholars may wish to ignore the claims of one or another of these groups, they would do well to be aware of what is at stake if they do, and, for humanities scholars, much will be increasingly at stake.

To a humanities professor in a large university, the society that most affects daily professional life has been the department. In a smaller college it may have been the college faculty organization as a whole or some more inclusive division such as the humanities. English departments, in particular, have not been identical with a discipline; they have been composed of many people representing many disciplines with different histories, conventions, and fundamental assumptions. Sometimes their interests overlap; most of the time they do not.

Departments will persist, but more scholarly work will be done in organizations that cross old boundaries. The tendency of some of these, of course, will be to become departments, keep changing focus, or die (some quite properly by intention, it would be hoped). What applies to departmental membership applies to these, which quickly form their own bureaucratic characters under the impetus of the inertia of the university itself. Wise administrators will make possible the birth of these units and the easeful death of those that have no longer any sensible purpose.

In large universities, the college, the faculty governing body (if it may be called that) and its committees often seem remote or occasionally comical. As universities have grown, their structures have become more complex, with the result that long ago an administrative class grew up and continues to grow. Many faculty, rightly or wrongly, see it as foreign to them or even antithetical to their interests. There is no question that in these larger institutions it is difficult for the individual faculty member's voice or even the collective voice (if one can say there is one) of a department to be heard. If a department does not bring in the research dollars, it is even more difficult.

Administrators, for their parts, often, rightly or wrongly, perceive the faculty as isolated, unrealistic, and intensely self-absorbed. Often they have good reason, for faculty are seldom intimately acquainted with administrative matters except when something suddenly impinges on their interests, at which point they enter the situation usually ignorant of its nuances, its history, and the larger internal (to say nothing of the external) political issues that contribute to its complexity. It has been said that administrators like solutions and faculty like problems. Few faculty members in larger institutions involve themselves in its politics beyond their departments; most think participation a waste of time and interference with their real work, which is usually regarded as research. Yet many are willing to criticize, sometimes savagely, administrative actions. The situation of alleged powerlessness is exacerbated by such attitudes; power comes only with responsibility. In spite of their primary allegiance to their scholarship or research, faculty are likely to need to be more involved in the workings of the institution, slow and creaky as these workings may be; the institution cannot be a collegial intellectual enterprise if they do not. But few universities let it be known to their faculty that they are expected to participate actively in its politics, and not many encourage faculty to do so. Indeed, many administrators actively discourage participation by withholding responsibility from faculty or acting against collective faculty will without at least seeking consensus. Under such conditions it is no surprise that individuals become bored by what seems the sham of faculty governance and withdraw into sullen passive resistance. There is a thing called "university service" that is usually listed among criteria for promotion, but it rates third far below research and teaching; and almost nothing is said about it as a responsibility during recruitment of a prospective faculty member, except at certain smaller institutions, where the matter is regarded as quite important. It is unlikely that the situation just described will change very much without the development of a new form of collective responsibility.

The institution is rarely identified in the public mind with its faculty.

Usually it is identified with the athletic teams, the physical campus, or the institution as a state budget item; or, it is regarded as a monolithic force affecting traffic, parking, rentals, and local zoning. When Dwight Eisenhower, as president of Columbia University, addressed the faculty as employees of the university, an offended professor replied that the faculty *was* the university. But it is also true that in public institutions, at least, the faculty are employees of the state and therefore of the people. This is a fact that many faculty have forgotten or never understood. It will become more important not to forget in a society where the university is increasingly involved in a myriad of social relations. For humanities professors, who have been moving toward the margins of the institution, it will become a matter of survival to reassess their role vis-à-vis the public and, particularly, primary and secondary education.

The public sees humanities professors almost entirely as teachers of young adults, though this view lags behind the fact that people of all ages are now attending college and more and more older people will. The public has little interest in literary scholarship, and often regards it as trivial. Since avoidance of teaching is a skill sharpened to a considerable art by a few scholars (or, rather, researchers), it will be well to remember that the public does not expect avoidance to be one of the arts professed. At the same time, faculty cannot be answerable to the public in a direct or passive way, for they ought to be exercising intellectual leadership in society. Answerability to the public, therefore, quite properly has its antithetical side, as does behavior within the institution. With respect to both societies, the intellectual gadfly has always been a necessity and will continue to be, though under greater pressure from forces already mentioned. Whether, in the future, humanities professors will be allowed to be gadflies depends to a great extent on their finding ways to support history, philosophy, literature and the arts in styles that the public can understand and respect. The most radical political critique has usually been tolerated by the academy with occasional grumbling and in the academy by the public if it is not carried on in adolescent ways, does not in itself suppress opposition, and is not taken into the classroom in a propagandistic way. Some may say that to take this view is in itself suppressive, for it domesticates and engulfs issues, trivializing any possible good effects. Although there is some truth to this, the reverse is generally true and certain styles harden resistance and generate needless opposition and suppression in return, to say nothing of occasional violence.

Humanities professors have always taken a major role in criticizing the academy and society. It has been in the humanities, appropriately, that substantial debate has occurred, but voices are heard only if they have platforms from which to speak, and Humanities professors will have to struggle to build a platform under conditions of diminished power. They will need to establish grounds for new power by advocating and pursuing ways to articulate humanistic study from early childhood through college. If the university comes to understand this need, the public will quickly understand it and respect the effort.

On the whole, university humanities faculties have not taken advantage of their positions in the larger academic society that includes primary and secondary education. Liaison, such as it has been and when it has existed at all, seems to have been limited to administrative levels, universities being inclined to create new offices for such matters instead of involving faculty members directly; it has been limited to a few faculty, usually connected with schools of education, which have often been part of the problem, not the solution. Humanities faculties could make a huge difference. They possess in the public eye, despite all I have already said, the prestige of their disciplines and arts; but this power is rarely harnessed in support of education as a whole. As a social force, humanities faculties will, out of necessity, I believe, have to pay more attention to their primary- and secondary-school colleagues. At present, few structures make possible such liaison, especially on the intellectual level, where it is most needed, and there are virtually no incentives for faculty to do anything to improve the situation. The larger academic society is fractured.

A few years ago I received a phone call from a local high-school English teacher asking me to come to her school to speak to the seniors there on the "humanities" in a program called "humanities week." She had called the university's speakers' bureau and got no help. She admitted in our conversation that she and her colleagues did not really know what the humanities were. I was curious about how, since no one seemed to know what the humanities were, such a program had occurred. It turned out that one of her administrators discovered in the state coffers funding for something called a humanities week in the schools, so he or she applied and got funds. The teacher was working in a high school that is among the top ten sending graduates to my institution and is rated one of the best in the state. Her seniors had never seen a college professor. I went, spoke, found everyone attentive, and may have done some good, or at least no harm. But few if anyone in my institution would care that I went. I suspect that if the behavior of university scholars does not voluntarily and systematically change with respect to this activity, society will force some ineffective bureaucratic form of liaison on universities. Humanities professors should regard this matter as of prime importance and themselves find ways to foster a more intellectual, to say nothing of literate, attitude in primary and secondary teaching. It would be in their own interests to do so, and it might save what they do.

Most humanities professors have not been particularly aware of the fundamental relation between the university and the nation because that relation has apparently not impinged on their work to any great extent. They have perhaps read one of the many reports issued by acronymic organizations, the full names of which are hardly known at all. These reports, when they have treated the humanities, have discussed literacy or the lack of it or have intoned high-sounding phrases such as "knowing what it is to be human" and leave things pretty much as they were. Occasionally noises meant to be inspiring and, not too long ago, noises more or less punitive issued from the national Department of Education and from a director of the National Endowment for the Humanities who is now blessedly gone. Task forces, blue ribbon panels, and commissions have come and gone. Organizations of various sorts have been established, seminars given, and fellowships granted. People in high places have written essays about preserving our heritage.

The situation has been quite different for scientists, and it is important for humanities professors to understand this clearly, since it helps to explain the mores of their distant colleagues, into whose departments the bulk of funding flows. The influence of these mores appears in criteria for professional advancement university-wide. As I have already indicated, most large academic institutions have survived on the margin provided by overhead from government-supported scientific research, this and the immense cost of supporting the scientific enterprise having been the single greatest influence on the life of academic institutions. Young scientists have had little hope of advancement without the ability to attract a steady flow of government dollars. Indeed, this criterion for promotion has sometimes had priority over what a humanities scholar is likely to think of as accomplishment. To the phrase "publish or perish" has been added "get grants or perish."

But in the climate of technological boom, and with governmental resources waning, it is techno-business that is becoming the patron of university scientists, who may often rise to partnership. The influence of this change has its dangers (as has government support). As I have already suggested, the spectre of utilitarian need is the greatest of these — at least from the perspective of the humanities. The saving grace, always belated, will be business's realization, which has occurred cyclically in the past, with the university passively entering the spiral, that their hirees, despite their university degrees, are virtually illiterate, very narrow in imagination, and inept at communicating relatively simple information. Unfortunately the response to the mindless utilitarianism that turns the historical wheel is likely itself to be utilitarian and will work only for a short time unless professors of literature can convince people (often administrators) that the literary is the only practical way to the kind of literacy desired. Antithetical to the utilitarian spiral, humanities professors will have to mount a stronger attack on the cyclicity I have mentioned. This means that they will have to resist aggressively trends toward making higher education into a bureaucracy producing, in the easiest and most economical way, phalanxes of whatever sorts of skilled workers some economic motive calls for. Such trends would not be quite so bad as they always have been if they did not bring about backlash and overproduction. There is nothing wrong with universities producing specialists, so long as they are effective ones who can think and communicate, preferably in more than one language, and have learned enough to function as thoughtful citizens of the world. Specialization is a contemporary necessity. The degree of literacy needed cannot be taught as if one were demonstrating how to take apart an automobile engine. It also cannot be achieved without a continuum between primary and higher education.

# 9.

All scholars, of course, belong to the society of scholars itself, replete with its disciplinary subdivisions and official organizations. The humanities scholar's responsibilities are not so much to these societies as they are to scholarship itself. In the future, these responsibilities will, of course, be exerted in new circumstances, but they will remain what they always have been and should be: to address one's subject seriously, to respect the rules of evidence and rational thought, to seek awareness of and to criticize one's own premises. There will be temptations, some of which are quite familiar. One that has often been deplored is the tendency to popularize one's scholarship at the expense of its integrity. This is a danger, but the future will require the literary scholar to be more sensitive to the presence of the public and the need to defend the scholarly enterprise in ways that people will understand. Academic busy work in the form of uninteresting scholarship ought to be less tolerated, if only because the academy has not known how to dispose of such refuse any better than it knows how to dispose of nuclear waste. Almost every university has had a faculty committee fretting over the apparently infinite expansion of the library stacks. On the other hand, technology may take care of that — in its own way — by making it possible to preserve in a small space absolutely everything ever written. That may be a prospect more frightening than one of libraries growing into what Blake called polypuses.

Most scholars of literature believe they have a responsibility to the society of writers and artists, but it has been observed bitterly more than once that literary scholars must not like literature or they would not do to it what they often do. The observer is usually a novelist or poet writing from a different perspective, smarting from a bad review, or expressing writerly anxiety over what some scholar might turn up. It is true that the society of scholars does seem at times intent only on its own professionalism and not service to the arts it studies. Indeed, in recent times there have been scholarly claims that literary theory stands at the same level as so-called creative work, though I know of no one other than some theorists who believe it. Throughout history there have been eloquent defenses of and attacks on poetry, drama, and prose fiction. The defenders well known to us have usually been poets. Scholars have edited and taught from these defenses and have made occasional theoretical defenses of the whole literary realm or of individual poets or works or schools. If literature is something to be studied, then it must have potential social value worth enunciating; this seems to have to be shown anew to every generation, which will be impatient with the defenses of the past, now threatening to become cliché-ridden. New defenders will, no doubt, arise, but in an atmosphere in which the tendency of scholarship has been to be simply descriptive and, where not that, overtly politicized, the need for defense may not be recognized. Furthermore, the defenders will have to be more open than in the past to forms of verbal and composite expression that are strange and to new technologies that are bound to clamor for admission to "literature" and will establish their own turf if barred. Also, given the vast amount of material available to study, scholars will be even more seriously charged with determining what is worthwhile and what is not and why, and with championing writers of value who may have been overlooked.

The last society I shall mention, but by no means the least, is the society of students. Professors both belong and do not belong to this society. It is a commonplace to say that the scholar is always a student, but it should be the reverse as well. The student ought to be a scholar. To bring students into the society of scholars for a time, where they can come to understand its values, responsibilities, and (sometimes antithetical) social function, is of fundamental importance. To seek such an end in one's students involves a myriad of practical activities in addition to giving vent to the dramatic instinct in the classroom. One must be available as an intellectual source; one must try to make students feel engaged in inquiry. One must search for connections with other disciplines and for their differences. More and more, students themselves are becoming involved in forms of scholarship, working in groups, critiquing each other's work by e-mail, and so on. Their impatience often with lectures is not just simply childish rebellion or the result of a diminished attention span. It involves the way they see the world and imagine the future. Probably as much as any change occurring, the formal relation of teacher to student is affecting the life of scholarship. The engagement of students in cooperative scholarly and creative ventures in the humanities is really just beginning, mainly as a result of technology that enables it in new and easier ways. The main danger will be the assignment of slavish activity helpful only to a professor's scholarship. The connection to personal research works better in the sciences; it is not likely to work nearly so well in the humanities.

I come now to take account of the usual oppositions that plague scholars and of which they frequently speak: scholarship (and research) vs. teaching; careerism (professionalism) vs. purism (amateurism), specialization vs. generalism. There are also some opposed loyalties: to the profession/to the university; to one's subject/to one's students, the latter being responsible for the hollow claim "I don't teach [supply the subject], I teach students."

In his *Marriage of Heaven and Hell*, Blake took note of oppositions he especially disliked and which in practice he regarded as dulling themselves and suppressing or "negating" each other, thus contributing to cultural stultification. He proposed active opposition to these oppositions. Yeats named a similar stance "antithetical." The oppositions I have just mentioned are pernicious when not opposed by a third force. There may be some difficulty for a young scientist in doing both research and teaching and making them complement and blend with each other. When, for someone in the Humanities, teaching and scholarship become separate, something is wrong either with the subject of scholarship or with the way the scholar sees the problem. It is indubitable that scholarship is a requisite for good teaching. Of course, scholarship in this sense does not have to result in publication, especially immediate publication, and much that results in publication is not scholarship. Publication, in whatever form it may take in the future, will continue to be a way as part of the ongoing conversation of scholarship.

Humanities scholars are by necessity slow learners. They have a lot to learn, seemingly an infinitude of texts, facts, thoughts, interpretations, and arguments. The problem for them is not the often alleged incompatibility of teaching and scholarship but an utter compatibility corrupted into opposition by academic society's decision to make judgments about promotion and tenure on a career model driven by the rhythm of scientific achievement. No one I know, however, has suggested, except in jest, that the trial period for humanists be lengthened and the retirement age for scientists be made earlier. If humanities scholars are going to survive with power and dignity, they themselves will have to rethink the grounds for advancement and insist on their adoption.

The careerist/purist opposition provides an uneasy refuge for scoundrels on either side or, rather, two categories in which to place those one wants to view with contempt. Faculty who actively participate in the larger society of scholars are often accused of blatant self-interest, while those who do not, or at least do so with restraint, are often accused of shirking scholarly responsibility or being out of touch. It is not necessary to copy either of these parodies. Scholars will best occupy a third, antithetical position in which they recognize the sometimes competing interests of activity in the larger world as well as the need constantly to evaluate the worth of such activities against the equally pressing need for rational distance. One can predict, in any case, that the day will continue to contain only twenty-four hours.

As the production of scholarship becomes ever more rapid and over-whelming in size, the tendency in all fields is toward specialization. As a result, it seems that the societies the scholar reaches decline in number; iso-lation and suspicion of uselessness threaten. I believe that society will more and more insist on demonstration that subjects professed are important and connect with societal concerns. It will ask what the point is of teaching them to undergraduates if they do not. We see this happening already in calls for assessment of results at every level, and in some cases the call for pun-ishments if the desired end is not reached. This is a characteristic result of American short-term utilitarianism and is not likely in our more and more materialistic society to go away. Faculties should pay serious attention to this trend. They must at the least define what the desired result is. If they do not themselves set the standards by which education in the humanities is assessed, someone else will. Blue ribbon panels? State legislatures? Parents feeling that they have not received enough return for their dollars? Students with grievances?

On the whole, faculties have not paid much attention to these questions. They haven't had to, but now they will. It will not be fun. It will be tedious and take up much time. The whole concept of practical, definable ends has been, if not anathema, at least an irrelevance. No more, I'm afraid, and recourse simply to high-sounding statements will not do. Results are what will be assessed, and faculties had better begin to defend of their territory, defining the aims and ends of their work, success and failure.

For literary scholars teaching has involved the careful reading of texts and then their relation to other texts, in order in part to address the role of literary art in culture. Over the past century we witnessed a cyclical move-ment that privileged now the single text as an object, now the text as cultural or historical phenomenon. But there has not been a lot of success in attempt-ing to encompass both at any one time. This opposition is a negation like those mentioned above, and it seems to fall into an historical cyclicity in which one, then the other, dominates. If one studies the history of literary criticism in the past century, one discovers that one movement begins by opposing a suppression, gains power, dominates, and becomes repressive and decadent, as did the old literary history, then the New Criticism, and more recently Deconstruction. From time to time, whole academic units have suf-fered internal disorders as a result. The danger is always present for every gen-eration of scholars, each of which is inevitably trained in the dominant fashion of its time and risks carrying that fashion into obsolescence without recog-nizing that the fashion was not itself Truth. All of this happens more rapidly than in the past. The most important social role of the scholar will, there-fore, continue to be to learn anew; to continue to regard oneself as a student in the larger sense of the word.

The relation of the scholar to society is inevitably going to have what, begging your reverence, I shall call a public-relations aspect. This is not exactly new, but it will become more evident as greater demands are made. Traditionally, scholars have not been very good at or prone to public relations, and universities have been almost as bad. On the whole, public relations have been left to the development and university affairs officers, lobbyists, and the president, who sometimes wonders whether he or she is not the victim of a concerted effort by faculty to frustrate reasonable effort. The main obvious societal responsibility of faculty, as I have suggested, ought to be (and may very well become) to foster effective cooperation with the society of teachers in secondary education. Whether or not this will be the case, there is certainly a great deal that needs to be explained about what and why professors are doing what they do. This chore has generally been left to others, who do not do it, cannot do it, do it badly, or occasionally do it well but cannot concentrate their energies on it.

In the last analysis, the social roles of faculty need to be defined ethically, but not by some moral code. Rather, the scholar's ethical stance must be that of looking more deeply, more widely, and with a certain distance, so that culture and power come under constant scrutiny. This involves an activity that has had a recent beginning and will develop more fully: looking closely at the culture of scholarship, the university itself, and its history, how it came to be what it is, and how it might become better. In this way, the best scholarship will be antithetical to itself, insofar as scholarship belongs to its own culture and has a way of endorsing its own limitations and failures.

# 13

# L'envoi

Does the past simply melt away? No, it is gone with the moment, its place usurped by memory, fallible surely and selective, though who is to say? The past, when we think we have captured it, appears to us only as a fiction of our own making, cast in the symbolic forms human beings have evolved and in which they live. Recently I heard of a young woman who remembers everything. If you ask her what happened in her life on a certain day, she can tell you. My first response to learning about her was to imagine this remarkable ability as a burden hard to bear. My second was to remember an old joke: "My mother-in-law has a terrible memory. She remembers *everything*!" But even if one could remember everything one would be impelled or have to choose what to call up at any moment. Likewise, one couldn't put it all into a book, and to write a book one would be well advised to find some principle of selection.

Even with the decision to center this book on my academic experience, I have discovered that other things, many long forgotten, have arisen to accompany something deliberately recalled in order to express my theme. These uninvited guests have clambered for inclusion. We are siblings, they say, or at least cousins, of what you have intended to include, and anyway where does an education begin and end, where are its boundaries? You thought you had forgotten us, but here we are, old relatives come to stay.

I have nothing against them except their lack of respect for any order I might have imposed: theme, plot, beginning, middle, end. They make persuasive claims. Who can honestly say to them, you do not belong? You know that your plot, such as it may be, is a fiction. They declare that everything is potentially relevant and can be made so. With the ultimate impertinence they even quote Blake at me:

261

> ...every sorrow & distress is carved here
> In all their various combinations...

And so, when they have insisted strongly enough, I have given in and admitted them. The Daughters of Memory select at their own caprice.

These guests have not intruded into my excursuses, which have been my own quite different intrusions, though I would have called them asides until it became clear that Chapter 12 cannot be regarded as an aside. It is an example of habitual professorial behavior, a lecture of more than an hour's duration, quite long enough to make the students late for their next classes. Up to that point my narrative rolls along rather like the many trips I have made across America, the train stopping occasionally to take on water — Grand Forks, Minot, Whitefish, Spokane — or rather, in this case, to let off steam — a baseball game somewhere, some eccentricity of professorial behavior, something that happened at Parris Island, Dublin, East Lansing, someone telling a joke I suddenly remember. None are dismissed. They are part of a story less thematically neat, but I hope more entertaining, than I had intended to tell.

# Index